THE NORTH ATLANTIC

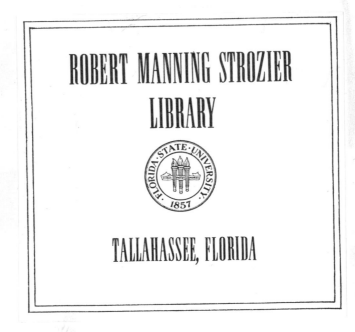

LAND TO THE WEST

GEOFFREY ASHE

Land to the West

St. Brendan's Voyage to America

THE VIKING PRESS
NEW YORK
1962

Copyright © 1962 by Geoffrey Ashe

Published in 1962 by The Viking Press, Inc.
625 Madison Avenue, New York 22, N.Y.

Library of Congress catalog card number: 62-9087
Printed in the U.S.A. by The Murray Printing Company.

To the unknown author of the

NAVIGATIO SANCTI BRENDANI

this footnote to his extraordinary masterpiece

is most respectfully dedicated

Contents

CONTENTS

List of Illustrations

Acknowledgments

My thanks are due to Mr. Joseph O'Halloran, who greatly assisted my inquiries in Ireland; to Captain Donal O'Donovan, who devoted a large part of his leave to driving me to inaccessible spots and handling negotiations with the inhabitants of County Kerry; to Messrs. Jerry O'Sullivan, John Walsh, William Crowley, and Dan O'Connell, who taught me about curraghs; and to Dr. D. A. Reidy, the Dean of Tralee, who advised me on several scholarly matters.

I also want to express gratitude to Mr. Malcolm Pearson, Mr. Norman Doucet, and others associated with North Salem, for their hospitality and helpfulness, and to Mr. Frank Glynn for his copious information on that odd place; also to Dr. Manuel O. Zariquiey of Eastman Kodak for a most unexpected hint.

Among recognised authorities on topics discussed, I would like to thank Professor R. J. C. Atkinson, Professor John Evans, Mr. T. C. Lethbridge, and Commander Alan Villiers, for the time they generously gave me; and especially Señor Joaquin Meade of Mexico City. I have tried to indicate my exact debt to them by specific statements and references. They are not to be held responsible for anything else.

I indicate in the list of illustrations my indebtedness for permission to reproduce photographs.

Finally, a note of acknowledgment to Macmillan & Co., The Society of Authors and Mrs. Cicely Binyon for kind permission to include a long extract from Laurence Binyon's translation of Dante.

In order to penetrate ever further
into their subjects, the host of
specialists narrow their field and
dig down deeper and deeper till
they can't see each other from hole
to hole. But the treasures their toil
brings to light they place on the
ground above. A different kind of
specialist should be sitting there,
the only one still missing. He
would not go down any hole, but
would stay on top and piece all the
different facts together.

Thor Heyerdahl, *Aku-Aku*
(*English edition, pages* 357-8)

ICELAND

Reykjavik

N

Clonfert

Brandon Mt. *Fenit* *Ardfert*
Tralee
Dingle

CANADA

×*North Salem*
•*New York*

U.S.A

×*Teotihuacan*

Mexico•
City
+*Mitla*
Oaxaca

VENEZUELA

COLOMBIA

BRAZIL

ECUADOR

PERU

BOLIVIA

Lima•
×*La Paz*
Tiahuanaco×

**Places visited
by the author**

Towns···•   Ruins···×

Part One

ST. BRENDAN'S VOYAGE

CHAPTER ONE

The Prospect from the Peak

OUT ON THE DINGLE PENINSULA, where there is no parish beyond till you come to Labrador, Brandon Mountain confronts the sea. It is very nearly the highest mountain in Ireland. The cape which it dominates was Lindbergh's landfall; surprised and relieved at the precision of his reckoning, he left the peak on his port side to skim in low past Dingle, the most westerly town of Europe.

My own first sight of it was a beginning rather than a conclusion, and appropriately less clear-cut. I had come there with my son Tom expressly to climb it, on an August day which ought to have been set-fair but was not. Our host, driver and interpreter, Captain Donal O'Donovan of the Irish Army, manœuvred the car as far up the hill-side road as he could, but into a zone of doubt rather than certitude, and an increasingly overcast sky. At the last field he spoke in Gaelic to the older of two peasants leaning over a gate.

" God bless the work," he said.

" We are idle," the man replied affably.

After these salutations they came to business. The peasants were unhappy about our proposed climb and disinclined to show us the path. Visibility, they remarked, was poor, and indeed one had only to look downward to see cloud-front after cloud-front sweeping in from the ocean over the coastal flats. But Tom and I had no choice; we would not be in County Kerry long enough for a second try. So they gave us directions, Captain

O'Donovan wished us luck, and we started up into the greyness on a track that soon vanished. Once a shepherd waved to us from a long way off, otherwise the world was empty, a silent slope of heather broken by streams that flowed down gullies or dived into hiding to percolate through patches of swamp.

We surmounted the lowest crest and passed on along a wide rock-strewn ridge that fell away through the fog to the right and left. The usual succession of false summits lured us on up the gentle gradient; then suddenly, with an alarming momentary grandeur, the sun burst through and disclosed the far steeper citadel that hung ahead of us and above us. That too we tackled in its turn, zigzagging among the huge grey flakes of rock that stuck up edgewise like teeth, and observing meanwhile the dynamic sky, the irregular blue, the clouds rolling in from the relentless ocean and piling up against the peak. Eventually the rocks thinned out and the going became easy again. A white cross and cairn several hundred yards in front signalled that this was truly the top. On arrival we found a ruined stone oratory and a well of brackish water. In a trench lay a tin box containing a plastic bag containing another plastic bag containing a visitors' book, which, naturally, I signed.

Brandon Mountain presides over a spacious panorama of Ireland and the adjoining Atlantic, and nothing thereabouts comes up to its shoulder except its own satellite hills. Yet its isolation is not desolation. It is not one of those mountains that die away skyward in a cone of sterility. Its heather inevitably dwindles toward the summit, yet even within sight of the crowning cairn a hum of bees is still in the air, and horned sheep go scrambling over the rocks. The people of that district used to believe that no animal could be killed on the mountain without sin. If there is a spiritual presence it is a living one that befriends and encourages. After we had seen what we could, we groped down through ever-thickening cloud, but the ridge was our guide. Without ever going astray we reached the car less than four hours after leaving it.

Presence or no presence, the mountain's name is taken from life. "Brandon" is one of several forms of the name Brendan, and the person thus honoured is an Irish abbot with a singular attached epithet, St. Brendan the Navigator, who died in the sixth century but is still an important inhabitant of Kerry. The cross and chapel at the summit are his monuments; every priest from the parish goes up there to say his first Mass; and from a creek in the nearby coast, as my guide-book informed me (cautiously, but with a less guarded endorsement from the good lady in the adjacent cottage), Brendan sailed out into the ocean and discovered America.

That belief was what I had come to Kerry to investigate. I knew it to be based on a legend, or tradition, which told how the saint undertook a quest for a land beyond the Atlantic, and how, after years of sailing and numerous adventures, he did finally beach his vessel in an immense and wonderful country an immense distance to the west. Such in substance is the famous yarn of St. Brendan's Voyage, and many have pardonably deduced an Irish discovery of America in advance of Columbus and all other commonly recognised competitors. The French historian Gaffarel accepted it in his monumental *Découverte de l'Amérique;* the eminent Celticist Gougaud was not unwilling to say " perhaps "; and an oblique approval came in the 1930's from H. G. Wells. Tentatively sympathetic among more recent writers are Charles Duff, Jean Merrien, and T. C. Lethbridge. It goes without saying that Hibernian patriotism has done what it can. Dr. G. A. Little, for instance, has offered an extraordinary and ingenious reconstruction under the title *Brendan the Navigator;* while another gentleman has actually argued that the fundamental Irish-American stock is descended, not from immigrants, but from Irishmen resident in America since the dark ages. There on the Dingle peninsula at the outset of my own inquiry, I hardly supposed that it would ever conduct me to a Celtic beehive-cell in Boston or to an ogam inscription at the Manhattan end of Brooklyn Bridge. Nor did it. But it conducted me to places equally distant, indeed more so, along a trail extending through Iceland and Mexico to the tallest heights of the Andes.

2

Whatever it may be, this Irish discovery, it is not merely a speculative whimsy of modern romantics. The medieval map-makers bear witness to a tradition of some sort by depicting "St. Brandan's Isle" in the outer reaches of the Atlantic: as map succeeds map the Isle grows larger and drifts about, appearing at last as a major land-mass far enough west to be part of the New World. Again, there is Norse testimony, which is all the more arresting because the Norse were not given to extravagant fantasy in such serious matters as navigation. It is a familiar tale how the Viking longships conveyed settlers from Norway to the British Isles and the Faeroes, from there to Iceland, from there to Greenland; and sagas describing voyages farther on, to "Markland" and to "Vinland the Good," are now generally held to be founded on fact—on the fact of an exploratory traffic, about the year 1000, between Greenland and the North American continent. In short the Norse discovered America before Columbus, even if nobody else did. But strangely enough the oldest records referring to their forays across the ocean carry a plain implication that Irishmen were ahead of them, certainly as far as Iceland, possibly as far as "Vinland" itself. Even sceptics who treat the Vinland stories as pure fiction have been driven to search for sources of inspiration in Irish books; even total rejection fails, paradoxically, to exorcise that spectre of Irish anticipation. And it seems that the notion was not incidental in Norse eyes but of some significance. A twelfth-century Arab geographer, jotting down a few scraps of information reaching him from remote Scandinavia, includes a hint at Irish colonisation beyond Iceland.

Not all of these clues point directly at St. Brendan, but to

study them in their mutual relationship is to be led back constantly to the problem of his Voyage and thus to the Navigator
himself. Or rather to the vast but faint Brocken-image of him.
He emerges, in so far as he does emerge, from a misty background,
a background of tiny unmortared buildings and inscribed stones
and crude crosses such as you can see at Kilmalkedar near the
foot of his mountain, among the red fuchsia hedges and inter-
lacing lanes. He is accounted one of the great saints of Erin,
ranking almost as high as Brigit, and not immeasurably below
Patrick. He is the patron of Kerry, and he was born about 484.
" Brendan " (which means nothing in particular) is probably the
correct form of his name, the spellings with " a " in the first
syllable being corrupt, but documents supply several other
versions with fanciful etymologies. The saint was born in or
near Tralee; most authorities say at Alltraighe Caille, i.e. Fenit,
a few miles round the north side of the bay. He had a holy
foster-mother, St. Ita, who trained him well and encouraged his
religious calling. After receiving ordination in 512 he worked
among the priests of his native region. His virtues and abilities
attracted disciples, and he founded a monastery of his own at
Ardfert, north of Tralee. But seafaring was in his blood, and
accompanied by parties of monks he went to Wales, to the
Hebrides, and . . . wherever else he did go. At some point in
his wanderings he landed in Brittany and called on Gildas, the
celebrated British abbot and historian, who, it is said, gave him
a churlish welcome and tried to humiliate him by handing him
a missal in Greek—which, however, Brendan was able to read.
About 558 he founded another monastery at Clonfert in Galway,
and at some date after 563, despite his age, he revisited the
Hebrides. His death is put as late as 577: not incredibly, since
the Christian ascetics of that early phase of monasticism, with
their strenuous habits and spare diet, did often pass the three-
score-and-ten.[1]

That is the life of Brendan the Navigator, and even that is by
no means all unquestionable. He is commemorated by various

23

legends besides that of the Voyage, and by a swarm of church dedications and place-names extending from Brittany through Cornwall and Wales as well as Ireland, to the Hebrides and beyond—names such as Brandon Hill in Bristol, St. Brandon's Haven in Perthshire, Brendan's Retreat on the Isle of Mull, Kilbrandon near Oban. But these further details prove little more than the extent of his fame. The two religious foundations, Ardfert and Clonfert, are the most solid facts. Ardfert stands on a slight rise in a low-lying stretch of country; to the west is the smooth line of Carrahane Sands where Roger Casement was put ashore. One sees medieval walls much more recent than the saint, and the stub of a tower somewhat closer to his time, and an ogam-inscribed stone contemporary with him, the only thing there that is. As for Clonfert it has a church still serving a Protestant congregation, with a carved thirteenth-century arch but nothing more ancient.

In and around Tralee, despite the scarcity of tangible traces, Brendan is very much alive. The one person I met there who explicitly disputed his American trip was the Dean, Dr. D. A. Reidy, who gave me a courteous and erudite talk inside the impressive quadrangle of bookcases in his study. Dr. Reidy spoke as a former believer converted to incredulity. The tale of the Voyage, he declared, was written much too long afterwards to possess any value—three or four hundred years—and anyhow it was too fantastic in its details to take seriously. He stressed the hazards of manuscript corruption, and assured me that the saint's alleged birth at Fenit was the result of a mistake of this type, and that inspection of the earliest document revealed Tralee itself to be the spot truly hallowed by his coming into the world. As for his having sailed any farther than the Scottish Isles . . . no, no, no. It wouldn't do.

Nevertheless I noticed in Dr. Reidy's church a striking statue, conspicuously placed, of St. Brendan in the prow of a boat. Evidently the Dean was not at great pains to divert attention from the fable; and I thought no worse of him for that.

3

Within certain limits the sceptics are manifestly right. To span the gap of centuries which divides St. Brendan from the writings directly and indirectly concerning his Voyage is a daunting task. His full authentic career may well be irrecoverable. But the next step after considering him as a person is to recognise that he cannot in any case be considered alone. Before the narratives of the Voyage itself can be usefully examined or criticised one must recreate his setting, the Ireland in which he lived and laboured, the things which he might have known and believed and done. Furthermore, since the legend developed over such a long space of time, one must see Ireland developing also, and recreate, besides Brendan's own environment, the environment in which the writers of later days applied their imagination and learning to make him a literary hero and (at the very least) interpret his story. Only thus can the configuration of the legend be charted, only thus can the proper weight be given to its different features. The prime requirement in the upshot is to determine just what question to ask. It might be the obvious question, "Did St. Brendan visit America?" But it might be a question not so obvious.

The context, then, and the legend after that.

Ancient Ireland swims hazily into history as an isle called "Ierne" by the Greeks, "Hibernia" by the Romans, and "Erin" by its inhabitants, who are classified as Celts—Goidelic or Gaelic Celts—although in fact there were several superimposed ethnic layers. The Irish discernible in the early Christian era are certainly related to the Celtic nations of Britain and Gaul. Roman authors confusingly designate them as Scots, after one of their more vociferous tribes; the migration which gave Caledonia its modern name had yet to occur.

These unmastered contemporaries of the Caesars were a

headstrong, impulsive, generous folk with intense clan loyalties. Away behind them stretched prehistoric generations now only dimly perceived through legend and archæology—generations of fair-haired invaders and dark-haired invaders, tribes crossing from Britain and tribes crossing from Spain, and, back in the Bronze Age, stalwart megalith-builders exporting gold and other metals abroad. With the Celtic predominance came the power of that hierarchy of Druids which so fascinated inquiring southerners, an international brotherhood that was strongest in Gaul but had its chief colleges in Britain. The Druids everywhere were priests and magicians with great influence in most departments of public business, and their initiates learned a medley of secret lore regarding astrology, reincarnation, and the poetic art. Druidic human sacrifice and hostility to Rome provoked the suppression of the Order in Britain, and, as a result, its enfeeblement in Ireland, but it persisted there, as indeed its doctrines did even within the Roman Empire, taught unobtrusively by isolated professors.[2]

Throughout a long phase of acquaintance at arm's length, Rome and her provincials left Ireland practically alone. Agricola, Governor of Britain under Domitian, contemplated adding it to his superior's domains, and judged that a small force would be enough for its conquest; but he dropped the idea, wisely no doubt in view of the misfortunes of later conquerors. The Menapians, a maritime trading people from Belgium, planted a depot on the east coast which Ptolemy's *Geography* calls "Manapia," and it may have been here that Carausius was born, the admiral who made himself independent ruler of Britain for a few exciting years in the third century. About the same time there seems to have been a growth of trade between Ireland and western Gaul, and a trickle of Gaulish emigrants going across as fugitives from trouble or to serve as mercenaries in the free Celtic hosts beyond the water.[3]

However, Ireland's real entry into the affairs of the nations occurred in 367, when a horde of plunderers surged over St.

George's Channel to pillage Roman Britain in concert with the Picts and Saxons. Their attack petered out, but during subsequent decades more Irishmen followed, some only to pillage, but some to settle, especially in South Wales. This process of raiding and colonisation came to a climax in the 380's when King Niall-of-the-Nine-Hostages organised pirate fleets under his own command. Niall's warriors rode in curraghs—light seaworthy boats made of skins stretched over a frame—and perhaps also in hired ships, and they carried swords and spears and round bull-hide shields and curled war-horns. About 395 they sacked several British towns including Chester and Caerleon, taking away large quantities of loot, and slaves by the hundred. The Imperial Government took measures for defence, but was too much distracted by continental disasters to make them effective, and Irish buccaneering did not slacken off permanently till Niall's death at sea in 405. Hibernia, however intimidating, was by now a known country and a country to be reckoned with, and an increased seaborne commerce with the outer world continued even through the convulsions of the Western Empire in the fifth century.[4]

Among King Niall's captives was a British Christian youth named Patricius, destined to immortality as St. Patrick. After six years' slavery on a farm he managed to escape and make his way home, but a conviction took hold of him that his vocation in life was to convert his captors, and he was at last able to go back, middle-aged, and make the attempt. Between his first unintentional trip to Ireland and his second intentional one, some small Christian groups came into being there independently of him. Legends refer to Declan and other saints in this period, while Patrick himself, in his autobiographical *Confession*, speaks of districts in Ireland " where no one had ever come to baptise or ordain clergy or confirm the people," the implication being that in other districts somebody had. The original Christians were probably followers of the British heretic Pelagius. A papal emissary went to Ireland in 431, but met with an ugly reception

27

and retired. Patrick, consecrated as bishop through the agency of the great Gallic prelate Germanus of Auxerre, set off in 432, and his familiarity with the land and the language gave him a decisive advantage. By the time of his death thirty years later he had established the See of Armagh and a flourishing ecclesiastical body, and his success in winning over a series of chieftains had brought about the conversion of their subjects, to whom he ministered with tireless courage and kindness.[5]

Patrick's labours initiated a radical change in Irish society, a transition from iron-age paganism to a Christian civilisation which, while uncouth and backward in many respects, was for some centuries easily the best that Europe west of Byzantium had to offer. It was during the transition that Brendan the Navigator lived.

Two Britons, Pelagius indirectly and Patrick directly, seem to have been the first Christians to make any impression on the Irish; and the new Ireland was, to an extent not always appreciated, a creation of Romanised Britain and thus a last unexpected master-work of the classical culture. Toward the close of Patrick's life his own country was thrown into chaos by a revolt of Anglo-Saxon mercenaries and an irruption of their barbarian kinsfolk from across the North Sea, but in the 470's something of the Roman system was reconstituted and the onrush was checked. The British Celts learned belatedly to remember their status as Imperial citizens, heirs of a cosmopolitan world, and to look outward beyond their own hills and inlets. They colonised Armorican Gaul, transforming it to "Brittany"; and a sudden florescence of the Church in Wales, chiefly due to St. Illtud, inaugurated a sudden multiplication of contact with Erin. British clerics came over to instruct the Irish; Irishmen such as Finnian went to study at British monasteries, at Llancarfan, Glastonbury, Candida Casa in Galloway; and we are told that the "second order of Irish saints" received their liturgy for the Mass from Gildas and David, Britons both. British ecclesiastical influence was made possible by British military victory. A counter-offensive against the Saxons in the first quarter of the sixth century, ascribed by tradition to the resplendent Arthur, preserved the western communities from the heathen, and very probably saved Ireland itself, which the Saxons never molested except for a single brief raid long afterwards.[6]

The island which thus absorbed a fragmentary *Romanitas* from its shielding neighbour, yet made it very much its own, was parcelled out among seven kingdoms, each of them being itself a patchwork of petty sub-kingdoms or chieftaincies. Over all were the High Kings at Tara, descendants of the arch-pirate Niall, holding a title which was not effectually disputed after 513 but remained nominal rather than actual. In the absence of towns, or focal points of any kind, there was no coherent State. Society was built up from the bottom: families were the primary units and the repositories of most of the real authority, and a bundle of families constituted a sub-kingdom. Within the loose framework men were punctiliously ranked and graded, the principal classes being three—the landowning warrior-aristocracy, the commoners, and the highly honoured *aes dana* or professional group including jurists, poets, doctors, and skilled craftsmen. Custom, codified by the jurists, regulated local law and social duties and privileges. The Irish had many purely barbarous habits which Christianity took generations to extirpate —human sacrifice, for instance, and the military service of women —but the thing to grasp is that with their barbarism they combined an unusual respect for intellect, learning and imagination.[7]

Ireland's economy was agricultural and non-monetary. Cattle were extremely important, a treasured prize of war, and values were expressed in terms of so many cows or sometimes so many "bondswomen," a bondswoman equalling four cows. Other domesticated animals were sheep, goats and of course pigs. The larger and wealthier farms were often centred on a ring-fort or circular enclosure with an earth bank and ditch, palisades, and houses inside made of wooden poles with interwoven clay-plastered wattles. In some areas where timber was scanty, such as western Kerry, ring-forts were made of stone and formidably defended. However imposing the farm dwellings might be, the householders themselves lived in abysmal squalor, with refuse piling up on the floor till it became intolerable and a fresh stratum of clay was laid down to bury it. The smell was partly drowned by the reek of a fire, which heated, besides the building, its most notable inanimate object, the family cauldron. Sheep-dogs, terriers, and little wiry cats browsed in the rubbish.[8]

But again the vital contrast—these disreputable Celts were a gifted race and lovers of beauty. They wore colourful cloaks and knee-length tunics, finely embroidered and secured with flamboyant brooches. They wrought in iron and copper and bronze, and they employed the lathe, the chisel, and other sophisticated implements. They raised pillar-stones with inscriptions in their ingenious ogam alphabet, a kind of Morse code scratched down the edge. They constructed bagpipes and harps and interesting board games. After the sixth century, under the impulse of the new religion, their genius developed fast. Freedom from invasion enabled them to take up the Celtic art of Britain and carry it further; and the simple but quietly progressing craftsmanship of previous ages exploded abruptly into superb achievement, into a multiple splendour of metalwork and book-painting and stone-carving all over the land.[9]

Nor were the Irish sedentary or physically inactive. They hunted the boar with spears, they competed in foot-races and horse-races, they played at "hurling," in those days a sort of obstacle-race in which the competitor had to drive a ball with a stick past opponents who tried to tackle him. In general there was not much reason to travel, but travel was practicable. Half a dozen types of boat had been invented, and there were inland roads, and chariots to go on them. The roads were used by the numerous royal and semi-royal personages, by members of the professional set, by roving minstrels and jugglers . . . and as time passed, increasingly by monks.[10]

That time of transition, Brendan's time, has been called the heroic age of Irish monasticism. Deeply affected by the itinerant saints of Britain, the Church shaped itself in a peculiarly Celtic manner. Though Patrick had formed dioceses on orthodox lines, his hierarchy was growing unsteady even before his death, and by 500 the bishops were subordinates and the abbots had risen to supremacy. A secular clergy still existed, but it was not noticeable, and the monks were the effective priesthood. Various reasons might be suggested: that monasticism suited Irish society, with its emphasis on the small family unit and the personal tie; that whereas bishops on the continent were acknowledged successors of a strong pagan establishment, those of Ireland lacked any such dignity; or, again, that missionary needs gave the monks a special importance, while the thinness of population consigned the settled parochial clergy to a minor role. At all events the abbots like Brendan, with their monastic " families," did rise to dominate the Church, together with scholarship, the arts, and to some extent politics, through their kinship with the chieftains. Even when reform was at length demanded, the demand was for a reformed monasticism.[11]

Irish monks in the heroic age knew nothing of Benedict and his innovations. They imitated eastern models, mainly Egyptian, having received the pattern through Gaul and especially through the famous community of Lérins on the Riviera. They differed, however, from the Egyptians in two essentials, first in their devotion to learning and education (perhaps a druidical inheritance), and secondly in their freedom from geographical fixity. While many of them stayed on the same spot tilling the soil, many others went afield widening the scope of their action. From the pioneer foundations—Clonmacnoise, Derry, Bangor on Belfast Lough, and the rest—the white-gowned abbots and their disciples, and the hermits associated with them, roamed off into extraordinary places. In 563 St. Columba left Ireland altogether and

formed the memorable Iona community. At that period the
" Scots " of Erin had colonised only a minute corner of their
future realm. Northern Caledonia was still almost wholly a
preserve of the Picts, and Columba's monks, passing over to take
the Gospel to them as well as to the handful of Scots, were the
true vanguard of the national redistribution. They penetrated
not only the Hebrides but the Lowlands, and co-operated with
British priests at work in the same region. Equally enterprising
were the clerics who ventured on to the turbulent continent.
Columbanus, having begun in his religious profession at Bangor,
sailed to Gaul about 585, founded monasteries at Luxeuil and
Fontaine in the Vosges and at Bobbio in the Apennines, de-
nounced the corruption of the Burgundian court, and corresponded with the Pope. Gall, one of his companions, founded
the Swiss abbey subsequently known by his own name. A map
of these foreign expeditions shows them extending as far as
Austria.[12]

With the new institutions came a new architecture to house
them. The first Christian buildings in Ireland were circular
enclosures like ring-forts containing a dwelling-house, an
oratory, and a kitchen. When more elaborate monasteries
evolved, they kept the round form, with a girdling bank and a
boundary ditch outside it. Within, the chief building was the
church, which was normally rectangular. If the district was not
exposed to rough weather this might be simply a cabin of planks
or wattles; and the monks lived in scattered cells of wickerwork,
with room for only one or two occupants. There would be a re-
fectory, a graveyard, a guest-house, and in the bigger monasteries
a school. Later and more advanced ages saw the addition of
libraries and finally of the well-known round towers, used for
storage and as lookout posts. Many monks of the pioneer days
had a fondness for islands, and their hardy perseverance has
presented archæology with some dramatic relics, notably off the
west coast, where climatic rigour dictated durable structure. At
Great Skellig, the skeleton of Sceilg Mhichil (fittingly dedicated

to St. Michael the Archangel) hovers above a 500-foot precipice. It consists of two little stone oratories and six beehive-cells, quadrangular at the base but curving in toward the roof. The corbelling of the cells is most adroit, each course of unmortared masonry being smaller than the course below, till a single stone tops the edifice. Walls hold in and hoard a few patches of earth. The monks must have fed on herbs, fish and sea-fowl, and they may have kept goats.[13]

One feature of these monasteries deserves a moment's further attention, because it will turn out to be important. Adapting the pagan pillars with their ogam inscriptions, the monks cultivated a taste for incised designs on stone slabs—letters, geometrical patterns, and especially crosses. As well as setting up slabs they set up whole crosses hewn out of stone, and sometimes they combined both by cutting out designs on the crosses. Their cruciform convention began very early to tend toward the *patée* shape with spreading arms, commonly though inaccurately known as Maltese, and specimens showing that evolution in different stages exist up and down Ireland and even as far away as the Shetlands. The " Maltese " cross as a Christian emblem was not then found very often except among the Irish and people under their influence; they used it more than others. But they also went further, adding a hub or a circular periphery. These developments began in the seventh century. Toward the year 700, first seemingly at Slievenamon in the south-east, soon after at Ahenny in Tipperary, ecclesiastical sculptors started carving complete ring-crosses of the peculiarly " Celtic " type with a circle linking the arms together. The reason for this design is uncertain. It has been explained as a concession to the imagery of sun-worship, surely rather belated, and as an accidental inspiration resulting from attempts to stiffen big shaky processional crosses by bracing them. Somehow at all events the Irish did hit on the ring-cross, and it became a characteristic of their religious art, frequently covered with carvings and surmounting a tall shaft similarly covered.[14]

The Shetland crosses are among the legacies of the northward drift of seagoing monks and anchorites. Columba's generation explored the Western Isles, and they and their successors got to the Orkneys in 579, to the Shetlands before 620, and (thus far at least the evidence is reliable) to the Faeroes and Iceland. Sea-pilgrimage, often leading to settlement on some wave-beaten mound of rock and soil, was a monastic custom. Many Picts of the Isles were baptised by the wanderers, yet the motive of wandering was not, as a rule, missionary: a notion of penance might be present, or a longing for a secluded haven comparable to the desert retreats of Egyptian hermits. However far from home the monks came to rest and built their cells, some restless adventurer would always be pushing on beyond in his curragh in search of an ocean solitude—or, as they called it, a " desert in the sea "—even more remote. Brendan the Navigator is not a preposterous or inexplicable figure; he fits into a well-attested historical movement. There is in fact no serious doubt that the founder of Ardfert did go to the Hebrides, wherever else he did not go.[15]

Adamnan, Columba's biographer, speaks of two holy men whose quests for an ocean solitude drew special notice. One was named Baitan. The other was Cormac, and he undertook three voyages with his followers, rounding Cape Wrath and visiting the Orkneys. On one occasion he was caught by an irresistible wind and driven headlong north under full sail for fourteen days. Then, says Adamnan, the curragh was attacked by " loathsome stinging creatures " nearly as large as frogs. Though they did not exactly fly they hurled themselves against the skin of the curragh threatening to puncture it, and clustered horribly on the oar handles. Fortunately Columba, at Iona, happened to think of Cormac and pray for his safety, and the wind veered and blew him back.

Fourteen days of fast sailing would have carried the boat into arctic regions. T. C. Lethbridge has suggested that the stinging creatures were Greenland mosquitoes swarming low over the water. The story has obviously improved in transmission, and anyhow everybody exaggerates mosquitoes. In parts of the United States, I am told, they resemble dive-bombers.

4

The Irishmen who voyaged so far, both on the Continent and into the wild north, were not illiterate fanatics but the finest scholars in western Europe. The root cause was the fact that their country had not been overrun by Teutonic barbarians. As a result, a virtual confinement of warfare to civil skirmishing had allowed the conservation of two gains. Early in the fifth century the trickle of migration from Gaul had brought over a number of professional scholars in flight from the invading Vandals, and some of them applied themselves to the education of the Irish.[16] Alone they might not have accomplished much, but a little later came the series of missionaries and teachers from Britain. Their religious zeal induced, perhaps, a certain friction with the pupils of their less ardent forerunners—St. Patrick refers to hostile " rhetoricians "—but the Irish inherited the learning at least of both groups. These men imported a classical culture in decay, but they did import it, and while most of them were certainly worse endowed than either their predecessors or their eventual successors in the mere number of their books, they were better off than we are now in the possession of what should never be underrated, a still unruptured tradition of comment and interpretation. Once planted in Ireland the Imperial heritage was never torn to shreds as it was on the continent. Through the universal Church, moreover, Ireland maintained a tenuous contact with the Byzantine East: there was that line of communication through Lérins, by which the monastic communities could obtain manuscripts from Egypt and Syria; and Irish pilgrims were still reaching the Holy Land in the darkest ages.

Schools founded early in the sixth century sent out graduates like Columbanus, who read Virgil, Horace, Ovid, Juvenal,

Prudentius and many more, and himself wrote competent Latin prose and verse. Irish monks did not know as much Greek as they knew Latin, but they were practically the only people left in the West who knew any at all. There seems to have been some study of Homer, of Aristotle, of Plato perhaps, of the Greek Fathers of the Church; and the theologian Erigena was familiar with Neo-Platonic philosophical texts. The Irish who visited the Continent as Columbanus did, assembling communities and evangelising Germans, were surprised to discover how far Europe had declined, and their part in the recovery under Charlemagne and his successors was a distinguished one. A Frankish author speaks of " Ireland emigrating almost *en masse* with her crowd of philosophers to our shores." [17]

For their literary labours the clerics of the heroic age used wax tablets in wooden frames. The National Museum in Dublin has a waxen copy of psalms dating from the time of Columba. But real books were already being made on a small scale, and the monks were already evolving a distinctive national style and script. This latter had nothing to do with ogam, which they tended to view as heathenish and a trifle suspect. On inscribed stones at such places as Kilmalkedar we can catch them at grips with the Roman alphabet. They learned, indeed, wherever they could, even adopting a method of gathering pages from the Coptic East, and in due course their perfected art created illuminated manuscripts of an astonishing beauty of design. Monumental volumes grew up, compilations of scripture and history and saga and much else—the Book of Kells, the Book of Leinster, the Book of Lismore; some of those that survive are medieval in date, but all are ultimately products of that brave feat of education in the first centuries of Christian Ireland.[18]

Armed with such equipment, the Scottish-Irish apostles of Iona spread their Celtic Christianity over an ever widening area. In 632 the Anglo-Saxon prince Oswald of Northumbria arrived in the island as a refugee from a Welsh invasion. He was converted, and when he went back to Northumbria as king, the saintly monk Aidan went there too under his aegis. Aidan was soon governing a Northumbrian Church combining Celtic and English features, and managed in Celtic fashion from an island community on Lindisfarne. Anglo-Saxon and Scottish-Irish influences entered into a fertile interplay, and the great scholar Bede united all the available learning of his time, both Celtic and continental. Similar events were going on in Wessex, where the Irishman Maelduib taught Anglo-Saxon priests like Aldhelm, and Irish monks established themselves at Glastonbury. But meanwhile direct papal authority had returned to the British Isles through the mission of Augustine and the foundation of the See of Canterbury. Between the pro-Romans and the Celts there were sharp divergences in outlook and practice, and when the former tried to assert control over the Church in Northumbria, their efforts precipitated a crisis which came to a head at the Synod of Whitby in 663. That dispute is at once enlightening and mystifying, and of a kind to raise questions about the implications of Irish religious writings generally and the alleged exploits of St. Brendan in particular.

The young Christianity of the Irish was at least as lively as that of other nations and much better informed. But it had idiosyncrasies, arising in part, it seems, from a more friendly treatment of the pagan inheritance. This was to some extent historical accident. Christians in the Mediterranean zone remembered a grim struggle with entrenched priesthoods and established theologies; these had fortified the Empire before Constantine and helped to persecute the Church, and were therefore held to be satanic. But in Patrick's time the Irish had not known such things since the decomposition of the Druidic Order. The surviving Druids were unorganised medicine-men; the surviving cults, though sometimes homicidal, were only locally effective; and there was no long tradition of anti-Christianity on the part of the old native religion, because the old religion had scarcely had to deal with Christians at all.

Naturally the Church strove to eliminate the remnants of

Irish paganism, and there are few signs of a revival. But the remnants were viewed at worst as superstition rather than devilry, and in the upshot, disinfected, they lingered on, inspiring a respectable corpus of saga and myth. The prophesyings attributed to the seers of the past were not reviled but explicitly recognised as valid. The kaleidoscopic mythical figures of the old dispensation—gods of a stature not immeasurably above humans; gods who took human shape, like the sea-ruler Manannan who gave his name to the Isle of Man; wonder-working chiefs like Cuchullain whose powers blurred the distinction of human and divine—prolonged their existence as beloved heroes or fairy-people or mysterious immortals, in an intensely topographical folk-lore. Druidical reincarnation persisted as a theme of romance, tumuli became fairy hills with strange occupants, haunting presences brooded over islands and across water generally, and the Church never objected with any vehemence.[19]

Everywhere, not only in Ireland, Christians adopted the shrines and myths of paganism and transferred them to new incumbents; but whereas on the Continent there was normally a clear-cut change and a suppression of what had gone before, among the Irish there was not—at any rate, not always. Moreover, they went beyond tolerance. Their Christianity itself had a twist to it. Pagan and unorthodox notions repeatedly glimmered on the fringe of their thoughts. The monks preserved apocryphal books which Rome disliked, such as the *Acts of Pilate*, destined to be a source of the ecclesiastically distrusted Grail legend. They anatomised the hierarchy of angels with a profusion of names and details reminiscent of the heretical Gnostics of Roman days, even giving formulae for conjuring the spirit realm. They devised acrostics and cryptograms and freakish vocabularies, likewise reminiscent of Gnosticism. Once at least the pagan strain in their hagiography overleapt acceptable bounds. St. Brigit, the namesake of a pre-Christian goddess, acquired attributes possessed by no other saint in the calendar. She was spoken of as " the Mary of the Gael " and as a female priest or

bishop in some mystical and assuredly uncanonical sense; she
was praised even more hyperbolically:—

> Brigit, mother of my high King
> Of the kingdom of Heaven, best was she born.

Elsewhere a poet calls her " the one mother of the Great King's
Son." What can these passages imply but that St. Brigit, a true
daughter of the druidical world, was the original Mary rein-
carnate? [20]

It was in the north, among the Scottish-Irish who evangelised
England, that eccentricity in the Faith seems to have gone farthest.
The clash at Whitby with Roman Christianity was in some
degree a clash of collective temperament, between the lucid
holiness and informal ways of the Celts and the legalistic, administrative outlook of the pro-Romans. But the violence with
which the latter sought to impose uniformity was symptomatic
of a more subtle cleavage. They uttered the fearful word
" heretic " with an air of conviction, yet never justified its use.
The Celtic Christians of the sixth and seventh centuries were
neither schismatic nor proto-Protestant; they accepted Roman
supremacy in principle and affirmed every essential Catholic
doctrine. What the pro-Roman spokesmen emphasised, making
it the test of obedience, was a demand for conformity on two
disciplinary points: the dating of Easter and the shape of the
tonsure. The Celtic Easter was calculated by an obsolete method,
so that it was kept on a different day from the Roman. It was
reasonable to press for agreement because of the confusion in
areas where the observances overlapped, but the language of
Roman advocates like St. Wilfred was so offensive that one
scents a symbolism in the business. So also with the tonsure.
All western monks except the Celts shaved a round patch on
top of the head, the Celts shaved a broad band from ear to ear.
This difference in itself should not have caused any difficulty at
all. Both the disputed points were probably tokens, battle-cries,
not the matters really at issue.

We do not know the truth. The Roman party prevailed at

Whitby, and perhaps its general triumph in the ensuing decades was simply a triumph of ignorance and witch-hunting, of uneasy authority elaborately smashing a mare's nest. Its leaders confronted something which they could not quite get the hang of—an atmosphere, an attitude, an irritating combination of holy anarchism with smiling hints at a deeper insight and special principles of spiritual order. Doubtless much of the Celtic eccentricity was a species of poetry rather than a species of heterodoxy, and a slight acquaintance with Gaelic folk-song will reinforce that impression. The strangeness was largely an enrichment, not a revolt. Nevertheless it was there. Irish sanctity was profound, Irish scholarship was faithful to its origins, but both took unfamiliar hues from the ancient dye of Irish imagination.

When written literature in Ireland grew up, as elsewhere, under clerical auspices, it had a predictable difference of tone. Editors and copyists in the monasteries transmitted not only the religious matter but most of the secular matter also, the Bangor and Movilla communities on Belfast Lough being active in both fields; and many manuscripts immortalise pagan oral traditions of high antiquity, which, as set down, exhibit a good deal less censorship than they might have done, and a fusion of Christianity and paganism rather than an outright conquest. Myths and poems and sagas, floating in the air from generation to generation, settled on the pens of the monks and so found permanent haven. Abroad the pagan literary heritage was passed on in the monasteries as something distinct, in Ireland it was passed on as something (so to speak) digested.[21]

The traditional corpus had hitherto been the concern of the *filid*, the professional bards. They were key functionaries in early Irish society, uniting the roles of seer, poet and scholar, and they formed a carefully stratified caste within the *aes dana* or educated élite. The plan of the High King's banquet-hall at Tara allocated seats to " first-grade poets," " second-grade poets," and so on in half a dozen degrees. It was the duty of these

ranked craftsmen to perpetuate, among much else, the family
legends and genealogies of the minor royalties whom they
served and the local lore of the districts where they lived. In the
sixth century some of the more rigid abbots demanded their
banishment, but they were spared, thanks, it is said, to St. Columba. From then onward, clerics of a more liberal sort were
tapping their memories—those astounding memories of the
pre-literate—and creating a literature marked by vivid imagination, unconventional freshness of outlook, and a sense of colour
scarcely matched except in the literature of their Celtic kindred
in Britain.[22]

To the handling of verse they brought the resources of their
own classical learning. A few scraps of purely indigenous poetry
have come down, in rough alliterative rhythm without rhyme.
The monks, however, improved on this, introducing the syllabic
metre and rhyming of late Latin verse while keeping their native
alliteration. Columbanus and others composed Latin poems of
their own, sometimes on the theme of exile suggested by their
wanderings; and vernacular verse finally found its way into the
manuscripts in a form resulting from the fertilisation of the old
by the new about the eighth century, with rhyming and fixed
numbers of syllables per line, though still a very free rhythm.
The recorded secular poems in Irish are notable for an observant
love of nature hard to detect anywhere else in Europe at that
period.[23]

From the filid came several kinds of prose literature—law
tracts, and heroic sagas, and vast cycles of ostensible history
reaching back through Roman times into the pre-Christian
centuries, sometimes supposedly recounted by sages who could
recall their past incarnations. When the monastic scholars committed these chronicles to parchment they tried to graft them on
to the scheme of general history, and to synchronise the Irish
events in parallel columns with the annals of Greece and Egypt.
Nebulous race-memories of remote migrations were worked up
into fanciful miniature Aeneids connecting the first settlement of

Ireland with people in the Bible and Greek mythology. But the original character of the cycles was not effaced.[24]

Partly from lay sources and partly from clerical there also emerged several related classes of popular story important to the literary fortunes of Brendan.

An Irish trait which has been called the desire to " penetrate the unknown and make the unseen world actual " produced a crop of adventure yarns dealing with quests in alien regions best defined as Otherworlds. These Celtic Otherworlds were variously conceived, sometimes as abodes of the dead, sometimes as homes of gods and fairy-folk. A carefree aristocratic Elysium quite like its Greek counterpart was pictured under many names, and sometimes located in the ocean: such was Tir-nan-Og. In a romance probably written by a monk of Bangor the Celtic god Bran, transformed into a more or less human hero, was made to visit a place of this kind, and his fame helped to inspire a series of voyage-romances describing tours among imaginary western islands—quests, in a sense, likewise, but with a shift of emphasis.

Besides recording and elaborating such tales, the clerics developed literary forms of their own. They wrote, for instance, apocalyptic " visions " anticipating Dante. Also, when the heroic age was left behind, the monks of later centuries compiled masses of fact and fable about their own spiritual ancestors. Some of the saints of Erin were commemorated briefly in calendars like the *Félire* of Oengus, begun about 800. Others, including of course St. Brendan, were favoured in addition with individual " Lives " of varying bulk, in Latin or Irish. A " Life " of this type usually had a biographical nucleus in the shape of a tradition handed down in the saint's community or the area where he lived, and if the author had direct access to this and worked not too enormously long after the saint's death, he might achieve a book of historical value: Adamnan's *Life of St. Columba* is a good specimen. Objective truth, however, was liable as a rule to be smothered under a heap of unlikely miracles, Christianised myths, and extraneous fantasies. Most of the Saints' Lives, though not all, are would-be edifying ecclesiastical fiction based on a few authentic names and details.[25]

But whenever the Irish monks touched literature they exposed Celtic materials to knowledge and ideas drawn from a grander world, meaning principally the classical world, both pagan and Christian. And as we shall see, the story of St. Brendan's Voyage is one of the most impressive consequences of that exposure.

5

Throughout this age of travel and erudition and civilising activity there ran a significant thread. The rare scholarship of the Irish, and to a less extent their wide journeyings, gave them fuller and sounder notions of geography than almost any of their contemporaries. In particular, some at least of them knew that the Earth was round.

During the Roman era, thanks to several centuries of debate, this had become a widely accepted proposition. The first known advocate of the globe was Pythagoras, about 530 B.C. He favoured it on religious grounds, urging the " perfection " of the spherical form, and he was imitated in this by Plato, who adopted the idea from Pythagoreans in Sicily and gave it a larger public. But authorities of a more scientific temper came afterwards bringing verification. Aristotle endorsed the round Earth, and so did the famous geographer Eratosthenes, and the Stoics.[26] In the fifth century A.D. two Latin authors, Macrobius and Martianus Capella, reasserted the theory in passing while dealing with other topics, and it was their books that more or less accidentally kept it alive, in places, through the period of decline that followed. The decline was catastrophic and the places were few. After 500 even Ptolemy, the greatest classical geographer of all, was nearly forgotten; most scholars leaned toward the opinion that the world was flat; while St. Augustine's testimony to its true shape was too curt and casual to lend the rival opinion the weight of his prestige. Nevertheless we find

Bede reaffirming the sphere in the eighth century, almost certainly because of his Celtic studies, and Bede's younger contemporary the Irishman Ferghil creating a scandal on the Continent by doing the same.[27]

Ferghil, otherwise St. Virgil of Salzburg, is a figure who compels one last preparatory pause. Born some time before 709, he became an abbot while still young, but went abroad in his thirties and stayed for a while at the Frankish court. Then he moved to Bavaria, which was under Frankish tutelage, and found himself embroiled in a feud between Duke Odilo and the English missionary St. Boniface. After some preliminary skirmishes, Ferghil's administration of the see of Salzburg, to which Odilo had appointed him about 748, led to a clash and an appeal by Boniface to Rome. The main point of complaint was Ferghil's Celtic practice of governing the Salzburg diocese from a monastery in the town; but Boniface also accused him of teaching the sphericity of the Earth and the existence of Antipodes, doctrines which the Englishman rashly pronounced heretical. While the Pope inclined toward Boniface personally, his official action in the affair was cautious. Ferghil was gently persuaded to conform in the administrative matter, but there is no evidence that he recanted or was ever pressed to recant in the geographical, and his recognition as a saint makes it likely that the charge of heresy was not seriously entertained. To the Frankish and English priests of his day he appeared as a bold thinker, but probably he was merely repeating what many of his compatriots took for granted.[28]

If the world was round, what might you discover by sailing westward? Irish story-tellers—and not only Brendan's biographers—loved to speculate on that theme. Here too they had classical antecedents, although for classical minds the question had never possessed the practical interest which it had for a nation on the brink of Europe. Aristotle had hazarded the guess that there were many islands in the Atlantic, Eratosthenes (perhaps) had discussed the possibility of reaching another continent round the far side. Occasional Greeks and Romans had even risked the final step, arguing that it was theoretically feasible to close the long curve and circumnavigate the globe. The Stoic Posidonius had maintained as much, and Seneca, the Cordovan who was Nero's tutor, declared that India could be reached from Spain in a few days by sailing westward with a fair wind.[29]

In 825 a slow geographical renaissance was set on foot by Dicuil, an Irish scholar at the Carolingian court. His treatise *De Mensura Orbis Terrarum* is mostly copied from classical sources, but it includes some unique data on the Faeroes and Iceland taken from the reports of seafaring monks. Proof that geography was a living science again during the following century, in England as well as Ireland, is supplied by an Anglo-Saxon world map which is much better than anything else that has survived from the same period. By now geographical studies were making progress also among the Arabs, and the road was being cleared for the return of knowledge that came with the Crusades.[30]

But in Ireland itself Dicuil's own lifetime brought a momentous widening of horizons in a fresh quarter. The violent expansion of the Norse peoples of Scandinavia penetrated the Atlantic; the heathen vigour which was carrying Danes to France, and Swedes down the Don to Constantinople, hammered fiercely against the British Isles. After Norwegian raids on the Irish coast, the Viking Turges landed in 832 and began a campaign of conquest that raged on into the middle of the century. It slackened at last, but then an influx of Danes near Dublin led to new disasters and the complexities of a triangular war. The Irish called the Norwegians "White Foreigners" and the Danes "Black Foreigners," perhaps because of a difference of clothing, but both kinds assailed the native inhabitants when they were not assailing each other.

Yet their inroad was not, after the inaugural onslaught, a mere orgy of plunder and enslavement. The Norse too were a gifted race, and no fundamental prejudice prevented their learning, during lulls, from the Celts among whom they had come to live . . . learning, or teaching. Their enmity to the Christian religion died away fairly rapidly. Churches continued to be looted, but about 850 we glimpse a Danish leader exhorting his men to invoke St. Patrick for help in battle, and over the generations there was a slow movement of conversion. In 873 the entire invasion halted, and the ensuing forty years' truce fostered an Irish recovery. Early collaboration and mixed marriage had already produced a hybrid crop of " Gall-Gaidhil " folk, and the truce was marked by assimilation and interaction. The Norse had been receptive to Celtic influences even before they attempted any settlement, and now their receptivity took them further, especially (and this also will prove important) into a spell of literary discipleship when their poets sat at the feet of Irish bards.

Ireland in fact was not so much subdued as drawn into the temporarily far-flung Scandinavian system, with its lines of communication extending into Russia and the Mediterranean and out into the northern ocean. Many of the Norse who went to populate Iceland were emigrants from the Irish colonies. Some were of mingled blood, some bore Celtic names such as Kormak, and some took Irish companions with them, often indeed as servants but not always. By the early tenth century these comings and goings over sea had opened the eyes of Irishmen on to almost illimitable vistas, not merely speculative as with Bishop Ferghil, but real. Fresh wars and tragedies were to follow, and a chaotic dispersal of their splendid achievement. But they had that respite of cosmopolitan vision, and it was roughly then that the tale of St. Brendan's Voyage was moulded into its definitive form.[31]

6

Back through the central Irish landscape, with its green levels and its hills apparently dropped at random, my train rolled toward Dublin. I had already realised that my undertaking was more complex, and also more challenging, than it had once looked.

When I first approached St. Brendan more than a year before that visit to Kerry, I supposed that the problem of his Voyage had been fully defined, and that my only task was to work up other writers' sketches into a finished picture. At that stage I was disposed toward the narrow and naïve view, that he did cross to America; or at any rate, toward the hardly less narrow and naïve view that the question to ask was whether he had crossed or not. Some further delving into the background, some experimentation with boats of the type he might have used, would surely equip me to say all that could be said.

However, the subject broadened out, as the facts I have reviewed in these first pages became clear to me in their proper perspective. There was the fact, which no arguing could circumvent, that the legend of Brendan in its extant literary shape was not written down till long after his death. There was the allied fact that for "interpreting" and embroidering the tradition of a voyaging saint, the Irishmen of that later period had rich resources and well-adapted habits of mind. I knew enough not to succumb to the academic fallacy that considerations like these could prove a legend to be baseless. But they did indicate a better way of stating the issue. One had to acknowledge the literary conventions in which the saint's biographers worked, and recognise that they might have overlaid the truth so thickly as to conceal it for ever, by crediting him with all sorts of feats he never accomplished. Yet a query could still remain as to how they came to imagine those feats, where they gathered the stuff of their narratives.

To ask "Did St. Brendan visit America?" is to restrict the topic much too tightly, and invite a negative or agnostic reply evading what is actually the main point. The question I eventually set myself to answer was more inclusive: "Does the story of St. Brendan's Voyage imply that Irishmen knew of America before the Norse got there from Greenland?" The Norse discovery took place about the year 1000. My attention, therefore, had to be focused on accounts of the Voyage composed earlier. If these turned out to show any such knowledge, it still might have been derived from a crossing made by Brendan himself. The romantic theory was in no sense ruled out by the framing of the question. But it might also have been derived from a crossing or crossings performed by other Irishmen, either in Brendan's time or in the next three or four centuries, or, again, from a crossing or crossings performed by people of other nationality, but reported to Irishmen. The really interesting question—whether Europe made contact with America before the Norse—depended on evidences of *knowledge*. If the Brendan legend disclosed these, then contact must somehow have occurred, an exciting lost chapter in the annals of exploration.

The mainspring of the argument which I shall try to develop is a personal story. It is the story of my efforts to unravel a problem, or at least to get it into shape and come to terms with its peculiarities. The problem raises so many heterogeneous issues, and draws in so many curious topics, that to embed it frankly in autobiography is the only honest method of handling it. To lift the argument to an impersonal plane would be presumptuous, because, as things stand at the moment, no two people would be likely to piece it out in quite the same way, not is there any strong reason why they should. All I want to do is to sketch my own tentative path toward clarification, and present the data in a more or less logical and chronological order, as objects met *en route*. If others can map out a surer path, good luck to them. They are very welcome.

CHAPTER TWO

Saint and Curragh

ON INSPECTING THE LEGEND, and surveying the growth of St. Brendan's fame as an explorer, I found certain things which I will summarise.

In the first place, since the growth was so gradual and the writing-down so late, "legend" is certainly a legitimate word, so long as it is not made to prejudge the whole business. The tale belongs to that fascinating body of literature which enwraps unknown quantities of tradition in unknown quantities of fiction, and has a way of upsetting documentary scepticism by turning out to be sounder than it looks. Greek epic poets and northern minstrels, Arthurian romancers and Vedic hymn-singers, have been vindicated so often by archæology as to create a slight presumption that Brendan's saga has a tincture of truth in it. Whether or not archæological support is here likely to be forthcoming, the presumption remains. Oral transmission being in any case customary in dark-age Ireland, and the evidence being so much in favour of a developed and conscientious artistry, the mere absence of early documents is not in itself decisively adverse. Because the tale was only set down at a certain date, it was not necessarily invented then; and experience shows that the historical lore of a rooted, pre-literate, story-telling people should not be brushed aside.

As Freeman wisely said in another connection, a legend may not be a record of facts, but the existence of the legend is itself a fact, and requires explanation. Of St. Brendan we can state with moderate confidence that he was always famous for seafaring, and not without cause; that he was known as " Brendan the Navigator " or something like it from early days; and that the romance of his Atlantic venture grew round this reputation, whether or not it corresponded at all closely to the actual achievement on which the reputation rested.

To a small extent, the process can be traced. Brendan makes his first documented appearance as a voyager in Adamnan's *Life of St. Columba*, the same book that relates Cormac's accidental discovery of the Farthest North. Born about 624, Adamnan joined the Iona community and became its ninth abbot. He was an energetic traveller and accomplished scholar. His *Life of Columba* (which cannot be later than 704, the year of his own death) is the sort of production we might expect from an author of his attainments in such an age. It is a series of anecdotes rather than a consecutive history, and it is full of marvels, but the scrupulous detail regarding people and places and the monastic profession makes it a most informative work. It includes two Brendans among the sea-roaming Irish monks— the Navigator himself, and a roughly contemporary namesake associated with Birr. In Adamnan's eyes it is Cormac rather than either of the Brendans who is the doyen of sea-pilgrims; but he does mention a Hebridean expedition which brought Brendan of Ardfert to visit Columba in Cormac's company.[1]

After this fairly trustworthy statement we get a medley of miscellaneous references, none of them very helpful. Legends of the Navigator were doubtless passed on by his spiritual descendants at Ardfert and Clonfert, and in other communities where he left his mark, but no such legend seems to have been widely spread in the generations immediately after his death. The references to major excursions by sea belong to that later period when the route to the Orkneys, Shetlands and Faeroes, and beyond them to Iceland, had come within the purview of Irish geographers, and interest in the remoter ocean was correspondingly enhanced.

Oengus's *Félire*, about 800, still does not allude to any voyages performed by St. Brendan. Its silence warrants the deduction that even in Oengus's time no such story was familiar or popular. But allusions do begin to appear soon afterwards. Ninth-century liturgical matter in the *Martyrology of Tallaght* commemorates, under 22nd March, the *egressio familiae Brendani*—that is, the going forth of Brendan's " family " or group of monks. It is palpably assumed that the reader knows where they went. Brendan is spoken of in an early work on St. Brigit as " sailing the sea " and " seeking the Land of Promise "; he is spoken of as " journeying far from home," and visiting wonderful islands, in the Lives of St. Flannan and several other saints. One beloved and recurrent feature of his adventures, a disembarkation on the back of a whale, occurs in a poem attributed to Cuimmin of Connor. Cuimmin was a contemporary of Adamnan, but the poem in its existing form is not so early; the whale passage in it may derive from the full written version, to be examined in a moment. The same is true of a litany incorrectly ascribed to Oengus, the author of the *Félire*, which contains the words: " I invoke unto my aid the sixty who accompanied St. Brendan in his quest of the Land of Promise." [2]

We find the beginnings of a connected story in the Breton *Life of St. Machutus*, i.e. St. Malo, which has Brendan in it as a prominent character. He is portrayed as living for a while at the South Welsh monastery of Llancarfan, and Malo joins him in a voyage in search of Yma, the Isle of the Blest. On the way the monks discover a giant lying in a death-like trance on another island; Malo revives and baptises him, and he wades into the sea and tows the boat, but the cable snaps. Easter is celebrated on the back of the famous whale. Owing to doubts about the manuscripts, this Breton version cannot be accurately dated, but it is supposed to have been written by a deacon named Bili between 866 and 872. The author avers that he has drawn on an older text. Since the Brendan episode must be an offshoot

51

of an already current native form of the Irishman's legend, some
sort of voyage-narrative would seem to have publicly attached
itself to him before, say, 850. The introduction of Llancarfan is
noteworthy: there is evidence that this Welsh house preserved
genuine historical information dating from as far back as the
sixth century.[3]

The probability is that a Brendan tradition long confined to
a small circle acquired new interest through the Icelandic voyages
of the monks and Vikings, and was being worked up into a sort
of saga towards the middle of the ninth century. Dicuil's geography was published in 825, a symptom, perhaps, of the same
trend. The saga was at first mainly or entirely oral, and we
cannot be positive as to what it then contained. It may have
been spectacular, it may have been meagre, it may have expressed nothing more substantial than a dim recollection that
Brendan went on long trips by boat. But let me recall our terms
of reference. Granted, we cannot follow the thread directly back
to its origin. What we can do is to look at the surviving accounts
of the alleged Voyage, and ask whether they are pure flights of
fancy, or whether they have anything in them that implies out-
of-the-way knowledge. Then, and only then, it may be worth
probing for the antecedents, in Brendan's authentic exploits or
somewhere else.

All the basic material of the developed and written Irish
legend belongs to the tenth century and to a period prior to the
Norse Vinland discoveries.[4] A Life of the saint was then compiled, and also—perhaps a few years after it—a separate account
of the Voyage, the *Navigatio Sancti Brendani*. The *Navigatio* is a
most remarkable Latin work which exists more or less intact in
its original form, together with many later editions. The *Life*
is less effective and exists in later editions only, some in Latin,
some in Irish. In all of these but one the chapters on Brendan's
voyaging are contaminated with borrowings from various
versions of the *Navigatio*, and the lone exception is heavily cut.
Hence the proper content of the *Life* narrative has to be dis-

entangled and reconstructed; but the material is full enough to make the reconstruction fairly convincing.

2

I have no wish to get heavily involved in minute comparison of these texts, partly because others have done it better than I could, but chiefly because the main point lies elsewhere. To justify treating them as historical or geographical documents, even in the most provisional way, one must make out a *prima facie* case for doing so.

The obvious arguments of the devil's advocate are that they are vague, full of mythical elements like the whale and the giant, and far removed in date from the events which they profess to report. These arguments in themselves are insufficient. They can all be used, and have all actually been used, against the Norse accounts of the Vinland voyages.[5] The sagas of Leif Ericsson and Thorfinn Karlsefni describe puzzling visits to a puzzling and indeed incredible America, several centuries back from the time of writing. While the interval is shorter and the infused fantasy less pervasive, the difference from the Brendan saga is of degree rather than kind. Yet these accounts are probably based on truth; Leif and Thorfinn probably did visit America. In medieval travel books such as " Mandeville," as in other writing including, conspicuously, the legends of saints, we have to re-concile ourselves to an uncertain separation of fact from fiction. Extravagance is the rule; so is the repetition of tenth-hand hearsay; and a tale of travel or a saint's life must never be excluded from consideration merely as being hearsay, or merely as being extravagant.

But the real adverse argument is more specific. It consists in the aforementioned fact that there are other Irish voyage-stories, the " immrama," with incidents like those in which Brendan figures. Since these are fictitious, it may be urged that the Navigator's adventures are only fictions of the same class, woven round the name of a popular saint; so that the search for fragments of historical truth or geographical knowledge is a plain blunder, contrary to the spirit of the saga.

Well, before looking at the Voyage in detail, let us look at these immrama. That the Brendan stories have some relationship with them, and belong at least partly to their broader tradition of maritime romance, there can be no doubt whatever.

They describe fabulous wanderings from island to island in the mysterious Atlantic beyond the horizon. A rough modern parallel is space-fiction of the earlier and more naïve kind inspired by Verne and Wells. Immram literature too was an outgrowth of technology: specifically, the Irish development of the curragh or skin-boat early in the Christian era. Its long phase of ascendancy, when it was used for the mass raids of Niall and the glorious ventures of the saints, left an imprint on their countrymen's imagination. To a people formerly almost circumscribed by their own horizons, it had given a new sense of possibilities, a new sense of marine mastery. Barriers had fallen: whereas the sea had imposed visible checks on the curiosity of past generations, there was now no definite limit. In consequence a voyage folk-lore grew up based on an extreme estimate of its powers.

For the elaboration of such a folk-lore the Irish were as promisingly endowed as any nation on earth. They faced the Atlantic, wondering; they watched for the weather that rolled in from its unseen solitudes; they explored the fretted coasts and complicated sub-archipelagos along the west of the British Isles; they looked out oceanward from their hills and saw other hills in the gulfs of sunset, which the prosaic might explain as clouds, but the imaginative construed as enchanted islands that came and went. Fishermen who sailed too far out, or were driven out by gales, returned to enlarge on their experiences, and hallucinations induced by hunger and thirst doubtless made those experiences all the more colourful. Sea-pilgrims like Cormac came home year after year to tell similar stories, with the added eloquence of trained preachers.

Such were the rich materials which lay to hand, and from these the immrama were fashioned, first (as usual) orally and later in writing. Much is assumed to have been lost, but several tales are preserved. Their preservation is due in part to the fact that sea romance was a mode of yarn-spinning fully in favour with ecclesiastical scribes; and indeed it is sometimes claimed that the legend of St. Brendan, especially in its *Navigatio* version, is nothing but a " Christianised immram." This is the simplest form of the literary case for total rejection. It is against the grain of Irish literary evolution, since the clerical tended to influence the secular rather than the other way round, but it needs to be examined.

Immram romance can be seen taking its characteristic shape in the *Voyage of Bran*. Bran is a figure of many manifestations. Once a Celtic god, he enters more or less humanised into British legend as well as Irish: there is a fort called Caer Bran near Land's End, and his severed head, buried on Tower Hill, is said to have protected the land against invasion till Arthur injudiciously dug it up. In a medieval poem he becomes Brons, St. Joseph of Arimathea's companion who bears the Grail to Avalon. The Irish tales know nothing of this, but they agree with the British in drawing him into a rather cryptic relationship with the Christian world. Though himself a pagan of the unfathomable past, he is favoured with prophecies of Christ.

Bran's *Voyage* is a mixture of verse and prose. It may be dated, by allusions and linguistic clues, somewhere toward the year 700, and it was probably composed at the monastery of Bangor on Belfast Lough.[7]

Bran is walking near the shore when he hears enchantingly sweet music. He sees a magic apple-bough covered with white blossom, and takes it to his hall. Thereupon a woman appears in strange raiment and sings of a realm across the sea which knows neither death nor decay, only simple human joys going on perpetually without care.

There is a distant isle,
Around which sea-horses glisten:
A fair course against the white-swelling surge ...
A delight of the eyes, a glorious range,
Is the plain on which the hosts hold games ...
Lovely land through the world's age,
On which the many blossoms drop.
An ancient tree there is with blossoms,
On which birds call to the Hours ...
Splendours of every colour glisten
Throughout the gentle-voiced plains ...
Unknown is wailing or treachery
In the familiar cultivated land,
There is nothing rough or harsh,
But sweet music striking on the ear.
Without grief, without sorrow, without death ...
The sea washes the wave against the land,
Hair of crystal drops from its mane.
Wealth, treasures of every hue,
Are in Ciuin, a beauty of freshness,
Listening to sweet music,
Drinking the best of wine.
Golden chariots in Mag Rein,
Rising with the tide to the sun,
Chariots of silver in Mag Mon,
And of bronze without blemish. ...

She goes away taking the white branch. Full of longing, Bran
launches three curraghs carrying nine men each, and they row
out westward for two days and nights. Then they meet the sea-
god Manannan riding over the waves in a chariot; he is the
guardian of this Otherworld. Manannan foretells his own future
incarnation as Mongan, an Irish chief. Bran presses on and soon
comes to the Island of Joy, and after that to the Land of Women,
where the queen escorts him ashore and keeps him for a year,
as it seems. On his leaving for home he is warned not to dis-

embark. The curragh reaches Ireland, but centuries have slipped away; one of the crew who steps on to the beach crumbles instantly to dust; Bran turns seaward again and vanishes from mortal ken.

Although this tale conveys the reader to only two islands, quite close and not very big, it is made clear that many more exist and that Bran barely touches the fringe of Atlantic geography. His charming visitant tells him of a whole New World lying beyond the outposts which he actually reaches:

> There are thrice fifty distant isles
> In the ocean to the west of us;
> Larger than Erin twice
> Is each of them, or thrice.

Bran does not explore. But Mael Duin, the second prominent immram hero, does. Mael Duin's *Voyage* is our other good piece of evidence as to the content of the earliest immram literature. Tennyson's amusing version introduced him to English readers, but with a new set of adventures; the poem does not follow the immram, which may however be found in translation in Patrick Joyce's *Old Celtic Romances*. Its composition is attributed to Aed Finn. One of the surviving texts is all prose, the other is a mixture of prose and verse.

A bandit murders a chief in sanctuary, and Mael Duin, the chief's son, returns to his country intent on vengeance. Since his enemy has fled away over sea, a Druid advises him to build a curragh and go in search. Mael Duin accordingly builds a " triple-hide " curragh of gigantic proportions, with room for sixty men. Just as he is embarking, his three foster-brothers join the crew.

They sail for nearly two days and come to a couple of islands, on one of which is the murderer. But the wind drives them off, because there are too many aboard, three in excess of the round sixty prescribed by the Druid. The consequent frustrated roaming goes on for a long time. In the course of it, Mael Duin and his companions see twenty-nine wonderful islands and a few incidental wonders between. Sometimes putting ashore, sometimes not, they visit an island swarming with huge ants; an island of terraces and bright-coloured birds; a sandy island with a monster guarding the beach; a flat island where a demonic horse-race is going on; an island with an empty palace; an island with a ridge all round it and a giant apple-tree in the centre; an island with animals that devour each other; an island with a circling wall and a monster rushing madly along it; a large beautiful island which is hot to the touch and inhabited by red-hot swine; and an island with a palace and a magical cat, which destroys one of the foster-brothers.

Then the voyagers visit an island bisected by a brass wall, with a giant shepherd who tosses sheep to and fro across it, turning them alternately black and white; an island with a mountain, a burning river, giant people and giant oxen; an island with a hellish miller who grinds up wealth improperly used; and an island of mourners, where the second foster-brother remains, weeping with the rest.

After that they visit an island of enchanted sleep, quartered by walls of metal and crystal; an island with a palace and a beautiful woman who receives them hospitably but disappears; an island of talking birds of various colours; an island occupied by an aged sea-pilgrim covered with white hair; an island of enormous blacksmiths; an island surrounded by a wall of water, where the natives pelt them with large edible nuts; an island with an arch of water above it and salmon falling out; an island standing on a pillar with a locked door in the base; a very great island with a palace, where the queen tries to detain Mael Duin by pulling him back with a magic thread; an island of intoxicant fruit; a large island with a rejuvenating lake, where a hermit says he is the last of fifteen who went on sea-pilgrimage following the example of " their master Brendan of Birr," and shows the travellers Brendan's satchel; and an island with a broad plain and people who laugh all the time, where the third foster-brother remains, laughing with the rest.

They go on to a small island of singers protected by a wall of fire; to a smaller rocky island where an old anchorite is fed by an otter; and to an island of greenery. But since the crew has now been reduced to its proper complement, the quest can be brought to a successful end. Mael Duin sights a falcon of Irish type, and sails after it south-eastward (the only mention of a direction) to another small island where he at last finds the bandit . . . . but instead of fighting it out, they make up their quarrel. With which Hibernian anti-climax the tale concludes.[8]

Attention is arrested at the twenty-fifth island by the reference to Brendan of Birr, the Navigator's namesake mentioned by Adamnan. It has been suggested that some sort of confusion between them, among readers of *Mael Duin*, prompted or accelerated the growth of voyage-romance round the greater Brendan. This conjecture is chronologically unlikely, but it is worth noting that the *Mael Duin* author seems to draw here on a monastic seafaring tradition earlier than the saga of his own protagonist. Incidentally Brendan of Birr's "satchel" is an authentic detail, strangely foreign to its delirious context. Handy leather cases, lovingly ornamented, were popular with the Irish monks for carrying their books and relics, and the National Museum in Dublin has several specimens.

Could St. Brendan's Voyage be a Christianised immram?

Those who say so are apt to give the impression that there is a large body of primitive immram matter, full of uninhibited pagan myth, with the *Life* narrative and the *Navigatio* limping along centuries afterwards as feeble monkish imitations. But the truth is almost the reverse. There are, to be precise, four surviving complete immrama. Besides the Voyages of Bran and Mael Duin, we have those of the Sons of Chorra, and Snedgus and MacRiagla. Now these tales are not " pagan " in contradistinction to " Christian "; on the contrary they are all Christian, even the first, with its prehistoric hero. Nor are they " lay " as opposed to " clerical "; Snedgus and his companion are monks of Iona, and holy anchorites living on islands are recurrent figures. The Brendan texts are more religious in emphasis, but there is no hard and fast distinction—Christianisation pure and simple is a chimera.

Moreover it is quite uncertain where priority lies. Of the four stories, *Bran* alone is indisputably earlier than the known Brendan narratives, and *Bran* only just qualifies as an immram. The stress is on the place which the hero visits, and the voyage itself is incidental and direct, with none of the wandering from island to island characteristic of the Irish voyage-romance proper. As for the others, only *Mael Duin* has any claim to be older than the accounts of St. Brendan. Its two texts are assignable to 920 or thereabouts, and have no archaic forms or scribal peculiarities suggesting a date of composition appreciably earlier. Parallels with the *Navigatio Sancti Brendani* itself have led some commentators to postulate a lost eighth-century version. But this postulate rests entirely on the question-begging assumption that where copying has occurred, the *Navigatio* author must be the one who did it. For several reasons this is very dubious, and it is hard to resist James F. Kenney's conclusion that in *Mael Duin* as we have it there has probably least been re-borrowing in the other direction. The primitive text of *Mael Duin* in fact is hypothetical; not a scrap of it actually exists, and nothing dogmatic can be affirmed about it. The *Sons of Chorra* and *Snedgus* both belong to the tenth century. While the former may embody some early matter, in its present form it draws on *Mael Duin* and on the *Navigatio* itself; and so apparently does *Snedgus*.[9]

It is therefore quite misguided to speak of St. Brendan's Voyage as cribbed from the immrama. Strictly on the manuscript evidence, it would be more plausible to say the exact opposite. Manuscript evidence is not everything; influences can be traced, themes of pagan descent are detectable, and there is no reason why the stories of Brendan should not be called religious immrama in a loose sense. But they may well give more than they receive. Typical of the interplay is the relationship between the name " Bran " and the " Brandan " spelling of the saint's name. It might be surmised that Atlantic sailing was attributed to the saint because his name happened to resemble the pagan adventurer's. But it didn't; " Brendan," beyond doubt, is the original spelling; the substitution of " a " for " e " seems to have come as a literary or even scribal piece of tinkering long after the Navigator's fame was established.[10] " Bran " means a raven, and Brendan is sometimes represented with a tame raven on his shoulder. But a development like this is something subtler than imitation, and more in keeping with Celtic Christian idiosyncrasy.

We must ask, not so much who copied whom, as what the merely literary tradition is—the mere sea-fantasy—and what, if anything, the Brendan stories contain that is special, not found in the true immrama, and indicative of additional sources of a more factual kind.

Behind all immrama, written and oral, was clearly that ancient dream of an Otherworld Quest. It was not peculiar to Irish mythology, but the Irish imagination with its interpenetrating planes of reality, its persistent striving to localise and actualise the unseen, pursued the vision of an attainable fairyland with a special ardour. The aristocratic Elysium, where favoured heroes feasted and sang with the immortals, was placed variously here and there, and divided and reduplicated. But it was identified in particular with a marvellous western island, or with a group of such islands: Tir-nan-Og and Tir-nam-Beo, Mag Mon and Mag Mell, where the climate was for ever warm and the soul for ever untroubled. Long before the *Voyage of Bran* was written, Celtic myths must have been telling of men who had to seek out some Otherworldly place, under a hill or across water, for some such purpose as obtaining a cure or fetching a treasure.[11] For these missions the potentialities of the Atlantic Island motif were especially alluring, and it was through the use of it that story-tellers drew the whole medley of oceanic themes into their repertoire: speculations about the range of the curragh and the secret regions of the west, phantasmal sunset visions, lore concerning the old gods, yarns spun by fanciful fishermen, reminiscences of the sea-roving monks and island-hermits. Immram literature resulted from the importation of all these things (the Ocean-Mythos, as it were) into the Otherworld Quest. But a shift of interest ensued; the Otherworldly goal itself faded into a problematical haze, and adventure by sea became a subject in its own right.[12]

We can thus trace at least a part of the literary process leading toward the epic of Brendan. Out of the clouds of daydream and folk-lore there is precipitated first, as one variation on the Otherworld theme, the story of a man who is summoned to an Otherworld across the Atlantic. This is the transitional *Voyage of Bran*. Bran's actual passage to the Otherworld is glossed over briefly, but he is described as hearing of many more islands, and this hint proves irresistible. A composite body of romance grows up in which the wanderings of voyagers through a western archipelago provide the main interest. Such is *Mael Duin*, a fully-fledged immram. Islands, and adventures among them, can obviously be multiplied without limit, and it may be granted at once that some of the fancies resulting from this multiplication will be found woven into accounts of St. Brendan's voyaging.

But let us note carefully what the pure immram picture is. It is a picture of Irishmen in curraghs paddling out to an archipelago that is not so very far beyond the horizon. Bran takes about two days to reach the first island, Mael Duin likewise. The archipelago in fact is simply an interminable extension of the British Isles. In the farther west there are rumoured to be land-masses comparable to Britain itself, but they are still regarded as islands with the sea stretching on past them; the tales give no hint of another continent, no hint of an opposite shore or a bound to exploration. Instead, a kind of Polynesia spreads away into the indefinite distance. Here Mael Duin beats aimlessly to and fro without compass-bearings, seeing preposterous things. He never demonstrably takes more than a week getting from one island to another. Even this might correspond to a fair space traversed—Scotland to Iceland, for example—but one suspects that he has simply missed the intermediate islands. There is never the feeling of a large expanse of water. The sea where this archipelago lies is only a medium of communication, a land-lubber's sea with no character of its own. Hardly anything is said about wind or weather, tide or current, sea-birds or aquatic life.

3

Now at last we are ready to begin anatomising the exploits of Brendan.

The *Machutus* narrative with the whale and the giant is the oldest extant, but as a mere by-product of the Irish legend it is not much use. Next to require examination is the *Life of St. Brendan*. Since this reaches us only in corrupt versions, overlaid with luxuriant fancy and broken up by copyings from the *Navigatio*, it may not seem to be worth studying either. But I·think it is: it has a crucial conception embedded in it.

As first written, the *Life* apparently told how St. Brendan prayed for a retreat in the ocean, went out in quest of it with a party of monks, failed to find the haven he longed for, tried again with sixty companions and did find it, but was then told by a heavenly messenger to go back to his divinely allotted tasks in Ireland.[13] The " retreat " sounds like the " solitude " which Adamnan portrays Cormac and others as seeking. In the *Navigatio* and its literary offspring the place becomes the " Land Promised to the Saints " and is sometimes identified with the Earthly Paradise; also the chronology of the voyaging is, or looks, different. The version of the *Life* which I shall take up here is in the Book of Lismore and was compiled during th twelfth century.[14] I choose it partly because it is accessible, partly because it is less inflated than some of the other versions with intrusive *Navigatio* scenes. Despite all the colourful embellishments of two hundred years, a good deal of the fundamental *Life* account is still discernible in it.

Brendan's seafaring fills about two-thirds of its text, constituting the last and longest episode. After his foundation of Ardfert, an angel comes to him in the night and tells him that God has granted him to visit a promised land which is clearly conceived as a retreat—a kindlier, happier retreat than the inhospitable rocks of Ireland and Scotland. Climbing up to the top of Brandon Mountain, he looks westward, and with miraculously strengthened eyes he glimpses the land across the ocean. Then he calls his monks together. They build three great curraghs equipped with sails and oars, each capable of carrying thirty, and set off into the perilous Atlantic, " over the loud-voiced waves of the rough-crested sea, and over the billows of the greenish tide, and over the abysses of the wonderful, terrible, relentless ocean," seeing " the red-mouthed monsters of the sea and many great sea-whales." Months accumulate into years as they pass from island to island. Every Easter their own special whale joins them and they go ashore on his back to celebrate Mass. He is not their only companion, since from time to time they are beset by the Devil, who tries to scare them with a vision of hell, and nearly tricks them into drinking poisonous water which flows from a rock. They also encounter the floating corpse of a gigantic mermaid.[15] There are few details, however, about the islands themselves. The one spoken of at most length is explicitly stated to be inaccessible. It is a beautiful place where the monks hear voices singing, but they sail round it for twelve days without finding anywhere to land.

After five unsuccessful years (the text is contradictory here, but five must be the correct number) Brendan returns. Ita, his foster-mother, urges that the curragh is the wrong craft for his quest, for he will never reach the sanctified country, where no blood is shed, in a boat made of slaughtered skins. He moves accordingly to Connaught and builds a large wooden ship. The chosen sixty embark, with a smith and a clown.

Brendan and his men take their ship over to Aran and strike out westward on the second instalment of the Voyage. Land at last is sighted, a lofty island where they are menaced by carnivorous beasts called sea-cats. The clown gives himself up to these creatures to save the rest of the crew, and through his self-sacrifice they escape. A second tragedy follows the first, since the smith also dies and they bury him at sea. Next they put in at a tiny islet inhabited by black pygmy demons, where they hover off shore for seven days and then go on, losing the anchor; one of the priests makes another. A further sail westward brings them to a small, delightful island with a solitary old man on it, who warns them against an exceptionally terrible sea-cat. Soon the monster comes swimming after them, its huge eyes and tusks rearing above the waves. Brendan prays, and a whale appears and fights the sea-cat till both sink together and are not seen again.

The monks go back to the island of the hermit, who explains that he is the sole survivor of twelve Irish pilgrims. He tells them the way to the promised land, and forthwith dies. They sail on uneventfully to their goal, the place which they have been seeking, in all, for seven years. It is " odorous, flower-smooth, blessed." Another venerable man advances to greet them, a dazzling apparition with a brilliant covering of white feathers. . . . But here the narrative breaks off, oddly anticipating Poe's *Arthur Gordon Pym*. Nothing is said about the homecoming. The concluding passage is a transcript from an Irish apocalyptic "vision": it has been suggested that this came after the *Life* in the previous manuscript with some pages missing, and the copyist failed to notice the gap, ploughing his way happily on into the next item.

What we have here is in essence a Saint's Life of the usual type, with sea-marvels replacing land-marvels because of Brendan's fame as a seafarer. It is thus that the immram elements must have infiltrated his legend, not originally in the Lismore text of the *Life* but in an earlier lost version. That is the view which the Dean of Tralee put to me, and I am sure he is right.

Very little of the story makes sense. It is almost as extravagant as *Mael Duin* and less engaging. As for geography, it has a shade more direction to it, and probably (as we shall see) a few echoes of travellers' tales founded on fact, but on the whole we get only the feeling of a long struggle westward over unspecified distances. Yet even this concoction has a touch that lifts it out of the immram world, the world of mere marine fantasy generated by the curragh. This touch, which is a part of the basic tenth-century material, is the change of boats. Brendan has a definite goal (the Quest-motif has reasserted itself in Christian guise), and he is driven by prolonged failure to give up the curragh as inadequate and try again in a big ocean-going vessel. True, the reason mentioned is of a magical type, but the change does take place. The immram literature offers no precedent or parallel. Furthermore, a difference of treatment matches the difference of plot. Everything is made more spacious, and the daunting wilderness of water impresses itself on the reader as it does on the saint. *Bran*, by contrast, emphasises the Otherworld, *Mael Duin* emphasises the islands. Their authors say nothing appreciable about the ocean itself or its animal inhabitants, but employ it simply as a setting for marvels. The writer or re-writer of the *Life of St. Brendan*, whatever his ignorance, is aware of the ocean as a phenomenon of nature; he tries to convey the awe of it; he introduces creatures that swim in it; he sees his islands as points on the map of it, even though he knows little or nothing of its configuration.

Hence, while the immram elements are admittedly there, they are not all. Somewhere in the background, at however many removes, is a realisation of maritime fact and an insistent murmur of the actual Atlantic. Somewhere behind the mist and spray loom the figures of real voyagers reporting real experiences. That authenticity comes surging, no longer muted, into the far greater *Navigatio*, to which we must soon turn, and which confirms at a glance the divergence between the Brendan tradition and the immram tradition. Brendan's ocean is always huge, always formidable. It is a ship-ocean rather than a curragh-ocean, even though he tries a curragh, and it has characteristics of its own. The same spaciousness, and the same sense of a map and a describable sea, persist. One edition of the legend sends the Navigator on his quest as a penance for doubting a geographical text-book.[16] Mael Duin, I think, would never have read a geographical text-book.

But a word more before the *Navigatio*. What about those boats? What precisely is supposed to be happening? The craft employed have as much right as the documents to a proper scrutiny.

4

As to the curragh, the immram vehicle, a fair amount is known. Skin-boat techniques probably originated in Central Asia and spread in two directions, attaining fullest perfection at the termini. Mongol tribes took them to the Eskimo, who devised the umiak. Indian and Iraqi boatmen learned to make coracles, and the methods were perhaps familiar in principle to the Celtic migrants who conquered Britain in the last centuries before Christ. The difficulty of pushing through British forests, however, gave these Celts a special inducement to go further and invent an improved coracle for coasting. They experimented with round tubs made of hides stitched together and stretched over wicker frames, but while these were suitable for ferry service on rivers, they were unsafe and unmanageable at sea. The next stage was the development of an elongated and tapered vessel, more toughly constructed. This may have been undertaken by the time of Caesar's invasion, since he mentions British skin-boats with ribs and keels of light timber. It was in Ireland, however, and somewhat later, that the skin-boat evolved into the finished curragh, and the reason was the same as the Eskimo reason—bleakness, and consequent scarcity of trees.[17]

In the third century A.D. British boats of ox-hide were getting over the Irish Sea quite regularly—though during the crossing, according to a Roman historian, the passengers " abstained from food." But the Irish retort was far more spectacular. The fleets which bore the raiders and settlers to Wales soon afterwards, under such leaders as King Niall, were predominantly curragh fleets, and Columba and his friends explored the Hebrides in the same versatile craft. The Irish curraghs were not simply glorified coracles. They took hints also from ordinary small boats made of planks, but wood was replaced by ox-hide. One hide could cover an area of frame about six feet by four, and many could be stitched together. It does not appear that the curragh normally needed a covering more than a single layer thick: the term " triple-hide" applied to Mael Duin's is thought to refer to multiplicity rather than superimposition. The curraghs of the ßeroic age varied in size, but the largest were very far from being mere cockles. Mael Duin's crew of sixty is exaggerated, but Columba's craft held thirteen, and there is a fairly plausible allusion to a twenty-five-seater.[18]

With their light wooden skeletons and greased waterproof skins these curraghs were capable, if well handled, of lying low in the water and weathering storms that would have overwhelmed anything of a more ambitious build. Some, though probably not all, had keels and rudders. They were driven by oars. However, the frame could support a mast stepped amidships, and Cormac was under sail when he was blown to the arctic. The sails were square and best fitted for running before the wind, but if we accept the experienced dictum of Commander Villiers we must suppose that sailing to windward might have been feasible; a square sail, he says, can always be adapted to that purpose if it is not hampered by fixed standing rigging holding the mast up. The important question of possible range remains undetermined. T. C. Lethbridge estimates that a big curragh starting from

Scotland could have reached Iceland in six days and Greenland in fourteen. But to go all the way to America, and then get back again, would certainly have required a great deal of luck.[19]

After the eighth century the prevalence of wooden ships, due to the Norse, consigned the curraghs of Erin to coasting and fishing activities in the west. But small ones are still being made to-day, the best of them in Brendan's own Kerry. They are put together bottom up. The gunwale is constructed first, with holes bored in it at intervals. U-shaped rib frames are arched over it; these have tapered ends which are inserted into the holes. Fore-and-aft stringers are attached to the outer sides of the frames, sometimes by nailing but sometimes by the older method of lashing. The ends of the principal stringers are also tapered and pushed into the appropriate gunwale holes. There is no keel. The frame is covered nowadays with cloth such as calico in one or two layers, saturated with tar. In Connemara the stringers are planks and the curragh approximates to a conventional boat. Oars are always used, pivoted on pins so that they cannot be feathered, and sails are used as well in Aran and in the Dingle district.[20]

My own direct acquaintance with curraghs is derived from a vivid hour or two on Tralee Bay. Captain O'Donovan drove me round to Fenit, St. Brendan's alleged birthplace, and introduced me to a friend of his, Jerry O'Sullivan, who was prepared to ask his fishermen neighbours to risk taking me out as a passenger. The appointed curragh was on the beach, resting on a couple of trestles with its black hull skyward, and stones attached to it by ropes to anchor it down. The rowers—John Walsh, William Crowley and Dan O'Connell, who for some reason kept calling me "professor"—placed the oars on the shingle like rollers and lifted the curragh down to slide it over them. These oars had no blades; they were simply poles with flattened ends. The object, they explained, was to reduce sheering. In such a light boat, without a keel, a stronger heave on one side than the other would swing you round, and broad oar-blades would magnify the unbalance. I saw what they meant when John Walsh stepped into the curragh alone and rowed her to the landing-stage. With a single occupant she bobbed and skidded comically, both ends curving up high out of the water. But when we were all aboard (the three fishermen, myself in the stern, young Tom squeezed into the bows) she settled down and became comparatively steady.

It was a splendid summer evening of blue and gold, with a breeze that made the sea choppy but not rough. Each rower sculled with a pair of oars. At first they did not move like a crew, but erratically and out of step, with a lot of laughter; the curragh weaved exhilaratingly to and fro. Later their co-ordination improved. The quickest tempo they reached, thirty-five strokes per minute, looked to me like a spurt. Mr. O'Sullivan, however, assured me afterwards that a team habitually rowing together could keep it up, and racers could manage forty-eight.

We rounded Samphire Island with its trim automatic lighthouse, and plunged back toward Fenit. Despite much spray and splashing and general bouncing about, the curragh shipped virtually no water. John Walsh gave me a fishing-line to troll with. They brought her in finally in the cool twilight, these generous and courteous men, pointing out the need to be careful not to hole the boat on the shingle getting ashore.

Everybody forgathered, of course, in the pub. I asked Dan O'Connell what would happen in rough weather.

" She'd ride the waves like a cork," he said cheerfully.

" How much water would she ship? "

" She shouldn't ship any. You turn her into the wind. Now if you were to *drive* her into the wind, that would be bad. But you take it easy."

" Could you cross the Atlantic in a curragh? "

" No," said Jerry O'Sullivan. " But in a big one you could go a long way."

Somebody produced a model and the discussion grew more

complicated, while the night grew darker outside and the usual snowballing group of Irish grew larger, talking, talking, talking. . . .

But enough; a line must be drawn somewhere.

While the curraghs of Brendan's period are fairly well documented, a search for that wooden ship of his yields less satisfactory results. Law-codes refer to sea-going "longships" and coastal vessels. The most valuable author is once again Adamnan, who, in the *Life of St. Columba*, mentions several types of boat besides the *curuca* or curragh. They include the *cymba* or skiff; the *alnus*, *caupallus* and *navicula* for river duty; the *navis oneraria* or freight-ship, in which the monks transported cargoes of twigs for their wattle-work; the *barca*, which could go on the sea; and *naves longae* or "long boats of hewn pine and oak." Some of these would seem to have been clinker-built. Few or none were of any bulk; many could apparently be hauled over land without much trouble.[21]

Brendan's ship is not to be found in that list, not convincingly anyhow, and the fact that Irish large-scale nautical terminology is mainly of Norse derivation implies that shipbuilding above the level implied by Adamnan was at least not a widespread practice before the Norse invasion. Attempts have been made to conjecture what a sixth-century Irish ship, if it existed, would have looked like. Broadly speaking it would probably have resembled the standard Roman merchantman, and, as such, would have been efficient and seaworthy. Roman sailors mistrusted the ocean with its towering tides and illimitable expanses, but they were as well equipped to master it if necessary as the Carthaginians and Greeks before them. The Roman merchant ship was rounded, high fore and aft, carvel-built, square-rigged. On the bows it had a small slanting mast called an artemon, where a sail could be hoisted to swing the ship through an angle. Its pattern recurs with variants in the Portuguese caravels of the age of discovery, in seventeenth-century Dutch craft, in modern

English West Country schooners and fishing-boats. There is unfortunately no proof, however, that Brendan's contemporaries possessed anything of the kind. Noah's Ark is portrayed thus in Irish sculpture, but the artists may have copied from pictures, not originals. Hence a note of interrogation.[22]

At all events, the nature of the boats themselves is the major practical question. Provisioning and navigation are secondary. The *Life of St. Brendan* mentions herbs and seeds as food; Mael Duin eats fish, both fresh and salted; Adamnan talks of a leather milk-bag. Drinking water would have been a more formidable problem than food, but not an insoluble problem for any real voyage credible on other grounds, though the months at sea in the legend as it stands are clearly fictitious. The monks had no compasses, but the tremendous odysseys of the Polynesians are sufficient warning against a low estimate of pre-compass navigation. Steering by the stars had been customary for thousands of years, as Homer shows, and much was known about the behaviour of wind and swell. Observation of migratory birds (such as ducks and geese on their way to Iceland and Greenland) would have furnished assurances that a sail in the same direction was not a leap into vacancy.[23]

So if we ask what Brendan or other Irish seafarers might have done, or what the Irish might have learnt by their own expeditions as distinct from their reading, considerations like these give no certain answer. There are limits and probabilities, but their exact statement is by no means easy; and the memory of the Kon-Tiki voyage is a powerful check to *a priori* denial.

CHAPTER THREE

Paradise Found

So WE COME to the *Navigatio Sancti Brendani* as the single real exhibit, on which the case for an Irish knowledge of America must depend. To describe the *Navigatio* thus is not to dismiss the *Life* in its various editions, or the Norse allusions and medieval maps. But if nothing can be gleaned from the one chronicle of the great quest that descends to us unadulterated by time, such minor clues are best shelved. It is only in terms of a reconstruction based on the *Navigatio* that they can acquire any weight.

This Latin narrative was written, almost certainly in Ireland, by an anonymous but highly talented Irishman.[1] It exists in a mid-tenth-century manuscript which has errors proving it to be a copy, not the original. A date of composition as far back as 900–20 would be perfectly in keeping. In other words the *Navigatio* may be earlier than *Mael Duin*, and (what matters more) it indubitably is earlier than the Norse voyages to Vinland. Therefore, if its author shows knowledge of America, that knowledge cannot be drawn from any discovery at present recognised by historians; and the Kerry cottagers are, in a sense, right, though they may not be right in giving the credit to their saint personally.

The *Navigatio* makes no pretence of being a " Life." It deals with nothing but the Voyage. Indeed it soon drifts entirely out of contact with the accepted career of the real abbot, and its complex mixture of European and eastern lore, which makes it an Irish counterpart of the *Odyssey*, accords with the picture of its

author as a poetic contriver rather than a biographer. Yet the
main issue which it raises is not affected: even if we must finally
decide that it is nothing but a mosaic of fables with a totally un-
historical Brendan as hero, we may still ask in all seriousness what
the author did know and how he knew it. We shall be encouraged to do so by a trait which shows him to advantage beside
some other Irish authors, his relative sobriety. The *Navigatio*
is a fanciful work, but there is nothing in it like the feverish
imagery of *Mael Duin*—colossal ants, demon horse-races, blaz-
ing rivers, regions of perpetual hysteria. Commentators
unwilling to accept sweeping claims for its geography have
conceded the authenticity of atmosphere, the haunting evocation of oceanic vastness and mystery, which set it apart from
the immrama.[2]

2

Here then is a summary of the *Navigatio Sancti Brendani*. The
section references are to the translation by Denis O'Donoghue
in his *Brendaniana*, pages 111–175. The line references are to
Schröder's edition of another Latin text in his *Sanct Brandan*,
pages 3 to 36; the first figure indicates the page, the second the
line on it—thus "9:12" means "page 9, line 12." I have
also used a third text published by Jubinal, and consulted the
oldest manuscript, which is in the British Museum. Where
discrepancies make a real difference I have sometimes noted it,
sometimes simply avoided emphasising one possible version at
the expense of the other. Nothing of importance, I think, is
based on a controversial reading, except for one passage which
is discussed in a note.

Sections I–II, *lines* 3:1 - 6:34
Barinthus, a monk of King Niall's race, came one day to visit
Brendan at Ardfert. In course of conversation he recalled a
journey to an island-monastery where his disciple Mernoc lived

as a hermit. Mernoc, he said, invited him on that occasion to sail west to the Land Promised to the Saints, " which God will grant to those who succeed us in the latter days." Entering a boat, they skimmed preternaturally across the ocean in a single hour, through thick darkness. The Land of Promise proved to be a vast island which they explored for fifteen days without reaching the farther shore. On the bank of a river that flowed from west to east[3] an angel appeared and told them that they had crossed half the island but must go no farther. They were treading the soil of the Earthly Paradise where Man, unfallen, would have dwelt. And so they came back again.

Such was the tale related by Barinthus at Ardfert. On hearing it, Brendan resolved to undertake the voyage himself. He chose fourteen monks to accompany him. They pitched camp on Brandon Mountain, and in a creek at the foot, using iron tools, they built a curragh with wicker sides and ribs, covering it with cow-hide " tanned in oak-bark " and tarring the joints. They put aboard provisions for forty days, with butter to dress the hides, and equipment for the voyage. At the last moment three more monks begged to join them, and Brendan accepted these late recruits.

II (*cont.*)–III, 6:35 – 9:12

Brendan set sail about the time of the summer solstice. The wind was favourable, and for twelve days [4] his boat drove across the Atlantic toward the Promised Land. Then, however, a calm descended and the sail dropped. After a few hours of rowing another wind sprang up, but by now the monks had lost their bearings. They ran on before the new wind, doubtful where they were going.

When they had been at sea forty days they sighted a steep rocky island to the north, with rivulets hurrying down cliffs that forbade access. They sailed round it and discovered a cove, where, three days after the original landfall, they managed to disembark. At first there were no signs of inhabitants, but by following a dog they came to a large building where they sheltered and rested for three days more. Harness and table utensils had been left by the vanished owners, and one of the three latecomers yielded to diabolic temptation and pocketed a fine silver bridle-bit; detected and exorcised by Brendan, he died penitent. As the monks were re-entering their boat, an islander approached and offered them food, which they accepted.

III (*cont.*)–V, 9:12 – 14:16

They now sailed " in divers directions " and arrived at another island. Its most obvious fauna were pure-white sheep of extraordinary size; the streams had plenty of fish in them. Brendan and his party spent winter here. In Easter week a man brought them bread and other food, and told them that the sheep grew so huge because they were never milked and had abundant temperate pasture.

(As to this person's identity, we are not clearly informed. But Brendan refers to him afterwards as " our good Procurator " —a procurator was the official agent of a religious house, a sort of bursar—and he is manifestly versed in the secrets of the ocean, since he acts as a guide. Hermit or angel, he is the principal character after Brendan himself, and the fact that his home is on the Island of Sheep needs to be borne in mind.)

On Easter Sunday the Irishmen put to sea to visit an islet in the neighbourhood, a bare scrap without sand or grass. To judge from the sequel it lay eastward from the Island of Sheep. They lit a fire to cook breakfast, but as the cauldron boiled the ground stirred underfoot, and they scarcely had time to scramble back into the boat when the whole islet slowly veered off and downward; though even when the distance had widened to two miles they could still see a remnant of their fire burning above water. Brendan explained that the deceptive islet was actually a whale—*the* whale, of course—and that its name was Jasconius.

After this misadventure they turned back toward the Island of Sheep and sailed along the coast for three days. Rounding its extremity (apparently the southern extremity) they sighted another island across a narrow sound to the west. It was grassy, wooded, and full of flowers. They put in on the south side where a stream flowed into the sea, and Brendan sat in the boat while his brethren towed her up between banks which were just wide enough for her passage. The stream rose a mile up country in a pool fed by a spring. Close by was a tree, low but with wide-spreading branches, and there were numerous white birds: this island, in fact, was called the Paradise of Birds. One of them spoke and told Brendan that they were spirits in disguise —intermediate spirits neither angel nor devil, involved in Lucifer's fall but not lost—and that they flew abroad and saluted God on holy days. The talking bird reminded Brendan that he had now been away about a year, and prophesied six years more of voyaging.

The monks remained on the island till Pentecost, with the song of the birds perpetually in their ears. Eight days afterwards (that is, probably, in June) they drew water from the spring and embarked. The talking bird predicted that they would come back.

VI–VII, 14:17 – 19:25

Then for three full months they " tossed to and fro," fasting on alternate days to eke out their provisions, and seeing nothing but sea and sky. At last another island broke the horizon. Driven off by the wind, they hovered in the surrounding ocean for forty days, getting ashore eventually in a tiny creek with room for only a single boat. They found two springs, one foul, the other limpid. An ancient white-haired man came to greet them and led them to a monastery, where they ate white bread with a community of twenty-four. These monks were also Irish, and this was the Island of St. Ailbe, their first abbot. They had lived here for eighty years since the days of Ailbe and St. Patrick, whom they called their patriarchs, and they were supernaturally fed and preserved in health. Normally they observed a vow of silence. Brendan admired their square chapel and its crystal altar-furniture, and kept Christmas on the island.

Leaving in the octave of Epiphany, early January, the voyagers drifted without oar or sail till the beginning of Lent. The next island was rich in vegetation, and once more they found a stream fed by a spring. But here the water was unsafe; several of the crew who drank too deeply were stupefied.

They sailed on, northward for three days into a calm, where the sea was like a " thick curdled mass." Again they drifted, for twenty days this time. Then Brendan hoisted the sail again in a wind which carried the boat east, aided by the sweeps, for several days more. A seeming cloud on the horizon ahead took form and substance, and revealed itself to be land. It was the Island of Sheep. They had traced an immense triangle and returned to the apex.

VII (cont.), 19:26 – 21:17

Lent was now nearly ended. The Procurator made Brendan welcome, and told him, immediately after Easter Sunday, to cross the western sound to the Paradise of Birds and stay there till the octave of Pentecost. First, however, the monks went to another island and recovered their cauldron, which had drifted ashore from the whale's back. Then they passed on to the Paradise of Birds as directed, and next Sunday the Procurator brought them food. The speaking bird declared that throughout his voyaging Brendan must continue to revisit the same points. He must keep Maundy Thursday on the Island of Sheep, Easter Sunday on the back of the whale (who would in future present himself for the purpose), Pentecost in the Paradise of Birds, and Christmas on St. Ailbe's Isle. This plan would mean, in effect, spending the late spring of each year in the island group where the Procurator lived, and the close of it with the distant ocean-community.

Again Brendan set sail, and now he went westward.[5] For forty days the boat held to her course. Then the monks were frightened to see a whale in pursuit, not the harmless Jasconius, but a predatory foam-spouting monster. Brendan prayed; the boat plunged about in waves that threatened to overwhelm her; the whale showed no signs of being shaken off; when suddenly another monster came rushing in from the west, head-on against the whale, which it killed after a terrible battle.

The danger was over. Next day the Irishmen put in at a large island with a spring on the south side. The whale's carcass had drifted ashore, and they cut off pieces to provision the boat, but were prevented from leaving by the weather. Storms, rain and hail persisted for three months. At length it became possible to put to sea, and laying in a supply of herbs and roots, together with drinking water, they sailed away to the north.

IX (*cont.*), 23:10 – 26:5

" One day " they saw an island far off. Brendan, either inspired or previously informed, explained to his companions that it had three classes of inhabitants, namely boys, young men, and elders, and he prophesied that one of the two surviving latecomers would end his pilgrimage here.

They approached. " The island was remarkably flat, almost level with the sea, without a tree or anything that waved in the wind; but it was of wide extent, and covered over with white and purple flowers." Three choirs drawn from the three classes of inhabitants were chanting hymns, the boys in white, the young men in violet, the elders in purple. Brendan went ashore, and two members of the second choir gave him a basket of purple fruit cryptically called *scaltae*, saying that this place was known as the " island of strong men." When the voyagers departed they left the second latecomer behind, by his own wish.

The *scaltae* were enormous, each one yielding a pound of juice.

Nevertheless, Brendan rationed it carefully. After twelve days at sea the monks ran short, and fasted for three further days. Then a bird of magnificent plumage flew to the boat with a bough of an unknown tree bearing a cluster of grapes, very red and as big as apples. For four days they ate these; for three days they fasted again; and then they reached an island. It was covered with the grape-trees, growing extraordinarily close together. There were no other trees, and no trees without fruit, in the whole island. Brendan went off exploring and noticed the wonderful fragrance of the air, like a house stored with pomegranates. At a place where six natural fountains welled up, and the vegetation was various and the herbage an intense green, they pitched camp and lingered for forty days. Putting out again laden with fruit, they were threatened by a gryphon, but in response to Brendan's prayers another bird assailed it and tore its eyes out.

IX (*cont.*), 26:6 – 26:12
They returned to St. Ailbe's Isle for Christmas (nothing is said here to specify distance or direction) and then " sailed about the ocean for a long time," calling at the prescribed places on the prescribed dates.

X, 26:13 – 27:2
" On a certain occasion," when Brendan was celebrating the feast of St. Peter at sea, the monks noticed that the water was marvellously clear. They could gaze down to the bottom and watch the great fishes moving like flocks of sheep. Brendan sang his Mass louder, and the fish rose from the depths and circled round him. Under full sail with a fair wind, the boat slid on for eight days over the pellucid ocean.

X (*cont.*)–XI, 27:3 – 29:9
" One day " the voyagers sighted an immense column in the sea. They took three days to come up with it. The thing seemed

to pierce the sky; it was all of crystal, and a silvery canopy overhung it. Shipping the oars and lowering the mast, they slipped through an opening in the canopy into clear water, through which they could see the base of the column in the sunshine. They stayed in the area for four days, estimating the column's dimensions. On the south side they found a crystal chalice and paten which Brendan took away. Then they rowed through the canopy to the north and put up the mast. A wind caught them and carried them northward, without rowing, for eight days.

They arrived next at a rugged island covered with slag. The landscape was one of bare rock, destitute of trees or grass, and from somewhere out of sight came a noise of gigantic smiths working at forges. One of the giants, a filthy, ugly creature, emerged menacingly with a pair of tongs, and tossed a lump of burning slag at the boat as the Irishmen struggled to escape. The mass fell in the sea and smoke poured up. More of the islanders gathered on the beach flinging slag, but the boat steadily pulled away, and they gave up trying to hit it and returned to their forges. The island seemed to blaze, and the water to boil; stinking fumes spread across the ocean for miles, and Brendan disclosed that this region was on the confines of hell.

XII, 29:10 – 31:33
" On another day " they saw a high mountain rising from the sea to the north, with mists clinging round it, and smoke pouring from the summit. They put in alongside a black vertical cliff, and the last of the three latecomers flung himself ashore crying out that an irresistible force was dragging him towards it. Demons seized him and carried him off. A wind propelled the boat away south again, and looking back, they saw that the mists had drifted aside and the mountain was shooting flames into the sky.

After sailing south for a week they saw a cloud shaped like a man, tossing to and fro on a mass of rock. Ice and restless waves were mingled in the sea round about. The apparition was Judas, who, it transpired, enjoyed a respite from damnation on Sundays. Brendan prayed on his behalf that this particular holiday might be lengthened a little, and as a result the boat was assaulted by angry fiends.

XIII, 31:34 – 34:17

They continued southward for three more days, and forty days before Easter they sighted a rocky islet. It was circular, only a furlong round, and quite bare, without soil. The sides were very steep and there was no place to bring the boat in, but Brendan saw a depression in the rock which would just take the prow, and there he leapt ashore. He explained that the islet was inhabited by a hermit named Paul who had been living for sixty years without food and for thirty years before that on food strangely brought to him by an animal.[6] After a difficult climb to the highest part of the islet, Brendan worked his way round to a patch of level ground on the east side, with two caves opposite each other and a spring of fresh water. Here he encountered the hermit, a venerable figure swathed in his own white hair. Brendan summoned the rest of the crew and Paul told his story.

For most of his life among his fellowmen, he said, he had been an inmate of " the monastery of St. Patrick " in Ireland, where he had charge of the graveyard. Patrick, on the day after his death, appeared to Paul and indicated the place where he wished to be buried; Paul himself, the saint went on, was to go to the coast where a boat was ready, and it would bear him to a retreat where he should await his own death. Paul complied, rowed for three days, drifted for seven with the wind, came to the islet and pushed the boat off. An animal walking on its hind legs brought him a fish to eat, and did the same regularly for thirty years. But sixty years ago this attention had ceased. Since then, Paul concluded, he had lived with no food at all, and he was now a hundred and forty. He observed that Brendan had endured six years of voyaging: in the year which he had now entered upon, the quest would be accomplished.

XIV, 34:18 – 35:6

During Lent they sailed away to the south. The boat drifted to and fro for some time, finally reaching the Island of Sheep on Holy Saturday. Accompanied by the Procurator, they sought out the whale and celebrated Easter Sunday on his back. He swam gently along and bore them round to the Paradise of Birds, where they stayed for the next few weeks. After Pentecost the Procurator instructed them to fill their water-skins at the spring. They were to steer once more for the Land of Promise. This time he would pilot them himself, and this time they would find it.

XIV (cont.), 35:6 – 36:19

Again Brendan set sail. For forty days the boat thrust ahead, passing at last into a thick cloud, which encircled the island he had sought so long. Emerging from the cloud into light, the monks beheld the Land of Promise.

It was warm, fruitful, bathed in a seemingly endless autumn sunshine. They disembarked and pushed up country for forty days, viewing the landscape on all sides but never glimpsing a farther sea; this island, though still so described, might perhaps have been better called a continent. Finally they stood on the bank of a great river which glided on into the interior.[7] It was too broad and deep to cross. Brendan said they could do no more and would not be able to discover how large the country was.

A handsome young man approached and ordered him to turn back. Christ had kept him wandering for seven years to show him the "mysteries in this immense ocean," but now the pilgrimage was complete. The Land of Promise would be revealed to Brendan's Christian successors many years hence, in time of tribulation. Later, when God should have united all nations under him, it would be made known to his Elect at large.

The monks returned to the coast laden with fruit, took leave of the Procurator, and sailed away through the cloud. After visiting the island of Mernoc they arrived safely home.

3

Such is the *Navigatio*. Perhaps the first topic to consider is whether it can be arranged in any intelligible relationship at all with the *Life*.

The main difficulty is that it conveys the impression of a single unbroken expedition, with no change of boats. Some of the medieval adaptors did read it in this sense, with resulting inconsistencies in their efforts to harmonise the material. But actually the seven years' wandering is in two instalments. On the first visit to St. Ailbe's Isle, in the late summer of the year following his departure from Ireland, Brendan is informed that the community has been there for eighty years since the time of its patriarchs (VI, 16 : 7-8). One of them is St. Patrick, who was therefore presumably alive eighty years before. The date usually given for his death is 17th March, 461, so that Brendan's visit to the community cannot be appreciably later than 540. Therefore his departure from Ireland cannot be appreciably later than 539. But in the last Lent he meets the anchorite Paul, who, by his own testimony, has been on his rock for an aggregate of ninety years since the death of Patrick (XIII, 34 : 6-7). It must now be early in 551, in other words almost twelve years after the latest possible setting-out. Since both these inferred dates depend on the same event, Patrick's death, they can both be altered by shifting that event, but they cannot be squeezed closer together. Nevertheless we are told unambiguously that when Brendan meets Paul he is only in the seventh year of his travels.

Somewhere between Ailbe's Isle and Paul there is an interval, a stretch of time not accounted for, and this missing or rather glossed-over piece of the story must be in the passage from 23:10 to 29:9. At 23:10 the continuous narrative breaks off —O'Donoghue's section-division is unintentionally misleading— to be followed by several disjointed and dateless episodes introduced by formulæ of the "one day" type: *quadam vero die* (23:10), *quodam vero tempore* (26:13), *quadam vero die* (27:3). Such formulæ are prefixed to other episodes, but elsewhere the "day" can be pinned down after a fashion, whereas these three passages are floating, unrelated to the calendar. Continuous narrative resumes at 29:10 and goes on to the end. The three unconnected episodes are all that the author gives for a period of at least nine years, and it is in this part of the text that the monks may be taken back temporarily to Ireland; doubtless in the vague passage (IX, 26 : 6–12) which describes them as "sailing about for a long time."

Hence the plan of the *Navigatio*, while not the same as the plan of the Voyage portion of the *Life*, is not downright incompatible with it, and the relationship of the two traditions needs to be thought about rather carefully. Some of the parallel passages and motifs in the Lismore text of the *Life*—the glimpse of hell, the combat of monsters, the bad water, the mysterious guide— are probably derived with much blurring and falsification from the *Navigatio* itself, but some, probably, are not. In particular the explicit and purposeful division of the Voyage into two parts must surely be prior to the camouflaged and pointless division in the *Navigatio*, which can only be explained as vestigial. It may be that there was an earlier common source, and the *Navigatio* author, however gifted, is enlarging on pieces of a saga with which he is not thoroughly familiar; he does not understand the chronology, and he misses the interesting conception of the wooden ship—though references to "sails," in the plural, show an awareness that the vessel must have been more than an ordinary curragh. While his book takes us as far back toward the roots as we can safely go, it is fair to try using the *Life* to interpret it and eke it out, because the *Life* may retain something of value from the common source of the parallel incidents. However, I doubt if this is seriously worth doing in more than a couple of places. For practical purposes the *Navigatio* can stand by itself. As what? That is the question. Scarcely as the literal record of a real voyage or series of voyages, whether by St. Brendan or by anyone else. Yet its bibliography reveals an enduring reluctance among its readers to set it aside as pure fancy. Sceptics like C. R. Beazley have condemned it as a farrago of nonsense, usually by laying a heavy stress on the whale; yet even sceptics, Beazley included, have tended to concede that there may after all be something in it.[8] Unlike the immrama, it leaves people with an insistent feeling that it would make sense if only the key could be found. It is so tantalisingly circumstantial, so scrupulous as to distances and directions and times and natural phenomena. The author is not dealing with a shapeless jumble of fairy-tale islets alongside Erin; he speaks of really long journeyings, of weeks and months on the waves; and when the Promised Land is attained after a colossal transoceanic sweep, it is not merely another island, but a land of continental dimensions that sets a limit to exploration. Both the long crossing and the continent itself are utterly unparalleled in *Bran* and *Mael Duin*. A long crossing does occur in the *Sons of Chorra*, but that tale copies it from the *Navigatio*.

Brendan's author seems to have amassed a collection of Atlantic lore and fitted it on to an artificial cyclic scheme: every Easter in the Island of Sheep and its environs, every Christmas in St. Ailbe's Isle. The Atlantic lore, the map, is our true concern. How far can we go toward elucidating this Voyage, and what can we infer as to the author's geographical scholarship? Does he or does he not confront us with a notion of America and the farther Atlantic which transcends guesswork, and therefore poses a problem because the *Navigatio* antedates the Viking discoveries?

A natural objection to any essay in reconstruction is that no place-names are given, so that there is apparently no point of reference, no origin of co-ordinates. Actually however we do get a name, or designation, and it occurs in the most obliging way possible. The focus of the quest, where Brendan keeps coming back for aid and guidance, is the Island of Sheep, and close by on the west is the Paradise of Birds. These are almost certainly Streymoy and Vagar in the Faeroes, Streymoy being the chief island of the group.[9]

The name "Faeroes" is derived from the Danish word for a sheep, and the animals are a staple of the islands' economy. They are said to have been imported by Gaelic-speaking colonists in the seventh or eighth century; a surprisingly mild winter and several bits of good pasture, much as described, have kept them flourishing ever since. Dicuil speaks of them, and also of the Faeroese religious community. The archipelago, he says in 825, consists of "small islands separated by narrow sounds, on which for about a hundred years there dwelt hermits who came from our fatherland; but even as these islands from the creation until then lay waste, so are they now, on account of the Norse pirates, deserted by these anchorites; but they swarm with innumerable sheep and an extraordinary number of sea-fowl."

Sheep, birds, Irish hermits, islands separated by narrow sounds —the combination leaves little room for doubt as to what place the *Navigatio* author has in mind. Nor need it be assumed that Dicuil's paragraph would have been the only source of knowledge available to him. Dicuil indeed may be wrong in his implication that the anchorites were the sole inhabitants, and it is not by any means certain that all the Celtic people departed or died off. Some may have survived into the tenth century or later to transmit first-hand information. Archæological traces of Irish occupation exist at Kirkjubøur in southern Streymoy, and a few place-names employed by the Norse who settled after Dicuil's time seem to hint at their presence. Dimon is Celtic, Baglaholm may be from *bachall*, a crozier, and Vestmanna means West-men or Irishmen. Near Kirkjubour it is interesting to find Brandansvik,

Brandan's Creek, a reminiscence of the saint, to whom a church was dedicated in 1420.

Vagar lies to the west of Streymoy across the narrow Vestmanna Sound. On its south side is a bay with sandy streams pouring into it from the hills, acceptable as the scene of Brendan's landing in Section v. Wild birds, though lacking in conversational powers, are very conspicuous; the avian life of the Faeroes is in fact phenomenal, and it grows more so toward the western part of the archipelago; the folk of Mykines, where the guillemots and puffins gather, live almost entirely by fowling. Even England can hardly match the Faeroese bird-symphony. Over two hundred varieties have been counted. From March onward the migrants are arriving, from May through the summer they are in possession, and late in August they leave. During the season there are golden plovers and oyster-catchers, meadow-pipits and hooded crows, gulls and skuas and many more. Patches of ground are white-carpeted with innumerable kittiwakes and arctic terns, probably the birds encountered by Brendan.

Whales abound in the waters round the Faeroes, even if they seldom behave like Jasconius, and the fishing in Faeroese streams is famous, the brown trout being especially notable. The items that do not fit are the woods and flowers. Heather perhaps will serve for the flowers; the colour of the landscape does visibly alter in spring. Trees, however, have not grown wild in the archipelago in historical times. The impression left is one which recurs, that the author's observation is seldom or never direct. He is embroidering the reports of others, an annoyingly common medieval practice.

Having, as it were, anchored his narrative, we must pass to the question raised by his more exotic offerings. Are we justified in looking for realities underlying these also? I think we are, and three instances may complete the preliminary case for reconstruction. These are the island of smiths, the crystal column, and the transparent sea. Each has mythical affinities,

yet each, despite the distorting medium through which it is seen,
is a real thing, the first and second at least having been recognised
as such by impartial students of the legend.
Here in full is the story of the smiths (xi, 28:7 – 29:9).

When those days had passed, they came within view of an
island, which was very rugged and rocky, covered over with
slag, without trees or herbage, but full of smiths' forges.
St. Brendan said to the brethren: " I am much distressed
about this island; I have no wish to enter it or even to
approach it—yet the wind is driving us directly towards it,
as if it were the aim of our course." When they had passed
on further, about a stone's cast, they heard the noise of
bellows blowing like thunder, and the beating of sledges on
the anvils and iron. Then St. Brendan armed himself all
over his body with the sign of the Cross, saying: " O Lord
Jesus Christ, deliver us from this malign island." Soon after
one of the inhabitants came forth to do some work; he was
all hairy and hideous, begrimed with fire and smoke. When
he saw the servants of Christ near the island, he withdrew
into his forge, crying aloud: " Woe! Woe! Woe! "
St. Brendan again armed himself with the sign of the
Cross, and said to the brethren: " Put on more sail, and ply
your oars more briskly, that we may get away from this
island." Hearing this, the savage man, above mentioned,
rushed down to the shore, bearing in his hand a tongs with
a burning mass of the slag, of great size and intense heat,
which he flung at once after the servants of Christ; but it
did them no hurt, for they were protected by the sign of the
Cross. It passed them at a furlong's distance, and where it
fell into the sea, it fumed up like a heap of burning coals,
and a great smoke arose as if from a fiery furnace. When
they had passed on about a mile beyond the spot where the
burning mass had fallen, all the dwellers on the island crowded
down to the shore, bearing, each of them, a large mass of

burning slag, which they flung, every one in turn, after the servants of God; and then they returned to their forges, which they blew up into mighty flames, so that the whole island seemed one globe of fire, and the sea on every side boiled up and foamed, like a cauldron set on a fire well supplied with fuel. All the day the brethren, even when they were no longer within view of the island, heard a loud wailing from the inhabitants thereof, and a noisome stench was perceptible at a great distance. Then St. Brendan sought to animate the courage of the brethren, saying: " Soldiers of Christ, be strong in faith unfeigned and in the armour of the Spirit, for we are now on the confines of hell; watch, therefore, and act manfully."

This is a volcanic eruption, worked over by somebody with a certain classical learning, who knows from Virgil and perhaps Homer the myths about Etna and the Cyclopean forge.[10]

As if to prove his familiarity with spectacles of that kind, the author goes on to portray another volcano without the adjuncts (XII, 29:10 – 29:29).

On another day there came into view a large and high mountain in the ocean, not far off, towards the north, with misty clouds about it, and a great smoke issuing from its summit, when suddenly the wind drove the boat rapidly towards the island until it almost touched the shore. The cliffs were so high they could scarce see the top, were black as coal, and upright like a wall. . . .

Afterwards a favourable breeze caught the boat, and drove them southwards; and as they looked back, they saw the peak of the mountain unclouded, and shooting up flames into the sky, which it drew back again to itself, so that the mountain seemed a burning pyre.

The first of the two volcanoes, reached after a long sail northward, is almost certainly in some barren coastal region of Iceland.[11]

To quote Professor O'Dell and his transcription of a striking medieval chronicle passage on Hekla:

> It has had over twenty periods of activity during the past thousand years. In the vivid words of the Logmann's Annal: "a fire broke out in Mount Hekla, so powerful that the mountain split in such a manner that it will be visible in Iceland so long as the country is inhabited. Large rocks moved about in this fire *like charcoal in a blacksmith's hearth* and crashed together with so much thunder and noise that it was heard as far as the North Land and in many other places. So much pumice stone was cast out on the Naefurhold farmhouses that their roofs were burnt off. . . . No man knew if it was night or day, inside or out, while the falling sand covered the ground completely. . . ." Hekla was regarded for centuries as *the region of chaos round the gates of hell.*[12]

And so Brendan thinks too.

Here next is the incident of the column (x, 27:3 - 28:7).

> One day, on which three Masses had been said, they saw a column in the sea, which seemed not far off, yet they could not reach it for three days. When they drew near it, St. Brendan looked towards its summit, but could not see it, because of its great height, which seemed to pierce the skies. It was covered over with a rare canopy, the material of which they knew not; but it had the colour of silver, and was hard as marble, while the column itself was of the clearest crystal. St. Brendan ordered the brethren to take in their oars, and to lower the sails and mast, and directed some of them to hold on by the fringes of the canopy, which extended about a mile from the column, and about the same depth into the sea. When this had been done, St. Brendan said: "Run in the boat now through an opening, that we may get a closer view of the wonderful works of God." And when they had passed through the opening, and looked

around them, the sea seemed to them transparent like glass, so that they could plainly see everything beneath them, even the base of the column, and the skirts or fringes of the canopy, lying on the ground, for the sun shone as brightly within as without.

St. Brendan then measured an opening which he found to be four cubits on every side. While they sailed along for a day by one side of the column, they could always feel the shade as well as the heat of the sun, beyond the ninth hour; and after thus sailing about the column for four days, they found the measurement of each side to be four hundred cubits. On the fourth day, they discovered on the south side, a chalice of the same material as the canopy, and a patena like that of the column, which St. Brendan at once took up, saying: " The Lord Jesus Christ has displayed to us this great marvel, and has given us two gifts therefrom, in testimony of the fact to others. . . ." Next day they rowed towards the north, and having passed out through an opening, they set up the mast, and unfurled the sails again, while some of them held on by the fringes or skirts of the canopy, until all was right in the boat. When they had set sail, a favourable wind came on in the rear, so that they had no occasion to use the oars, but only to hold the ropes and the tiller. And thus for eight days were they borne along towards the north.

The man who wrote this can hardly have seen the object himself. But such an object existed to be seen. It is not pure imagination. There are Celtic tales introducing towers of glass in the ocean, but these belong to an Otherworld type of myth which the author shows no sign of having in mind here, and the characteristics are quite different. No; when we strip away the trimmings, the object emerges as an iceberg—a large, drifting, disintegrating berg, sighted first under a low cloud-ceiling, with arches opened in it by melting, and some sort of overhang.[13]

We should note, not only the iceberg and the volcanoes, but their spatial relationship. The outlets of infernal fire are situated in the cold north, while the iceberg floats to the south of them in a much lower latitude: Brendan sails northward *from* the column *to* the island of smiths. This arrangement is essentially right, since the active North Atlantic volcanoes are in Iceland and Jan Mayen, while the zone of large melting icebergs extends far out to the east of Newfoundland. But would a wholly imaginative writer, especially a writer influenced by fables of Etna, have hit on the truth? With regard to the principal volcano the probabilities are of course more concrete, since the advent of Irish monks in Iceland before Dicuil provided a source of information. But the likely authenticity of the volcano makes the iceberg all the more challenging. Large ones are non-existent, or virtually so, directly south of Iceland or anywhere in the Irish neighbourhood. To accommodate the relationship even roughly as to direction and distance—to accommodate the iceberg at all—we must pass over toward Newfoundland. Then we can manage it. The effect is not of guesswork, but of shadowy semiknowledge grounded on obscure explorations.

Likewise, finally, with the other passage referring to a translucent sea (x, 26:13 – 27:2).

On a certain occasion, when St. Brendan was celebrating the festival of St. Peter, in the boat, they found the sea so clear that they could plainly see what was at the bottom. They, therefore, saw beneath them various monsters of the deep, and so clear was the water, that it seemed as if they could touch with their hands its greatest depths; and the fishes were visible in great shoals, like flocks of sheep in the pastures, swimming around, heads to tails. The brethren entreated the man of God to say Mass in a low voice, lest those monsters of the deep, hearing the strange voice, might be stirred up to attack them; but the saint said: " I wonder much at your folly. Why do you dread these monsters? . . ." Having thus spoken, he proceeded to sing the Mass in a louder voice, as the brethren were still gazing at the large fishes; and these, when they heard the voice of the man of God, rose up from the depths, and swam around the boat in such numbers, that the brethren could see nothing but the swimming fishes, which, however, came not close to the boat, but swam around at some distance, until the Mass was ended, when they swam away in divers directions, out of the view of the brethren. For eight days, even with a favourable wind, and all sails set, they were scarcely able to pass out of this pellucid sea.

Irish folk-lore notoriously delights in sunken cities visible through the waves, such as Kilstapheen, Skerd, Tir Hudi.[14] But this motif is precisely what we do not find in the *Navigatio*. No castles decorate the sea-bed. The description is nearly realistic . . . but with the reality of a coral sea, not a European one. It is as if the man who wrote it (let us cope with the shocking notion as best we can) had heard some rumour of the Bahamas.

Versions of all these episodes appear in *Mael Duin*, and a comparison is revealing. The immram lacks the second volcanic island completely, and, in the first, the interest has shifted to the smiths themselves. Instead of the graphic details which make everything clear to a reader having the classical background, there is a comic dialogue of ogres, a sort of fee-fi-fo-fum with no volcano discernible. The author has moved a step away from the object. So also with the transparent sea. In a corresponding passage *Mael Duin* begins in much the same vein, but the author cannot keep it up; the temptation is too strong; he introduces submarine mansions and submarine herds of cattle, and relapses into a fairy-tale world. Again there is a retreat from the object. So also, and most remarkably, with the column. The *Navigatio* author is dealing with a report which he cannot quite get the hang of, and he has not seen anything like this himself, but considering the obstacles he does not do badly. The *Mael Duin* author tacks on the detail of a voice calling from the top in an unknown tongue, but, more important, he betrays his incomprehension by a simple change that destroys the whole image: making the column silver instead of crystal. Yet again he has moved away from the object, this time disastrously. It need hardly be added that he also drops the vital geographical relationship between the column and the island of smiths.

In these three instances at least, there cannot be much doubt as to either the nature or the direction of any literary borrowing that occurred. The *Navigatio*, or some previous Brendan narrative on which it was based, supplied ultimately factual material which *Mael Duin* annexed and perverted into fiction.[15]

4

Encouraged thus far, we may try what can be done with the Voyage as a whole. The topic has been bedevilled in the past by fruitless argument over " what Brendan actually did." Some commentators dismiss the *Navigatio* because they see little solid reason to think that he, personally, went very far, while others extort amazing itineraries from it in an effort to show how he, personally, might have gone a long way. Both parties avoid the real issue. Whatever Brendan did, Brendan's author let his fancy roam over the ocean to some purpose. But where to, and with what implications?

On first fairly confronting this question, having provisionally ceased speculating about the historical saint, I realised that nobody could spell out a logical answer by a firm sequence of inferences from beginning to end. There was not enough to go on. My sole chance was to try a series of guesses—making grateful use of the ideas of my predecessors wherever these might be helpful—in the belief that the eventual test would lie in coherence, in the impression of a cryptogram solved or not solved.

It would not matter if a step looked risky or even absurd at the time of taking it. But how would it look in retrospect when the last step had been taken? It would not matter if the proposed identity of an island did not follow decisively from the frail clues available. But would the island, thus conjecturally identified, fit into the final pattern? Would Brendan turn out to reach it and sail away from it in a way that agreed with my other identifications and with the facts of geography? Could a string of hypotheses, each one intuitive rather than rational in itself, add up to a reconstruction having rational force by virtue of internal consistency?

I tried, and I offer the result, with such prior and concomitant notes as it requires at this stage. It presupposes the shedding of all preconceptions. The historical kind must go first: once again, it is pointless to ask either what Brendan did, or what anybody with Brendan's resources could have done; the problem is literary, and (to borrow a term from mathematics) topological. But beyond this, there must be no preconceptions as to what the author could or could not have known. To assert that the limitations of Irish geographical texts exclude this or that is to beg the question, since the *Navigatio*, however fictitious, is itself a geographical text. It is a fantasia on a map of the Atlantic. Perhaps it is not much more than a fantasia ... but the map, I think, is a provocatively good map. And if anyone feels inclined to retort that the proposed solution is arbitrary, and that the *Navigatio* is merely another immram, let him prove his contention by extracting an equal amount of geography from *Mael Duin*; or for that matter, by contriving a different exegesis of Brendan's own voyaging that fits the real Atlantic equally well.

The only point calling for comment at the outset is the recurrence of a period of forty days. Fair play demands that that period be taken literally as often as possible, but its exact duration should probably not be insisted on. It means, vaguely, a longish time, and its correspondence to Lent conveys the hint of a

Brandon Creek, Co. Kerry

Scenery in the Faeroe Islands (Koltur)

Iceland: Hekla in eruption

penitential pilgrimage. I have allotted dates throughout for convenience, but the actual years *anno Domini* matter very little. The month-by-month progress of the Voyage matters far more, and it will become evident that this is coherent and that the author's imagery of the seasons is seldom at fault.

I give warning at once that while most of the suggested geography is going to stand up under criticism, some of it is not, because an odd factor intrudes. But all further questions, however clamorous, may be postponed.

1–11, 3:1 – 6:34
Barinthus; the building of the curragh
" Barinthus " may be a Latinisation of Finnbar, and there are traces of an Irish sea-god with some such name. Brendan's doubtfully historical visitor has been equated with St. Barrind, who appears in Oengus's calendar under the date 21st May.[16] A preternaturally swift crossing, such as he recounts, is an ancient legendary theme. Odysseus returns to Ithaca from the land of the Phæacians between dusk and dawn. Procopius, a Byzantine contemporary of Brendan, refers to Celtic accounts of the ferrying of the souls of the dead from Gaul to Britain: the nocturnal voyage, he says, is accomplished in a single hour, whereas the normal time of transit from the same point is a night and a day. In the context of such ideas it is useless to speculate about the Land of Promise as described by Barinthus, beyond noting the shift to a paradisal concept. Brendan himself is the only navigator worth trying to follow.

The creek where the curragh is constructed is Brandon Creek, the inlet in the Dingle peninsula still pointed out by cottagers. Brandon Mountain towers above it. A narrow crack between cliffs, it is fed by a torrent coming down at right angles. Here a quay has been built, and the black upturned curraghs of fishermen, with tiny bottles for holy water at the bows, are descendants of Brendan's boat in a line of occupancy which is probably unbroken.

11 (*cont.*)–111, 6:35 – 9:12

Departure, toward the summer solstice; twelve days sailing with a fair
wind; calm; fresh wind of uncertain direction; at the end of
"forty days" (i.e. from embarkation), the steep island with one
landing-place; the theft

Brendan sails from his creek about 20th June in a year which
we may call 539. He makes a false start across the Atlantic and
is carried off his course by the prevailing westerlies, but in July
he reaches St. Kilda, the outermost of the Outer Hebrides.[17]

St. Kilda (or strictly speaking the chief island of the St. Kilda
group) is called in Gaelic "Hirta," the Western Land. It answers
well to the author's description. Three miles by two, it is almost
surrounded by immense cliffs, rising at Conachair to more than
twelve hundred feet. Disembarkation under sail is practicable
only in a rocky cove at the south-east, and then only when the
wind is right; for eight months of the year the island used to be
nearly cut off. Brendan's visit is placed in the best season, but
his long-drawn circuitous approach is in keeping with experience.
Shipwrecked sailors have reported rowing into one of the smaller
inlets and sheltering there for days from the weather.

Boswell records a discussion of the reason why all the St.
Kildans caught a cold when a stranger landed. The explanation
was said to be that before he could get ashore he had to wait till
the wind veered into the proper quarter, and the epidemic was
due to this change of weather, though of course the stranger was
blamed. In 1930 the last inhabitants were removed at their own
request, and nothing now remains of them but an arc of grey
cottages near the harbour. The R.A.F. is in possession.

One of the three old chapels on Hirta was called St. Brendan's,
so that if dedications are anything to go by we are on his track.
The deserted house where his crew sleeps may be a romanticised
reminiscence of the prehistoric settlement across the island at
Gleann Mor. Notice that the monks have to be led there; it
is not visible from the cove. The Gleann Mor settlement
consists of sixteen unmortared stone cells arranged round a

courtyard. St. Kildan legend asserts that Amazons lived there. Matriarchy, and the participation of women in battle, were customs that prevailed among some of the early tribes of outlying Scotland and the Isles.

No significance attaches to the affair of the pilferer and his end. This is the immram theme of the last-minute Jonah who enlarges the crew above its correct complement and has to drop out if the voyage is to attain its goal. It is the same with the buffoon in the *Life* and with Mael Duin's foster-brothers.

III (*cont.*)–V, 9:12 – 14:16
Sailing " in divers directions " to the Island of Sheep; the Procurator; the whale; the Paradise of Birds; departure eight days after Pentecost

As to the geography of this part of the Voyage enough has been said. Following the same generally northward course, by whatever zigzags, Brendan reaches Streymoy and winters there. The character of the knowledgeable Procurator is distilled from those Irish anchorites who explored the northern ocean from Faeroese bases in the eighth century.

The notorious whale episode in its *Navigatio* form is sometimes alleged to have been copied from *Sindbad the Sailor*, a theory which presents difficulties, first because there is little reason to think that oriental romances were read in Ireland, and secondly because the *Navigatio* was written before *Sindbad*. The only traceable influence of that kind is in the other direction, since Brendan traditions undoubtedly do enter into the Arab geography of Idrisi; moreover the whale's name, Jasconius, comes from the Irish *iasc*, a fish. But the adventure is a traveller's tale which could easily have occurred to various people independently, and while it may have literary sources, too much time need not be spent looking for them. Something similar is told of Glooskap, a demigod of the Micmacs of Nova Scotia, and a sculptured whale with a house on his back has turned up in Easter Island.[18]

All that the incident reflects is an awareness that whales populate the seas round the Faeroes; as they do.

After Paschaltide in 540 the monks pass over the Vestmanna Sound to Vagar and haul their boat up one of the streams that flow into the bay on the south. The hills have changed colour, and the bird season is fast advancing. Everywhere there are white terns and kittiwakes, and swarms of song-birds of many species. About the beginning of June Brendan sets sail. He has observed that the migratory wild-fowl come from the south and that Vagar, for most, is the limit of their flight. Mistrusting the seas beyond, he does not persist along his course of the previous summer, but turns back to explore another path.

Conversations with birds are not unknown elsewhere in hagiographic legend. St. Flannan is credited with the same feat, and even outside Celtdom we find St. Francis communing with them, and St. Antony preaching to fishes. The notion of neutral spirits in suspense between earth and heaven is more peculiarly Celtic; it reappears in the romance of the Holy Grail.

VI–VII, 14:17 – 19:25

Three months " tossing to and fro " to St. Ailbe's Isle and " forty days " trying to land; Christmas; drift to the island of stupefying water; three days sailing northward; calm; twenty days drifting; several days sailing and rowing eastward to the Island of Sheep again

This initial three months' passage from island to island is much the longest in point of time throughout Brendan's voyaging. In view of the indication of a wavering course, it cannot be singled out with complete confidence as the longest in point of distance also, but there seems no reason why the author should have given it such a vast duration unless he meant the boat to traverse a vast space of sea. By implication he gives a hint at Brendan's direction. As he says nothing of bad weather or downright contrary winds, a voyage of such length from Vagar toward the British Isles or the Continent is out of the question.

It appears moreover from what he says later that he would not put a holy place like St. Ailbe's Isle in the Arctic; it also appears that he regards the westward crossing as taking far less than three months.

Tentatively therefore (very tentatively indeed) we might conceive the long voyage from Vagar as predominantly southward, carrying the boat into the currents and winds past Spain and Morocco, the same used by the fifteenth-century Portuguese navigators. St. Ailbe's Isle would then be an African island, Madeira or one of the Canaries or Cape Verdes. Medieval cartographers who drew Brendan's own "Isle" on their maps generally drew it in this area; if tradition said anything at all about the way he went, this must have been the quarter to which it inclined. But positive evidence that the Navigatio author had the same idea must come from the sequel.

As it happens, the island of bad water can be identified quite plausibly. Not many in the Atlantic have springs that qualify. The most hopeful candidate by far is St. Michaels, the largest of the Azores, a volcanic ridge covering three hundred square miles. In the extinct crater-bed of the Furnas Valley, mineral waters of various composition gush through vents in the ground. Some of the water is cold, some boiling, and the sulphur and iron solutions have given Furnas the status of a spa. But among the comparatively mild springs are several of a more potent kind, which tourists are warned not to sample without medical advice.[19]

Despite the scarcity of competitors, it would be rash to infer from this fact by itself that the author has St. Michaels in mind. But here as elsewhere, details are linked in a way that strengthens the probabilities. Not far beyond this island Brendan is becalmed in obstructed water, a "thick curdled mass." The phrase tallies with early allusions to the Sargasso Sea, which seems to have been known after a fashion to ancient and medieval geographers. We shall examine what they say in due course; the immediate point is that the juxtaposition of overpowering water and "thick" ocean limits the search. Brendan is either in the general region of the Azores or in a Never-Never-Land with a chance resemblance to it—hardly, however, in any other definable place. The main Sargasso begins just west of the Azores, not north, but the weed spreads extensively, and where the area is so distant a slight inaccuracy of this kind cannot destroy the force of the juxtaposition.[20]

If the Azores identification is adopted as a working hypothesis, St. Ailbe's Isle is Madeira. Brendan drifts from there to St. Michaels in January. At that season the prevailing winds do in fact swing round and blow transversely from Madeira to the Azores,[21] whereas a corresponding drift from the Canaries or the Cape Verdes would be abnormal.

St. Ailbe has a legendary and mythical background apart from geography. In the first place, he is a real person, belonging to the cloudy interim period before the beginning of the heroic age of Irish monasticism. He is said to have been brought up in a British colony in Ireland and to have preached the Gospel there before Patrick. He is also said to have lived into the sixth century and to have obtained a royal grant enabling St. Enda to found a monastery on Aran. This doubtfully compatible action brings him into contact with Brendan, who, it will be remembered, goes to Aran in the *Life*.

The actual account of St. Ailbe's Isle gives few hints. The prolonged delay over landing, and general beating about in the area, is blamed on the elements rather than topography. If Brendan by-passed Madeira and then turned back, he might well have had the wind against him, and the drying-up of streams on the south side of the island during summer would have made his search for a creek more difficult; so a shred of genuine knowledge may underlie the passage. Certainly Madeira has springs in abundance. It is volcanic in its formation like the Azores, mountainous, wooded, well supplied with fruit and flowers, and altogether a place appropriate to such a long-lived and healthy community.

But what are Ailbe's monks doing there? It seems that the

Ailbe of Irish legend is a kind of preliminary sketch for Brendan himself. According to a reference in the Book of Leinster,[22] he too sailed in quest of the Land of Promise. We are not told which way he sailed. One story says that in his old age he desired to go to Thule over the northern sea. But he never went; the king closed the ports to prevent his leaving. Perhaps he tried a southward voyage from a port where the royal writ did not run. The implication in the *Navigatio* episode, which makes Ailbe an approximate contemporary of Patrick, is that he did not stop in the Isle himself, but planted his monastic " family " there. In the picture of the community of twenty-four, with its noble chapel and its eighty years of supernatural nourishment, there are touches of a theme which appears more fully developed in Grail romance. This also draws on the saga of Bran, and the entranced island of Ailbe's sons has a real if obscure literary relationship to those visited by the pagan hero.[23]

For the moment we may sum up this part of the Voyage and pass on. Brendan leaves the Faeroes in June 540, arrives at Madeira in the autumn, stays till January, then catches the changed wind and reaches St. Michaels in February. His subsequent course is pretty much what an imaginative author with a modern map in front of him might devise. He sails a little way into a rather unpredictable bit of ocean on or at least fairly near the Sargasso fringes, then enters the Gulf Stream Drift flowing north-eastward. He moves along with the current and wind till he finds himself in the latitude of the Faeroes again, picks up a westerly, sights the north end of Streymoy, and lands there in time for Easter 541. Irish acquaintance with the Gulf Stream is another topic best postponed.[24]

VII (*cont.*), 19:26 – 21:17
Easter on the Island of Sheep; meeting with the Procurator; recovery
of the cauldron; Pentecost in the Paradise of Birds
Brendan consults his adviser, and the monks keep Easter. After the short trip to another of the Faeroes to recover the cauldron

—a touch recalling the importance of cauldrons both in Celtic myth and in Celtic life—he goes to Vagar, where the birds have now returned. Their spokesman (symbolising Brendan's deductions from their habits) allots him a bird-like pattern of migration: he must spend every Christmas in Madeira, and come back to the Faeroes every spring. These are the two termini from which he is to probe the Atlantic routes.

VIII–IX, 21:17 – 23:10
" Forty days " west; battle of the whale and the eastbound monster; three months' confinement to an island by storms and hail; departure northward

Now, however, something goes wrong. Either Brendan makes for the Land of Promise too soon, or he attempts a reckless reconnaissance. The outcome at any rate is nearly disaster. His sailing from Vagar (to be repeated in the successful crossing in XI v) is westward along the Viking route, past Iceland and Greenland and into Davis Strait, where his troubles begin.

This is one of the few passages where the *Life* can assist. In the Lismore version the hazards of the first sail westward are assigned to the second, but the same happenings are clearly meant. The nebulous rival monster, by which also the monks are threatened, is specified as a sea-cat, and the tiny black fiends add a further peril.

Again we have an impressive collocation of details. Whales, to begin with, have always been plentiful in the seas west of Greenland. The black fiends are rather like the " skraelings " of Norse saga—small, dark, elusive trolls dwelling in Greenland and Markland, referred to in Latin texts as " pygmies," and doubtless to be understood as Eskimos seen through a haze of folk-lore.[25] Brendan meets them on an islet, perhaps off the south-west Greenland coast. The sea-cat is described in the *Life* as a powerful animal with huge eyes, bristles, tusks like a boar's, and a mouth like a leopard's, i.e. whiskered. It is recognisably a walrus. These are now purely Arctic creatures, but they used to come farther south, habitually to Nova Scotia in historical times, and into the Gulf of St. Lawrence as recently as 1765.[26]

Eskimos, whales, walruses, the latter unknown in Irish waters, and a sea far west of the Faeroes where all are available— the coincidence is arresting.

Brendan is trying to push on across Davis Strait when the whale chases the boat. The crew swing her round and double back in the hope of shaking it off. Then the walrus, swimming toward the Greenland shore, seems to come after them itself, but instead kills the whale. After this alarming combat the monks follow the floating carcass to another Greenland island or promontory, where they hack pieces off to eat (a practice learnt from the pygmy devils?).

It is now late June or July 541, and we are approaching the gap, where the story ceases to be connected. The author detains the monks on their island for three months of foul weather in summer and early autumn, a notion so implausible that its actual comparative plausibility is suggestive. To quote Professor O'Dell: "Most of the fall [of rain in Greenland] occurs in late summer and autumn. . . . Snow can occur at any time of the year. Fog or mist is very frequent in July and August." (*The Scandinavian World*, page 356.) The Irishmen are at last allowed to get off in October before the freeze-up, provisioning their boat with the herbs and roots proper to a high latitude. They go still farther north with the current and wind past south-west Greenland, then catch the contrary polar wind out of Baffin Bay and escape into more hospitable waters.[27]

IX (*cont.*), 23:10 – 26:5

The flat treeless island of the three choirs; twenty-two days to the wooded island of giant grapes; "forty days" camping there; the gryphon

This is the first of the episodes with a prefatory "one day" that is wholly indeterminate, and some of Brendan's sailing has been omitted. He is now in a region of luxuriant fruit, resplendent birds, vivid colours. The reiterated "purple" is probably important, being very peculiar. The purple flowers are *calthi*, marigolds (if O'Donoghue's reading is right—Schröder however has *scaltae* here); the purple clothing of the elders seems insufficiently contrasted with the violet of the young men; and if the purple *scaltae* which are certainly mentioned later were only yellow, it might be easier to guess what they are meant to be. One could wish to believe that the word was originally *aureus*, "golden," and that at some stage in manuscript transmission somebody wrote the word with an initial flourish, after which a copyist read it as *pureus* and took it as a contraction of *purpureus*. Golden-coloured marigolds, golden-coloured garments, golden-coloured oranges or possibly grapefruit: all would be satisfying. But I think it more likely that "purple," though regrettable, is correct, and that the author is recalling the Purple Islands, which were supposed very confusedly to lie somewhere west of Africa. This impression is reinforced by other legendary features of the same episode. The giant grapes on the next island are the fruit proper to the classical Fortunate Isles, where the vines were said to tend themselves; and the gryphon or griffin (a mythical monster part eagle and part lion that guarded treasures) may well be a reminiscence of the dragon who watched the apples of the Hesperides. Both the Hesperides and the Fortunate Isles, like the Purple, were located at an indeterminate distance westward from the African coast.[28]

Almost certainly that is the direction in which Brendan's author is taking him here. But the flat island at least cannot be in the Canaries or in any of the groups on the nearer side of the Atlantic, with which the Fortunate Isles and Hesperides were sometimes identified by classical writers. The groups on the near side are all mountainous. The superficial effect of the whole passage is West Indian,[29] yet even in the West Indies candidates for that first island are not plentiful, since nearly everything thereabouts is mountainous likewise. With the whole ocean at disposal, it is curiously hard to meet the simple requirements. To pick out anything anywhere that will serve, one is driven to look for coral formations; and these are rare.

Bermuda, by no means flat and famous for cedar forests, is hopeless. The Bahamas supply a better field. They are all low, and several extend far enough to be called extensive. Yet few are entirely satisfactory. It would be absurd to insist on absolute treelessness or absolute flatness, but any island chosen must be such as to create both impressions. Several of the Bahamas, Cat Island for instance, would have to be disallowed as too hilly; others, Andros for instance, as too densely wooded. The most promising is perhaps Long Island, which Columbus called Fernandina. It is seventy miles in length and three in breadth. Most of it is exceptionally flat, even for the Bahamas; much of the vegetation is modern; and the natural bush is sparser than usual. Outside the Bahamas altogether there is one other interesting coral formation, Grand Cayman in the Caribbean, which is also very flat, and noted for flowers.[30]

The three classes of inhabitants bring in an immram element and need not detain us, though the fact that Brendan finds a Christian community in this particular spot is worth bearing in mind. As for the second island it has idiosyncrasies not drawn from recognised myth, for example its unparalleled multitude of springs. Now the name "Jamaica" is the Arawak Indian *Xaymaca*, "abundance of waters"; and the colourful bird, the close-packed forest, the fragrant air, the various and intensely green vegetation, are all characteristically and even especially Jamaican.[31]

These adventures might just be fitted into 541 between October and the Christmas return to St. Ailbe's Isle in that year, but such a procedure would prompt inferences as to intended times and distances. As a reminder that such inferences are not warranted, it is safer to imagine the gap as a fairly long one, and place the episode loosely in 542. Brendan is exploring the West Indies. He visits, perhaps, Long Island (or another of the

Bahamas, or Grand Cayman), drops the second Jonah, and goes on to Jamaica.

IX (*cont.*), 26:6 – 26:12
Back to St. Ailbe's Isle for Christmas; then " sailing about the ocean for a long time "
Brendan reaches Madeira at Christmas in 542. There follow several years with only three definite incidents, all of which are important and have already been quoted. Somewhere in this period is the gap indicated in the *Life* between the two portions of the quest. After his unrecorded return to Ireland Brendan starts out again, let us say, in the spring of 548.

X, 26:13 – 27:2
The transparent sea on the feast of St. Peter and for eight days thereafter
I do not know which feast of St. Peter is meant here, or on what date the Irish kept it, but the episode may be assigned to 548. The only considerable sea of this kind in the Atlantic is among the Bahamas, which Brendan is presumably revisiting. Coral dust is responsible; and as in the Greenland episode, we get a significant convergence of detail—the flat island and the translucent sea are both of them un-European and both of them suggestive of coral. The great surfacing fish can be seen at Bimini, where modern anglers go after them—dolphins, tuna, sailfish, swordfish.[32]

X (*cont.*)–XI, 27:3 – 29:9
The crystal column; eight days northward to the Island of Smiths
The season for icebergs is in spring, when they drift down from Greenland and Baffin Bay. To provide for the northward sail to Iceland, we shall want to give this particular berg as long as possible a south-easterly journey before its dissolution. Also we must leave time for Brendan to get from Iceland to the Faeroes for his Easter appointment. Hence the beginning of this episode is best placed in the spring of 548 or 549 or 550, whichever year

would have had the latest Easter by the assumed method of reckoning. Brendan sights the berg somewhere in the fifty-north-forty-west area, examines it at close quarters, and sails before the prevailing wind to Iceland, witnessing an eruption and then steering southward for Streymoy and the Paschal feast.

XII, 29:10 – 31:33
The northern mountain of smoke and fire; seven days south to Judas
Here, after the *altera vero die* marking a break, the author reverts to straightforward narrative. It is February 551. The doom of the third Jonah, the Judas incident, and the apparition of demons, manifestly belong to the confines of hell, already fixed as the Iceland zone. The graphically portrayed volcano, rearing through mist in a remote and appalling north, suggests the Svalbard of medieval Icelandic geographers. This was probably not the modern Svalbard, namely Spitzbergen, but rather Jan Mayen, which lies in desolate seas between Norway and Greenland.[33] The most conspicuous part of Jan Mayen is the huge lava cone of Beerenberg, seven thousand feet high. From it a long, narrow and much lower promontory, not visible so far off, stretches twenty miles to the south-west. Clouds and fogs are the rule. Beerenberg has not been active in historical times, but an eruption of one of the lower cones was observed in 1818.

Jan Mayen seems to be a good choice and the only one available. The island must be in a high latitude, because there is ice on the sea a full week's sail to the south of it. Judas's rock with its frozen fringe is perhaps a cloud-wrapped promontory of Iceland; the demons who attack the boat recall Cormac's Arctic mosquitoes, and also the small black fiends of the *Life*.

Brendan sails southward from Jan Mayen before the polar wind[34] along the 10th meridian or a few degrees west of it.

XIII, 31:34 – 34:17
Three more days southward; the precipitous islet of Paul the hermit
The account of Paul's retreat adequately fits Rockall, which

rises from the Atlantic beyond the Hebrides, on a line drawn approximately south from Jan Mayen past Iceland. Rockall[35] is a granite cone with a portion split off, and, from most angles, looks more or less circular. Even the *Navigatio* measurement is somewhat too generous. The greatest diameter is a hundred feet, the smallest eighty, and the tip of the cone is about seventy feet above water. Almost totally barren, Rockall has only algae and lichens on its face. Landing is very tricky, and impossible on the sheer eastern cliff; elsewhere it has been accomplished, though (as our text says) there is no indentation deep enough to admit the whole of a boat, and Paul's action in kicking his own away is an accurate touch. In 1811 Lieutenant Basil Hall led a party of sailors from the frigate *Endymion*, who got ashore and managed to scramble to a ledge near the top. This, now known as Hall's Ledge, extends from the western side round to the south-east. An expedition in 1955 used a helicopter to reach it. There are no caves, no springs, no mammals, but the description of the rock and Brendan's ascent is very much what might be imagined by somebody acquainted with Rockall's appearance from a boat. The line of Hall's Ledge, where the hermit dwells, is traced at a distance by the guillemots and gannets that settle there.

Paul himself, the white-maned, preternaturally long-lived exile, is a figure of a type that recurs in the immram literature. The monks encounter him forty days before Easter, ninety years after St. Patrick's death—that is, in March 551. Six years of voyaging lie behind them, and the seventh is advancing.

XIV, 34:18 – 35:6

Departure southward; " drifting to and fro " for some time; arrival at
  the Island of Sheep on Holy Saturday; across to the Paradise of
  Birds on the whale's back, accompanied by the Procurator; depar-
  ture after Pentecost with the Procurator as guide

After leaving Rockall, Brendan is borne slowly to the Faeroes by the Gulf Stream Drift and the westerlies. His starting direction is puzzling, since he seems to be making for his Easter rendezvous without trying to go anywhere else first. But the author perhaps locates Rockall too far north. If the Judas scene does belong to Iceland, the brief "three days" from there to Paul supports the conjecture.

Brendan is about to repeat the long westward sail of VIII, but with a pilot.

XIV (cont.), 35:6 – 36:19

"Forty days" sailing; the dense cloud; emergence near coast; "forty days" exploring the Land of Promise in autumnal sunshine; the large river flowing towards the interior; the celestial messenger; return to Ireland

Again Brendan follows the Viking route.[36] But this time, advised by the Procurator, he swings round into the fog on the Newfoundland Banks, passes Nova Scotia, and lands at last on the Atlantic seaboard of what is now the U.S. For the second part of the journey no duration is given, and his actual landing may be well on in August, so the exploration can be stretched into autumn.

Brendan· and the monks "traverse" this gigantic island on foot, "viewing it in various directions," a choice of words that suggests a fairly direct march through hilly country. The wide river that flows on toward the centre does not sound like the one reported by Barinthus, and the fact that Brendan's experience does not reproduce his or even confirm it (since in fifteen days Barinthus was half-way to the other side) tells against any merely literary interpretation. But it is none too clear why, when Brendan reaches his own river, he is so determined on the necessity of crossing it, and regards his failure to do so as a fatal check. We might picture him coasting down America and landing in Chesapeake Bay, then pressing forward through Virginia and Kentucky, passing over the Appalachians, and turning gradually north to make a circuit, but finding his path blocked by the Ohio near Huntington.

The celestial messenger tells Brendan of Christ's wish to disclose to him the " mysteries in this immense ocean ": thus the author conveys his geographical purpose. The prophecy of the future is double. In a day of trial for Christians, the land will be revealed to Brendan's successors—presumably to his Irish monastic successors, and as a place of refuge. Afterwards, when the Church's warfare is won and persecution has ended for ever, the same knowledge will be imparted to Christians generally.

Of these predictions the latter is hypothetical. It is the former that concerns the author's contemporaries. During the ninth century the Irish monks were being repeatedly hounded from their retreats by the heathen Norse. They had to flee from the Scottish Isles and from the Faeroes and Iceland, and the *Navigatio* drops a plain hint at a haven farther off still.

Brendan's return to Ireland is quickly disposed of. The final point of interest is that the Procurator stays in America.

5

The following, it would seem, is arguable. I do not say that it is proved; I do not say yet that it is even clearly probable, since the *a priori* unlikelihood is a potent objection. But the interlocking consistencies and coincidences are surely striking enough to justify continued inquiry, and an attempted approach along other lines.

It may be argued that the author knows the Atlantic to be exceedingly large, and that he has some notions of its oceanography and meteorology. That he knows of the prevailing westerlies, and of the Gulf Stream Drift as moving approximately south-west to north-east. That he knows also of the currents and winds past Portugal and Africa.

It may be argued that he knows of St. Kilda with its cliffs, its solitary cove, and its empty ruins; Streymoy with its sheep, pasture-land, temperate winters, and whales; the narrow Vestmanna Sound; Vagar with its southward-flowing streams

St. Kilda: the bay

Bahamas: aerial view of Berry Islands,
illustrating the flat formation

Rockall, showing Hall's Ledge near the summit

and flocks of white birds. That he knows about the huge icebergs that float east of Newfoundland in spring, and the prevailing winds that will sweep a boat from this region to Iceland in its much higher latitude. That he knows Iceland's volcanoes, and what their eruptions are like. That he knows Jan Mayen with its mists and volcanic cone; the polar wind that can carry you south from it past eastern Iceland; and the possibility of arriving at Rockall by persevering on roughly the same course. That he knows that Rockall is small and bare and round and steep, and has a ledge near the summit running toward the east side.

It may be argued that he knows, if dimly, of Madeira and the Azores; of the January wind blowing from the former to the latter; of the mineral springs on St. Michaels, and its approximate whereabouts, a little to the south of the Gulf Stream Drift and near the Sargasso. That he knows the Bahamas: the flat flowery coral islands, the translucent coral seas, the great fishes that break the surface. That he knows Jamaica, with its abundant water, its crowded forests, its gorgeous birds and fragrant atmosphere and very green herbage.

It may be argued that he has some conception of the northern route to America, the Viking route, from the Faeroes past Iceland and the tip of Greenland. That he knows of the whales in Davis Strait (the *Life* tradition adds Eskimos and walruses). That he knows the stunted sub-arctic vegetation and the bad Greenland summer and autumn. That he knows that a boat leaving southwest Greenland and following the trend of current and wind will go north before she goes south.

It may be argued that he knows the fog on the Newfoundland Banks and the way in which a voyager will emerge and sight land. That he knows that the land sighted is of continental extent and has a hot summer and autumn, that a man marching inland can overlook wide expanses, and that a considerable distance up country a broad river flows away from the Atlantic.

I doubt whether pure guesswork could yield so much, fifty items of information at least. If the reconstruction covered only a fraction of the story, leaving the rest nonsensical, then these apparent successes could be ascribed to luck. But it covers the entire Voyage. Every island has been accounted for, every incident except a few which are palpably mythical has been given a factual basis; and most of the details used are specific, they are not generalities that could apply to any island or any stretch of sea. The volcanic islands cannot be in the Hebrides or the Faeroes, and since they are explicitly northern they cannot be located in any other volcanic zone. The flat island with the flowers and enormous fruit cannot be fitted into the mountainous groups closer to Africa. With the island of bad water we get only that solitary distinctive feature, yet it does distinguish; it is enough to exclude the vast majority of Atlantic islands other than St. Michaels. The reconstruction, then, may be as fanciful as you please, but what are the chances that guesswork would produce a story on which such a reconstruction could even be forced? Once again, try it with *Mael Duin*, or try reconstructing the *Navigatio* itself in a different way without loss of descriptive aptitude.

I have held over one further consideration, the question of distances and the implied shape of the map. How badly does the author distort?

He never quotes a distance in miles. It must always be deduced from the number of days' sailing recorded, and as the wind is sometimes favourable and sometimes slight or erratic, all such deductions are most uncertain. However, this practice of measurement in so many days' sail used to be customary. The problem is to judge what mileage is represented, on the average, by a day's sail in the *Navigatio*. Can it be shown that any of the distances specified were known in the early Middle Ages? If it were established that the distance from Island A to Island B was known to be 300 miles, and our reconstruction made Brendan traverse it in six days, we would have the provisional equation

1 day's sail = 50 miles,

which could then be tested on the other distances mentioned. The answer is that none of the distances were known in that way. But one of them was measured quite early, very possibly as early as the tenth century, in the " day's sail " unit of the Norse. This was the distance from Jan Mayen to north-east Iceland, which is given in the *Landnamabok* of the Icelander Ari Frode (1.i) as four days' sail. The *Navigatio* as interpreted here makes it seven days from a point at sea where the top of the cone is still visible, perhaps a substantial part of another day's sail off, so that the author may be supposed to imagine Brendan's heavily laden boat as travelling approximately four-sevenths or four-eighths as fast as a Viking ship. Unfortunately the *doegr* or day's sail of Norse writers is an indefinite measure which may vary from 70 miles to fully 100. Arguing from the structure of the longships themselves, T. D. Kendrick suggests an average of 75 miles a day; for this particular voyage from Jan Mayen to north-east Iceland, the implied average would be greater.[37]

Hence we might infer, tentatively, that the *Navigatio* " day's sail " corresponds to an average of somewhere between 35 and 50 miles. Durations are specified or indicated for twelve phases of the Voyage:

1. Out into the Atlantic from the Dingle peninsula with a favouring wind . . .   12 days
2. . . . then back by an uncertain course to St. Kilda, reached after a total of 40 days from embarkation   28 days
3. From the Faeroes to Madeira, " tossing to and fro " on a devious course   90 days
4. From Madeira to St. Michaels, drifting without oar or sail   40–50 days
5. From St. Michaels by a curving course to the Faeroes, mainly drifting   30 days?
6. From the Faeroes to Davis Strait off south-west Greenland   40 days
7. From the flat island to Jamaica   22 days

8. Sailing through the Bahamas   8 days
9. From the iceberg to Iceland   8 days
10. From within sight of Jan Mayen to eastern
     Iceland   7–8 days
11. From eastern Iceland to Rockall   3 days
12. From the Faeroes to the fog off Newfoundland   40 days

We must discard Nos. 4 and 5 as largely taken up with drifting at unknown speed—though No. 5 does not work out at all badly. The rest are tolerable if inconclusive. A start south-westward with a " favouring wind," followed by a wide circling sweep to St. Kilda, will accommodate No. 1 (420–600 miles) and No. 2 (980–1400 miles). No. 3 is doubtful, only implying that the passage is very long, perhaps the longest one in the story . . . as it is. No. 6 (1400–2000 miles) is satisfactory: the distance depends on the part of the Strait to which it is measured, but lies within these limits. No. 7 gives 770–1100 miles: if the flat island is precisely Long Island or Grand Cayman this is too much, but if the author is only measuring from " somewhere in the Bahamas " he need not be far out. No. 8 (280–400 miles) is reasonable. No. 9 (also 280–400 miles) is to-day too short, though changes of climate may have made a difference. No. 10 is the distance used as a basis and is therefore axiomatically acceptable. No. 12 (1400–2000 miles) is also acceptable, especially if the boat goes into Davis Strait and out again, a route followed by small sailing craft in modern times.[38] As for No. 11, which places Rockall only 105–150 miles from Iceland, a northward displacement of Rockall does at least explain the otherwise inexplicable southward direction in which the boat moves away from it.

A map, therefore, can be drawn without gross inaccuracy, and nearly all the places fit together to form an intelligible net-work. The first island with the cliffs, the Island of Sheep, the Paradise of Birds, St. Ailbe's Isle, the island of bad water, the curdled sea, the sea where the monsters fight, the island of stunted vegetation, the crystal column, the Island of Smiths, the isolated volcano, the rock of Judas, the islet of Paul, the fog-barrier, the Land of Promise itself—all these are linked by the descriptions and interconnecting sea-passages. They can be brought into a spatial or at any rate a topological relationship with each other. Only the "West Indian" episodes are detached; the author is not sure how to fit them on to his map. The anomaly is interesting.

6

To reject all this out of hand, it would be necessary to show that while the scoring of so many hits by pure chance is improbable, the possession of such knowledge by a tenth-century Irishman is still more improbable. That is the next topic to go into—what sources can be discovered, whether in books or in recognised explorations. However, it is worth remarking at once how much the historians of geography have already allowed to be within credence. All authorities admit an Irish knowledge of the Faeroes and Iceland; Beazley mentions Rockall, with perhaps Madeira and the Azores; Wright hazards St. Kilda and the iceberg zone; Babcock suggests Madeira and the Gulf of St. Lawrence.[39] Surveying all these confessed possibilities (and in aggregate they make an impressive possible gazetteer) we may take it as settled in principle that a tenth-century Irishman *might* have had a great deal of the knowledge attributed.

As I said before, counsel has too often been darkened by an obsession with trying to conjecture where St. Brendan actually went. The conclusion is that he may have gone to the Faeroes, or the Canaries, or wherever the writer prefers to send him. But whatever the selection, it leads either to wild dreaming or to an arbitrary restriction of the field, and this biographical mode of study must be given up if any real progress is to be made.

Obviously it is hard to believe that Brendan was reconnoitring Iceland and America before Columba got to the

Hebrides; that he was outdoing all the other monastic seafarers, not at the height of their activity, but before that activity had even fairly started. Cormac's unintentional Arctic trip must be placed later, and Adamnan, who describes it at length and calls it a voyage to the limits of human attainment, does not take Brendan beyond the Western Isles. It might be urged that Adamnan is concerned with people only as they figure in the life of Columba. Perhaps; yet he speaks of several sea-pilgrimages, and we would expect to find some allusion to anything spectacular achieved by another of Columba's friends. The continuing silence through the eighth century, the lack of evidence for public awareness of any discoveries by Brendan, makes the reality of his bolder exploits all the more dubious.

We may gladly grant him his voyages through the Hebrides, and a sojourn in Wales, in view of the popularity of British monasteries as training centres for Irish clerics. All else is speculation. Attempts to rationalise the grand tour by rearrangement or editing can never convince. I am thinking here mainly of Dr. G. A. Little, whose *Brendan the Navigator* I consulted for my first sketch.[40] To insist, like Dr. Little, on Brendan personally, is to expose yourself to a species of criticism that diverts attention from the true issue and discredits even such ingenious and attractive ideas as Dr. Little's. Moreover, if anything like a credible voyage is to be carved out of the *Navigatio* the episodes must be reshuffled, an unwarranted change which obscures the character of the text.

There is a further difficulty over the large wooden ship which gives such a memorable flash of authenticity in the *Life*. It remains wholly inferential. We can say what it would probably have been like, but we cannot point to a sixth-century Irish ship and say, " There." No archæological traces have been found. If such vessels existed they must have been extremely few, and the art of their construction little diffused; the adoption of Norse shipping terminology long after Brendan's time, in the absence of Irish words, is a strong negative argument. As for his going

all the way to America in a curragh, and coming safely home . . .
well, I doubt it. Only practical experiment could fully establish
the probabilities here, but he would surely have needed extraordinary skill and extraordinary luck—double luck, in both
directions.

What then is the truth about Brendan the Navigator, the
man, that is, as distinct from the legend? We don't know. It is
a pity, but we don't. Literary allusions do point to a tradition
connecting him with an Atlantic quest; yet the actual key
characters in the *Navigatio* may be Barinthus and the Procurator.
The Brendan of legend is not so much a pioneer by whom lands
are discovered as a good listener to whom the report of them is
passed on, and, in several of the places he visits, he finds that
others have come there ahead of him. St. Ailbe's monks have
been in possession for eighty years, the three choirs are Christian
and therefore of Old World provenance, and the Book of
Leinster even preserves a story about an anchorite " whom
Brendan found before him in the Land of Promise." [41] A supposition which goes as far as any can go with a semblance of
plausibility is that the saint's Hebridean mission led him to take
an interest in Atlantic geography, real and fabulous; that he
collected data for which his community became the repository;
and that he made an exploratory foray—perhaps through the
Outer Hebrides probing the northern route, perhaps toward the
south-west where the later map-makers took him—but, in any
case, a foray that kept him away long enough for the growth of
rumours. Round these the legend crystallised.

What matters at the moment is not the lost truth about
St. Brendan but the nature of the geographical lore which he,
or his disciples, or at any rate somebody in Ireland, would seem
to have compiled. And at the end is the crowning question:
how to construe Brendan's America, what to make of the " West
Indies " and the Land of Promise itself. Did the *Navigatio* author
guess, or did he know?

Part Two

THE MAKING OF A MAP

CHAPTER FOUR

Pathways in the Ocean

To DRAW this clear if reluctant distinction between the Voyager and his attributed Voyage is simply to accept a conclusion toward which analysis of the problem soon drove me. On the one hand the historical element withered to a shred, but, on the other, the setting given to Brendan's travels acquired substance. With all its marvellous accretions the *Navigatio* contrived to stand up, not indeed as a proof but as a puzzle; in that character it confronted me, complete with its bewildering climax in the Land Promised to the Saints.

Pre-Norse knowledge of America did not strike me as being incredible in itself. Besides weighing the possibility of voyages by the Irish, I might see whether geographical matter from other nations supplied any clues; whether I could detect the New World (however disguised) in Greek literature, or in Arab literature, or anywhere else. But was it worth trying?

My solid datum was the fact that an intelligible map could be inferred from the *Navigatio*. That might be due to the author's actual use of a map, or of equivalent books, but it might also be due to sustained coincidence. If there was no real reason to think that anybody in that period could have known so much, then coincidence, however far-fetched, was the more prudent explanation, and the quest for a prototype of his apparent America might best be abandoned as the pursuit of a mirage. Strictly speaking, of course, the choice was not so rigid, because of items like the Island of Sheep for which the proposed interpre-

.tation presented no difficulty. But these did not account for a large enough section of the map to create a presumption that the rest was equally well grounded.

It appealed to me as a fair procedure to approach the harder part by way of the less hard. What I had already done in a glancing fashion I could go on to do more systematically. Following the fictitious Brendan outward from his home waters, I could examine the conjectural map feature by feature and see whether it could be documented, in the sense that a tenth-century Irishman could have filled it in from sources available to him. It fell into three divisions, a northern, a southern, and a western. If relevant information could be shown to have existed in those days for the first two portions, then, as far as they were concerned, the multiple-coincidence theory might be dismissed, in favour of the more natural view that genuine knowledge—however distorted and decorated—underlay them. The resultant case by analogy for genuine knowledge rather than guesswork underlying the third portion, the western or " American," would then justify inquiry into possible sources for that too, from which, perhaps, the shape of an unsuspected discovery would emerge.

2

Brendan's hypothetical northern sailing takes him most of the way along the northern route to America, the route gradually traversed by the Irish and Norse during the Dark Ages. I have construed the *Navigatio* as referring here to St. Kilda, Rockall, the Faeroes, Iceland, Jan Mayen, south-west Greenland, and the Davis Strait area; also to the prevailing winds. Let us ask, in more detail than hitherto, just what the potentialities are.

St. Kilda cannot be documented as far back as the tenth century, but a tenth-century Irishman could certainly have heard of it. The Hebrides were not a remote desert archipelago, nor was their exploration a thing of yesterday. They were known to the Romans, who sent a fleet round Great Britain on at least one occasion, and coins of the later Empire in the same area suggest that it remained within reach of civilisation.[1] Brendan's authentic voyages took him into that quarter, and, as we have seen, many of his people came after, one of whom dedicated the chapel to him on St. Kilda itself. No blind leap into the ocean would have been necessary to find the island: once Harris was known St. Kilda must have been known too before long, since it is visible from the hills above West Loch Tarbert.[2] The Gaelic inhabitants of whom the remnant left in 1930 had nothing definite to tell of their ancestors' arrival, but the community had lived there for a very great while.

Rockall is nearly two hundred miles farther out. Not explicitly catalogued in Irish works, or colonised except in imagination by Irish hermits, it raises an issue that will recur—what the *Navigatio* author might have learnt, directly or indirectly, from the Norse.

The importance of this Norse factor in the life and thought of the period must be re-emphasised. The Scandinavian explosion was due to much the same causes as the similar explosion of Bronze-Age Ægean peoples in which the Trojan War was an incident. Pressure of population in a country of barren mountains and cramped valleys, combined with skill in ship-building and daring in navigation, thrust the surplus inhabitants overseas. Their national adventure passed quickly through a quiet introductory stage into a far more formidable surge of conquest. First came a peaceable movement of peasants into Orkney and Shetland, then a wave—several waves—of predatory noblemen with their warriors, a pirate-aristocracy. These latter, the Vikings, poured from Scandinavia in all directions, into the British Isles and France and the Mediterranean, down the rivers of Russia to the Black Sea and Constantinople, and outward over the Atlantic to the Faeroes and Iceland. They invaded Ireland, as we saw, in 832, and for a time the carnage was fearful; but phases of peace, with the growth of trade and the mingling of blood and culture, brought an era of interchange before the ninth century was out. The Norse in short were available; any geography known to them through their wide seafaring could have been transmitted to educated Irishmen, and by the somewhat more tranquil tenth century it probably was.[3]

Rockall sticks up in a space of ocean constantly crossed by them in transit between Ireland and their more northerly outposts. They were not cautious coastal sailors. They struck out across the high seas, and it is far more likely than otherwise that some of them sighted the granite cone on the way, and compared notes about it afterwards. The same applies to the Irish slaves and others whom they took with them.

I have no wish to present inferences as certainties. Nothing in writing mentions St. Kilda, nothing in writing mentions Rockall. But their identification with Brendan's islands offers no difficulty. There is no need to postulate unproved expeditions. It is a question, not indeed of information specifically known to have been possessed, but of *information derivable from voyages known to have been made.* That is a criterion to bear in mind.

The Faeroes we have considered (pages 87-8), and with them the documentation is sound. One date suggested for the Irish settlement is 670;[4] Dicuil at any rate confirms that the archipelago was familiar—sheep, birds and all—in the ninth century, and could therefore have passed, fictionalised, into the *Navigatio.* Those who sailed into the northern Atlantic would have reported on the prevailing winds there. Streymoy, the Island of Sheep, is made a point of departure, and so it doubtless appeared to the Irish and their Norse successors. The Faeroes were still more or less Europe, but beyond lay mysteries; and it is here in Brendan's infernal Arctic that we encounter the great ghost of Thule, and, for the first time, come into contact with a tradition from classical antiquity.

About 330 B.C., the merchant Pytheas, a Greek from the

colony at Marseilles, embarked on a voyage of discovery. He took his ship out of the Mediterranean via Gibraltar, coasted round the Bay of Biscay, crossed the Channel, and circumnavigated Britain. On his return he wrote an account of what he had done, with a section about an island called Thule, which attracted much comment. Pytheas's account survives only in second-hand and third-hand fragments quoted by authors none too friendly to him, and even these, if they are quoted fairly, cast doubt on his reliability, since his estimates of distance are most peculiar. On the other hand he is known to have been an excellent astronomer, and some of his more significant statements depend on celestial observations unlikely to be far wrong.

Thule, he declared, lay six days' sail north of Britain. In summer it had nights of only two or three hours, and from somewhere in it, apparently, one could see the midnight sun. With allowance made for the slight change over the past two millennia, these data establish that the part of Thule described by Pytheas extended from about 64° N. to the Arctic Circle, which was then 66° 15′ N. Pytheas said he was told of Thule by British informants (a profoundly interesting fact, implying previous voyages), and it is sometimes asserted that he never went there himself, but merely reported what the Britons affirmed. He is quoted verbatim, however, as saying that " the barbarians showed him," indicating perhaps that he sailed to Thule with native pilots. It is sometimes asserted also that he spoke of this northern island as inhabited by people who ate oats and kept bees, a description which would make its identification easier, but there is no proof that the passage applied to Thule specifically. He did say that around Thule there was neither land nor sea nor air but a bizarre mixture of all three which impeded walking and navigation: we have visions of the southerner battling his disgusted way through snow, sludge and clammy fogs. Finally, a day's sail beyond Thule the sea was frozen.

This is a simplification of the problem, which has been

threshed out at considerable length. It is undetermined whether Pytheas's Thule was Iceland or a misinterpreted Norway. Prevailing winds and currents would have tended to carry him and his precursors to Norway rather than Iceland, but either could have been reached with good seamanship in six days.[5] The name affords no help; various fanciful Germanic and Celtic etymologies have not carried conviction.

But wherever Pytheas went, he fixed a permanent image in the classical mind—an image of land, " Ultima Thule," near the frozen frontier of the sea beyond Britain. Pliny speaks of a northern British island called Berrice, probably Mainland in the Shetlands, as " the starting-place for Thule." Seneca's tragedy *Medea* includes a choral passage which is said to have stirred the imagination of Columbus:

> *Venient annis secula seris*
> *Quibus Oceanus vincula rerum*
> *Laxet, et ingens pateat tellus,*
> *Tethysque novos detegat orbes,*
> *Nec sit terris ultima Thule.*

Freely, " The time shall come at length when Ocean will unloose the bonds he imposes, when the vast Earth will lie open, when the sea-goddess will disclose new worlds, and Thule will not be the last of lands." They had a copy of this play in the Irish monastery at Bobbio.[6]

Iceland must have been reached by someone in the fourth century A.D.; three coins of Diocletian have been unearthed in its south-east corner. The sixth-century Gothic historian Jordanes, who is the first author to make any significant allusion to Thule after that, is also the first to refer to it in terms that unequivocally denote Iceland. He locates it far to the west, and excludes any link with Scandinavia. Isidore of Seville, a seventh-century bishop through whom a large amount of classical learning was transmitted to medieval Europe, describes " Thyle " as the most remote of islands and places it to the north-west of Britain. Again it must be Iceland.[7]

Dicuil treats the Icelandic identity of " Thyle " as self-evident. After citing Pliny and others, he goes on to quote some of the Irish monastic seamen:

It is now thirty years since certain priests, who had been on that island from the 1st of February to the 1st of August, told that not only at the time of the summer solstice, but also during the days before and after, the setting sun at evening conceals itself as it were behind a little mound, so that it does not grow dark even for the shortest space of time, but whatsoever work a man will do, even picking the lice out of his shirt, he may do it just as though the sun was there, and if they had been upon the high mountains of the island perhaps the sun would never be concealed by them.

Dicuil indicates, however, that the monks never actually saw the midnight sun while they were in " Thyle." He adds: " A day's sail northward they found the frozen sea." [8]

As with the Faeroes, a doubt lingers as to how many Irish settled there, and when they did it, and whether the monks were the only ones. There are the same hints at a larger Celtic population of long standing—Gaelic names of fjords, rivers, mountains, and so on—though these may have been conferred by Irish or half-Irish who accompanied the Norse immigrants. The Vestmanna Islands off the coast near Hekla are said to have been named from some fugitive " West-men " or Irishmen shipped to Iceland as slaves in the ninth century by Leif Hrodmarsson, but it has been suggested that Irishmen inhabited the islands before, and that the story of Leif's runaway slaves taking refuge there was an etymological fiction invented later.[9]

One glimpse more, a very intriguing glimpse, in the twelfth-century *Landnamabok* of the Icelander Ari Frode, who spells the classical name " Tili."

Before Iceland was peopled from Norway there were in it the men whom the Northmen call Papar; they were Christian men, and it is held that they must have come over sea from the west [i.e. the western part of the sphere of Norse activities], for there were found left by them Irish books, bells, and croziers, and more things besides, from which it could be understood that they were West-men; these things were found east in Pap-isle and Papyli, and it is stated in English books that in those times voyages were made between these countries.[10]

Ari's English books no longer exist, but his quotation of them is interesting. Northern islands are shown on the fine Anglo-Saxon map already noted.

Thus Brendan's northerly isle with the pyrotechnic smithy falls into place as the product of a respectable tradition lately corroborated, Thule-Iceland being a thoroughly established fact. No early writer who discusses Thule says anything of volcanoes, but, by the tenth century, people had indubitably gone there and seen them: the Irish from about 795 onward, the Norse from about 860 onward. To the question why the volcanic island is not actually designated as Thule—why, in fact, none of Brendan's islands is given a proper name—the answer lies perhaps in the author's method. He portrays Brendan as groping his way to these places before the Norse and before Dicuil's monks; for the Navigator they are still *terra incognita* or virtually so, and we are shown them through his eyes, unfamiliar.

If the reconstructed map is correct, however, Seneca's prophecy has been fulfilled and Ultima Thule is no longer ultimate. Two more leaps have been taken beyond it.

I have argued that Brendan's second volcanic island is the same as " Svalbard." The *Landnamabok* (i.i) alludes briefly to that inhospitable shore, four days' sail northward from Longness in northern Iceland, and Professor O'Dell's identification with Jan Mayen is satisfactory. While nobody knows whether the Norse reached it as far back as the tenth century, they could presumably have done so at any time after their colonisation of the greater island in 874. Cormac indeed would seem to have gone equally far much earlier, and his " stinging creatures " may have supplied a hint for Brendan's demons, but Adamnan says nothing of any land sighted by him. It is worth repeating, however, that Dicuil speaks of the Irish monks who explored Iceland as also sailing north from it.

Lastly, Greenland. Its discovery is sometimes credited to Eric the Red, who sailed from Iceland in 982, having made the country too hot (figuratively) to hold him. He rounded Cape Farewell, followed the drifting ice to haven in the comparatively temperate south-west, christened the country with an agreeable name, and brought settlers over about three years after his reconnaissance. The *Navigatio* cannot be as late as this expedition of Eric. But he was not actually the first in the field, and when he set out from Iceland he was looking for something he expected to find. The real pioneer was Gunnbjörn, and it was a report of his voyage, as far back as the year 900, that shaped Eric's course. In transit from Norway to Iceland Gunnbjörn was driven by storms along the same path, seeing a large country and many small islands, " skerries." Probably he sighted and rounded Cape Farewell.[11] We are not told what else he saw, but Eric's enterprise after Gunnbjörn and his crew were all dead shows that they must have spread the news. Accounts of their experience could have furnished all that sounds authentic for this area in the *Navigatio* and in the *Life of St. Brendan* too: a long westward sweep, islands of different sizes, stunted vegetation, foul weather, winds and currents tending northward, Eskimos, whales, walruses. (There is, however, another possible source which we shall study later.)

If this view is accepted, by the way, the *Navigatio* can be dated with fair accuracy. It must be later than 900; but the *Mael Duin* adaptations of the volcano, the iceberg and the transparent sea push it back before the date of the immram, which is 920 or a trifle sooner. The implication is that it was written in 910 or within a very few years of that; the reference to

LAND TO THE WEST

" tribulation " might suggest a connection with a renewed Norse offensive which afflicted Ireland in 914.

At any rate it turns out that the northern sector of the proposed map is entirely credible. A tenth-century Irishman could have learnt of the places and their spatial relationship. He would have needed to be a good scholar, a good inquirer, a good listener, but he could most assuredly have done it. Except for the minor query suspended over Jan Mayen, all this part of the *Navigatio* can be put together from information known to have been possessed, plus information derivable from voyages known to have been made; information in a broad sense, including some misinformation, but rooted in geographical fact. Nothing merely speculative has thus far proved necessary, and no strong inherent improbability has thus far been demonstrated. It is simpler to suppose that the author drew on available data than that he guessed well.

3

Brendan's southern adventures are comprised for practical purposes in Sections VI–VII, lines 14:17 – 19:25. If the reconstruction is right, the author shows knowledge of Madeira, the Azores, the Sargasso Sea, and various trends of wind and current, notably the Gulf Stream Drift.

Information was available to him for this region also. Much of it, however, was classical rather than recent, and traceable in the first instance to the Phœnicians and Carthaginians who traded in the nearer Atlantic with Tartessus and Cadiz as bases, reached or at least knew the British Isles, and coasted far round Africa under such captains as Hanno. Diodorus Siculus, about 8 B.C., has this to say:

> There lies out in the Ocean from Libya [Africa] an island of considerable size, situated a number of days' voyage to the west. Its land is fruitful, much of it being covered with

mountains and the remainder a beautiful level plain. Through it flow navigable rivers, which are also used for irrigation. . . . In ancient times it remained undiscovered because of its distance from the known world, but it was discovered at a later period . . . by the Phœnicians who while exploring the coast outside of the Pillars of Hercules [Gibraltar] were driven by strong winds a great distance out to sea.

This is doubtless Madeira, a shade exaggerated.[12]   The same island is described in much the same language in the collection *De Mirabilibus Auscultationibus*, ascribed, falsely, to Aristotle. Diodorus adds that the rulers of Carthage stopped an Etruscan project to found a colony there, partly because they wanted to prevent an exodus of their own citizens, partly because they wanted to have a refuge in case of catastrophe.   The paragraph gives documentation not only for St. Ailbe's Isle but for the winds blowing towards it from the north-east.

Madeira and the African archipelagos became entangled, in classical imagination, with myths of the " Fortunate Isles " or " Isles of the Blest " as old as Homer and Hesiod and indeed much older.   Plutarch, in his *Life of Sertorius*, says that when the rebel leader was at Cadiz he met some sailors lately returned from those islands, which were two in number, inhabited, with a gentle climate, and ten thousand stadia away—roughly a thousand miles.   Sertorius wanted to retire there, but was prevented.   One of them was undoubtedly Madeira and the other Porto Santo, its small neighbour.   In Pliny's *Natural History*, however, and in the geographies of Strabo and Ptolemy, the Fortunate Isles are the Canaries, discovered by the Carthaginians and rediscovered toward the beginning of the Christian era by the Moroccan king Juba, who may have had access to Punic records.   Ptolemy runs his basic meridian close by the group, and lists Madeira separately.   Late-classical and early-medieval authors give further variations on the same theme.[13]

So Madeira and the waters around it can be admitted.   The

Azores and the Sargasso Sea are more problematical. Besides referring to the Canaries, Pliny gives an obscure and diffident description, drawn partly from Carthaginian sources, of a group called the Gorgades or Gorgon Islands (inhabited by apes) and another called the Hesperides, neither seemingly very far out from the coast of Africa.[14]   While it is quite possible that the Carthaginians did go to the Azores, their habitual secretiveness, and the ruin of Carthage and its commerce, left a haze of doubt hanging over their exploits.   No one can tell how much they passed on: very little to academic geographers, but perhaps more to practising seafarers and collectors of maritime folk-lore.

The Azores, being mountainous, can be seen a long way off. The case for the Carthaginians having sailed over to them rests upon antiquarian evidence which has annoyingly vanished. Attention is concentrated on Corvo, the most westerly of the group, a little island named after the sea-crows or cormorants. It is said that when the Portuguese first arrived about 1450, they climbed to the highest point and found a statue of a man on horseback without a saddle, his left hand touching the horse, his right extended westward.   On the pedestal they made out an inscription in unfamiliar characters.   They carried the statue off downhill and . . . lost it.   Those who treat this tale with respect urge that the Carthaginians used to set up commemorative columns, and that the twelfth-century Arab geographer Idrisi mentions statues on pillars at Cadiz, in the Canaries, and elsewhere; but a natural rock formation on Corvo resembles a figure pointing west, and the story may have grown round it.

More important and far more perplexing is the circumstantial account of a coin-hoard on the same island.   In November 1749, it is said, storm damage uncovered a vault, and searchers picked up a broken vase with gold and copper money in it.   The hoard was taken to a monastery and nine of the coins were sent to a Father Flores in Madrid, who gave them to a Swedish numismatist named Podolyn.   Some were inscribed with horses' heads, others with complete horses.   In 1778 the publication of reproductions by the Gothenburg Royal Society led to the realisation that the coins were North African, eight of them being Carthaginian and all being assignable to the third century B.C. It sounds authentic enough, but the coins have seemingly disappeared, and owing to the recurrent exposure of alleged coin finds as errors or fakes, no conclusion is justified without the originals. There for the moment the matter rests. Archæological work on Corvo might conceivably yield something to show its real date of discovery. Idrisi describes an island of cormorants with which Corvo has been tentatively identified, but on weak grounds.[15]

Vested interests have combined with the gaps in testimony to raise difficulties about the Carthaginians' supposed voyages toward the Sargasso as well as the Azores. Wishing to keep a monopoly of Atlantic trade, they spread reports, which many Greeks including Plato and Aristotle accepted, of clouds and darkness and dangerous shoals; thus anything from them implying a bar to navigation is suspect.[16] However, some of them refer to seaweed in a style that rings true. The Sargasso Sea is an immense patch of ocean chiefly west of the Azores, where the sargasso weed (the only species that grows unattached in open water) flourishes in vast quantities, and the winds and calms are unpredictable. Greenish-brown floating algæ spread across the surface in parallel bands, cluster during tranquil weather in patches covering several acres, and close up when herded by the breeze till a ship seems to be surrounded by prairie. The effect is more alarming than the phenomenon warrants, and the yarns of derelicts trapped in a sort of jungle, while unfounded, are quite excusable. Though the Sargasso proper lies well to the west, weed is sometimes encountered over a wide area stretching beyond the Azores and as far as Madeira and the Canaries. Hence allusions to it in matter derived from the mariners of Carthage must be handled with care, if anything is to be deduced about the extent of their sailing.[17]

The *Periplus* of "Pseudo-Scylax," composed in the fourth

century B.C., speaks of Cerne, "which island, it is stated, is twelve days' coasting beyond the Pillars of Hercules, where the parts are no longer navigable because of shoals, of mud, and of seaweed." Cerne, a Carthaginian depot, was an islet just off the African coast; there is no implication here of a long voyage outward. On the other hand, fragmentary reports of an Atlantic voyage by the Carthaginian Himilco survive (in an uncertain state of preservation) in the *Ora Maritima* of Avienus, a Latin versifier of the late fourth .century A.D., and these are more apposite:

> No breeze drives the ship forward, so dead is the sluggish wind of the idle sea. He [Himilco] also adds that there is much seaweed among the waves, and that it often holds the ship back like bushes. Nevertheless, he says that the sea has no great depth, and that the surface of the earth is barely covered by a little water. The monsters of the sea move continually hither and thither, and the wild beasts swim among the sluggish and slowly creeping ships.

That description may refer to the Sargasso proper, or it may not. It occurs in a brief sketch of a four-month voyage out and back toward Brittany of which Avienus knows hardly anything. Both the weed and the sea-creatures—whales and tunnies—are unfortunately said by Pliny to be met with fairly close to Europe. A second passage gives a direction but still not a distance:

> Farther to the west from these Pillars [Gibraltar] there is boundless sea. Himilco relates that . . . none have sailed ships over these waters, because propelling winds are lacking . . . likewise because darkness screens the light of day with a sort of clothing, and because a fog always conceals the sea.

This impenetrable frontier zone is a composite picture, projected by the Carthaginian hope of deterring competitors. It is built up from reefs off the coast of Africa, weed-masses farther west, fogs farther north, and calms in various places;

Greek myths of a gloomy hell at Earth's limit may have contributed to it, and the thickened and frozen seas described by Pytheas eventually became involved in it also.[18]   Whether the true Sargasso near and beyond the Azores was an original ingredient, it is impracticable to decide.

Avienus himself, however, is a noteworthy person. He may have got whatever he learned of Himilco through lost Greek intermediaries, or he may have got it from Carthaginian manuscripts preserved in North Africa.[19]   But wherever he did get it, his flourishing in the last phase of the Western Empire shows that a tradition of Punic explorations endured into the dark ages, sustained by writings of some kind. There are signs that others were pursuing similar researches at about the same time as Avienus, and even that their findings were supplemented by renewed sailing, unrecorded because of the chaos of Europe. Martianus Capella, who practised law at Carthage in the fifth century, was the author of a philosophical work in which—besides affirming the Earth to be round—he repeated Pliny's statements about the three groups of Atlantic islands, but with the unexpected addition that the Hesperides lie beyond the Gorgades " in the most secret recesses of the sea "; a phrase echoed by Isidore of Seville, who speaks of " secret gulfs." This rearrangement of Pliny's island-groups into a chain stretching away from Africa—to Madeira? to the Azores?—becomes still more explicit in Dicuil, who says that the Gorgades are farther out than the Canaries and the Hesperides are farther out than the Gorgades.[20]

The sinister image of the dead choked ocean recurs in writers from the fourth century onward, and the locale is accepted to be westward, without Arctic or African confusions; the concept has been in some way sorted out. Texts that give indications of distance and latitude make the distance considerable and the latitude roughly that of southern Spain, as the reconstruction of the *Navigatio* requires. Martianus Capella was known to Cassiodorus, the secretary of the Gothic king Theodoric, and a lost book by Cassiodorus himself supplied much material for Jordanes, the same in whose *History of the Goths* an acquaintance with Iceland is first definitely implied. Jordanes may have learnt, through Cassiodorus, of the fourth-century visits to Iceland implied by the coin finds, and concerning the warmer zone he makes some tantalising remarks:

> The impassable farther bounds of Ocean not only has no one attempted to describe, but no man has been allowed to reach: for by reason of obstructing seaweed and the failing of the winds it is plainly inaccessible. . . . This same Ocean has in its western region certain islands *known to almost everyone by reason of the great number of those that journey to and fro.*[21]

It looks as if the Punic and other matter used by Pliny and Ptolemy was not only preserved in the fifth and sixth centuries but actually augmented by new exploration, possibly by victims of war or persecution in quest of a refuge. A sprinkling of late Imperial coins along the African coast may be relevant here.[22] Jordanes, it will be noticed, gets rid of the Carthaginian accretions and hits off the Sargasso more or less rightly.

One more witness, Idrisi the Arab. In the twelfth century he gives a paraphrase of the lost narrative of the brothers Magrurin, which outlined a voyage undertaken before his own day but after the Arab occupation of Portugal, i.e. between 712 and, say, 1100.[23] The brothers resolved to find out " what it is that encloses the Ocean, and what its limits are." They assembled a party of eight, all of their own kindred, and set out from Lisbon. Eleven days' sail westward with a fair wind brought them into a sea " of which the thick waves " (the adjective used in the *Navigatio*) " had a fetid odour, concealed many shoals, and were dimly lit." They turned south and, after further adventures, worked their way back to shore at a promontory of Africa. Some of the story, perhaps all of it, is fictitious, and Idrisi insists here and elsewhere on a super-Carthaginian myth of complete darkness in the farther Atlantic; but the place assigned to the zone of impediment is no less interesting for that. An eleven-day sail puts it about 1000 miles west of Lisbon, near the Azores—that is, in the exact area suggested for Brendan's "thick waves." Honorius of Autun, an author probably read by Idrisi, states in 1130 that the " curdled sea " adjoins the Hesperides and covers the site of lost Atlantis, which lay west from Gibraltar. His Hesperides can hardly be anything but the Azores, a fact which slightly increases the probability that the same group is meant by Martianus Capella and Isidore.[24]

Whatever its factual background, therefore, the thick becalmed sea of the *Navigatio* can be documented both as to nature and as to general situation, with only a subsidiary query arising from the doubtful date of the material drawn on by Honorius and Idrisi. Many able Arab geographers were active from the ninth century onward, and one of these may have been the source.[25]

To sum up, the southern part of the map survives the test evolved for the northern part. It too can be pieced together from information known to have been possessed plus information derivable from voyages known to have been made; or— if " known " in this case is sometimes too strong—surmised fairly plausibly. Some of the sources are more distant in time and space, and some of the channels of transmission to Ireland are less easy to define. Classical items, however, could always have percolated through, and as for Arab items, Irish pilgrims to the Holy Land could have brought back anything current in the Islamic world. Once again it is simpler on balance to suppose that the author collected existing data, or tapped the researches of some precursor, than that he wove such a story out of his unaided fancies.

Lastly a word on the subject of the Gulf Stream. No classical or dark-age authority directly refers to it. In the immram *Snedgus*, however, the monks' boat is made to enter a tepid current three days' sail north-west of the British Isles. The eminent Celtic scholar Zimmer concluded that the Gulf Stream was known to the Irish; the eminent explorer Nansen dissented.[26] But, in any case, a note-book left by Columbus discloses that the phenomenon was observed in his own day by sea-watchers in Ireland, and as they never bothered to publicise it, one may guess that they had been similarly observing and similarly not bothering from time immemorial. Objects, in fact, were drifting continually from across the Atlantic on to their beaches. Columbus describes a dead man and woman of non-European race who had been washed ashore in Galway lashed to some wreckage, and the hard brazil wood that wandered over from Mexico was plentiful enough for regular trade. " Irish wood " was exported to France in the 1460's, and a library in the Louvre was panelled with it. Besides his Hibernian data, Columbus gathered many accounts of artifacts and corpses picked up at sea and on the Atlantic islands, always coming from the west. While there were more people to pick them up in the fifteenth century than in previous ages, similar finds must have occurred far earlier.[27]

4

When I found the *Navigatio* conforming to the real map with such curious pertinacity, I was struck first, let me recall, by the unlikelihood that the author would have scored so many hits by chance. Further thought suggested the only viable counter-claim, namely the still greater unlikelihood that a tenth-century Irishman could have learnt so much. This line of argument has now proved invalid. Most of the proposed Voyage could have been invented by an Irish geographer of unusual but by no means superhuman attainments: a student of Avienus and Dicuil, of Diodorus and the Arabs and other standard authorities, with a special journalistic flair for drawing out travellers in conversation. Herodotus is the obvious parallel, and Herodotus accomplished much more than the *Navigatio* would have required of its author, or of any scholar whose work the author plundered.

To accommodate St. Kilda, Rockall, the Faeroes, Iceland, Jan Mayen, Greenland, Madeira, St. Michaels, the Sargasso, and the prevailing winds and currents, it is seldom necessary to place any uncomfortable strain on the probabilities.

While the *Navigatio Sancti Brendani* is a romance—we must never lose sight of that—it turns out to be, as so many have felt it to be, a geographical text such as to excite curiosity. The chances are that the author had access to a map, or the equivalent of a map, a good deal more comprehensive than anything else that has survived from his period. This being so, the question of the western portion, the " American " residue, becomes a vital one. The air of basic authenticity here is no less impressive than it is in the rest. On the analogy of the rest, therefore, the western portion too should be a product of study rather than fancy; it too should be grounded on actual writings and actual voyages. But the attempt to trace these writings and voyages leads to apparently baffling results.

Brendan's western adventures are those involving the crystal column or iceberg, the fog which precedes his landfall, the continent and river, and the " Bahaman " and " Jamaican " scenes. While inquiry can make a start even here, it glides off quickly into the indefinite.

The iceberg has appealed to many readers as genuine, yet its genuineness is of an elusive kind. It might seem to derive readily enough from the report of some Viking blown off course like Gunnbjörn, and its relationship with Iceland is all in favour of such a view. But the truth is not so patent. The difficulty is that the actual word " ice " is never used. The description stands at a distance from the object, just as the adaptation in *Mael Duin* stands at a further distance, altering the object finally beyond recognition. What Brendan encounters is a large berg, drifting and distintegrating in warmer water, but a berg transfigured by the poetic imagination of a Celt, like Cormac's mosquitoes. How many removes away is the eye-witness? A practical Norseman would have known that the thing was made of ice,

and said so. Has the crystalline transmutation been wrought by
a succession of yarn-spinners none too easily fitted into the time
available; or was the fanciful Celt the original observer, in
which case the column could indubitably have sprung full-blown
into being, but we would have to inquire how the observer got
there? To postulate an enslaved Irish bard in a Viking's off-
course ship is to heap conjecture on conjecture.

So with the fog. There are antecedents, but their nature is
doubtful. If it really is where it seems to be, on the Newfoundland Banks, it is hard to account for by any accidental wanderings
likely to have occurred before the tenth century . . . so far as
our information goes. But it may be a merely literary fog, with
its ancestry in Avienus's paraphrase of Himilco or even in Greek
mythology. Adam of Bremen, a schoolmaster who is the first
writer to refer to the discovery of America by the Norse, quotes
a Danish king about 1070 as saying that "beyond this island"
(Vinland) "no habitable land is found, but all beyond is full of
dreadful masses of ice and boundless fog." Since Vinland was
in fact part of the North American continent, the king's statement
must have been founded on mythology rather than observation.
Similarly Idrisi calls the outer Atlantic the Sea of Gloom, saying
that there is no inhabited place in it and nobody knows what lies
beyond. (Brendan's author, like Bernard Shaw, feels the need
to affirm that there *is* a beyond.) [28]

Breton and Basque fishermen are thought to have ventured
far out toward the Banks in pursuit of cod long before the days
of Columbus and Cabot, and possibly to have sighted Newfoundland.[29] They preferred to keep the secret of the rich
fishing-ground to themselves, and cared nothing for any coast
they happened to see. But there is no way of ascertaining
precisely where they did go, or in what century they first reached
the Banks, if they went there at all. It is interesting to find
Brendan associated with the Breton Machutus in the oldest
recorded form of his saga; but not more than interesting.

Apart from one topic which demands special treatment,

I think we have now wrung the last drop out of the recognised geographical authorities. The rest of the *Navigatio* with its " American " glimpses cannot be explained, at any rate from obvious sources. Classical geography, strictly so-called, is a dead end.

The naïve solution is that the American portion of the narrative is true in substance after all: Brendan did visit the West Indies and the mainland, and came back to tell the tale, which is the source of these items and the nucleus of the whole romance. I have not ruled the possibility out and do not intend to, but the objections previously stated look very grave. There would seem to be some justification for trying to trace a pre-Norse discovery of America, but little or none for ascribing such a discovery to the saint himself. Indeed, as I have stressed, his own legend disclaims it. Barinthus passes over the ocean before him; the Procurator knows the way; the island of the three choirs is a Christian colony already established; and the Book of Leinster mentions that anchorite who preceded Brendan in the Land of Promise itself. Even to take the legend seriously is not to make Brendan the discoverer of America, but to remove the discovery back beyond him.

In that particular sense I decided after a while that I was willing to take it seriously: to rummage about behind the Irish, to sift the traditions of other and older nations, to seek out literary and archæological oddities of however ancient a date, in the hope of uncovering fresh clues to this cryptic West. That search, in the end, was not entirely vain. But there was also one more acknowledged Hibernian possibility to try, and its investigation blended with the next phase of my travels, to which I was already committed for reasons that will transpire in their place.

CHAPTER FIVE

Great Ireland

SUITABLY within the octave of Pentecost, I boarded a plane at London Airport. It touched down at Glasgow and then headed obliquely toward the Arctic Circle, along a line passing not too far from the Paradise of Birds and terminating in an obtuse angle to port, off the coast of Iceland. Beyond that angle lay Reykjavik and America. This was the veritable northern route, the way of the small craft, Irish and Norse; I was making my own first reconnaissance of it.

Dusk descended as we flew over the Highlands, still so extraordinarily bare and vacant, while on the left Brendan's Hebrides appeared fitfully as sombre strips of land with pallor between. The Scottish mainland ended in a dark jagged edge and fringes of foam. The clouds were gradually closing beneath, but at intervals a rift exposed a grey sheet of sea overprinted with rippling lines. Here it was that the curraghs toiled northward.

My watch said half past ten. A red sunset glow hovered above the dense cloudbank in the sky ahead. Accustomed to the nightfall of my own latitudes, I unthinkingly foresaw darkness, and wondered how much I would see of Iceland after all. But then I recollected Dicuil's monks picking the lice out of their shirts: in June, surely, it would not be dark up there? But if so, what was going to happen on the way? Would night fall as usual and then, so to speak, lift again? I kept an eye on that sunset as we advanced north-westward, and presently became aware that it was making no progress. Red still showed above white in front; the cumulus floor solidified and piled up, till grey hills were silhouetted against the crimson light; but always the light was there, growing brighter if anything and more golden, like a sunrise. By eleven o'clock it was shining over a phantasmagorical skyscape, illuminating a stratum of cloud drifting across a lower stratum, and picking out bluffs and cliffs of vapour in a muted chiaroscuro. Sometimes it pierced clean through to the underlying Atlantic, spreading an immense diffused luminosity over a surface now variegated by criss-crossing waves, but only seldom flecked with white.

At 11.15 contemplation was interrupted by the arrival of tea, our approach toward the New World being signalised by the use of tea-bags and a floury powder called Instant Sugar. At half past eleven we began to traverse a lucid gulf between clouds. Puffs of vapour hung in it, seemingly without motion, casting purplish shadows on the mottled and glowing sea. It had certainly grown no darker, and the sky was blue overhead, but the horizon near sea-level was a mystery of shadow and grey. In that eerie stabilised twilight there was no telling what was, or was not, a real island. Towards midnight—an ironic term—I almost fancied that I did see the Faeroes as a gently undulating line far away to the east . . . but there was no telling. This was a region of illusion, to be respected as such. A mere three miles' removal upward, it seemed, had opened a window on the visionary archipelago of Mael Duin.

Rapid transit, with its changeproof pressurised cabins and its universal standardisation, may to some extent have demystified the world. You would not anticipate finding giants or demons in a country separated from your own doorstep by a single meal and the reading of a paperback novel. But one bizarrerie gives way to another. Over the North Atlantic, if speed and direction combine rightly, Joshua's prodigy is a literal fact, and the prosaic aircraft becomes a pocket Laputa with a hesitating sun of its own. In an immram, a flying island with that characteristic would be skimmed over as simply an incredible figment like the rest.

The mind is governed by the laws of its context; and who can say through what customary symbolism, what conditioned apparatus of riddling imagery, the men of the past really saw their world? When a Hebrew writer relates a miracle or an Irish writer relates a marvel, what are they trying to convey? If one could get inside them and recover the key to their unintentional cryptograms, perhaps a book like the *Navigatio* would be neither far-fetched nor obscure at all. One lacks resources.

Soon after twelve the inverted sunset was manifestly brightening, a flaky jigsaw of pink and gold and azure. The pink faded, and a pastel-tinted westerly dawn brought a spectral and outrageous daylight. But I had dozed off, I believe, when a voice behind me said: "That's Iceland." Recalled, I looked at it. The Thulian littoral had already come round to starboard, and by losing altitude we were leaving some of the clouds above us and getting more and more frequent glimpses of the map. Coastal Iceland presented itself to me as a low-lying expanse of palish green and grey-black, veined like a gigantic leaf with small rivers cutting through it. Peaks of snow lined the horizon. In the middle distance, ridges and craters of intermediate size kept shooting up unexpectedly, ruffling without breaking the quilt of black and green. It struck me that in such a random landscape the Irish monks might have felt at home.

Down at Reykjavik Airport the atmosphere was cool and dank, refreshing to step out in. While the sky was overcast, there would have been no trouble in tracking down those lice. Of an airport waiting-room, however, what can you say but that it is an airport waiting-room? Souvenirs and postcards and feeding disposed of, the flight continued by way of Keflavik into the zone of speculation. With morning, the true morning, we sighted Labrador, and the gap still dividing us from Idlewild narrowed rapidly.

Over the sea off New England the sun threw a shadow of the aircraft on to the mists below, with a prismatic halo round it. I wish I could claim to have had the bardic insight at the time to perceive the omen I perceived in retrospect afterwards. Nature herself was fashioning a Celtic emblem: a cross in a circle.

The Vikings, having seized the Faeroes, reached Iceland in force about 874. Close behind the pioneer Ingolf Arnarson came a mob of settlers, and within a few generations all the more habitable lowlands were parcelled out. Meanwhile others were sailing farther still. Gunnbjörn's Greenland excursion was not imitated at once, but Eric the Red's expedition planted Norse colonies there toward the close of the tenth century. From Greenland Eric's son Leif, nicknamed Leif the Lucky, and Leif's brother Thorvald, and their kinsman by marriage Thorfinn Karlsefni, groped their way on to "Helluland" and "Markland" and "Vinland the Good," all apparently parts of North America. Medieval sagas which tell the story give no hint that any of these adventurers stayed for long, or penetrated far inland. But the voyages were accomplished, and northern minstrels and chroniclers passed the word on.

In doing so (as I said before) the Norse made several statements which imply that the Irish were ahead of them, and which can be taken as implying that the Irish kept ahead all the way, as far as the New World. If the second inference is correct, the *Navigatio* author might have learnt of America, not from explorations before Brendan or by him, but from explorations after him—Irish ones nevertheless. And that is a possibility which requires looking into.

2

Life for the Irish sea-pilgrims was not only migratory, but sometimes more migratory than they planned. Established in the Hebrides from Brendan's time onward, in the Orkneys and

Shetlands from 579, in the Faeroes from about 670, and in Iceland from about 795,[1] they were afterwards compelled to run before the oncoming Norse. Their flight from the Faeroes took place early in the ninth century. A doubt may be admitted as to whether the islands harboured a Celtic lay population also; a doubt may be admitted as to whether any of such a population stayed there; but assuredly there was a flight. So also with Iceland. Some Irish monks (perhaps the same who abandoned the Faeroes) made their home at Kirkjubaer in the Sida district of the south-east, where, for a time, their community maintained itself. In this case too it is open to question whether there were larger lay settlements, and whether Celtic place-names such as Dimunarvag and Katanes carry any implication; but in this case too, just as assuredly, there was a flight. When Ingolf beached his ship, he found only the church furniture which the vanished *papar* had left behind. A strange spell seemed to linger over the spot. No heathen ever succeeded in living there, and it was not till a Christian came that it was reoccupied, first by the convert Viking himself, and later by a house of nuns. But while a new wave of Irishmen came in the baggage of the invaders, their predecessors never returned.[2]

The history of the Norse absorption of Iceland, of its sharing-out and its republican constitution, is told in such works as the *Islendingabok* of Ari Frode, and in the already cited *Landnamabok*, written about 1130 and attributed in the main to the same author. However, we are not given the slightest clue as to the destination of the fugitive *papar*, or of any lay companions they may have had. Did they slip off southward again, unnoticed, and into Viking-infested waters? Or did they prefer to follow precedent and push on farther into the unknown? The Norse did the latter, and we get a first glimpse of their discovery of Vinland —Nova Scotia or Massachusetts or whatever it was—in Adam of Bremen. Adam's hearsay description does not enlarge on any of their voyages to it, or name any discoverer.[3] The *Land-namabok* mentions the place casually, but still gives only one account of an actual voyage out Vinland way. This account antedates all the sagas; it concerns a certain Ari Marsson, and startlingly accentuates the enigma of the departed Irish.

> Ari . . . was driven across the sea by heavy gales to *Hvitra-mannaland*, which by some is called " Great Ireland." It lies westward in the sea near Vinland the Good. It is said that one can sail thither [from Ireland] in six days. Ari could not escape thence, and was baptised there. This was first told by Hrafni Hlymreksfari, who had been long himself in Hlymrek [Limerick] in Ireland. Thorkel Gellisson stated also that Icelanders had told, according to what they had heard from Thorfinn, Earl of the Orkneys, that Ari had been seen and recognised in *Hvitramannaland*, from which he was not allowed to depart, but that he was otherwise held in great esteem there.

The bracketed words "from Ireland" are usually included, but they were not, it seems, in the original text.[4]

Ari Marsson's misadventure would have occurred about the year 983, when Eric the Red was reconnoitring Greenland, but before any Norse colonists had arrived there.[5] *Hvitramannaland* means "White-Men's-Land"; the alternative name given is *Irland-ed-Mikla*, literally "Ireland-the-Great." Ari's baptism implies a Christian population, neither Eskimo nor American Indian.

The *Saga of Eric the Red*, written in the thirteenth century, describes the voyage made to America about 1010 by Thorfinn Karlsefni with three ships and 60 or 160 Norsemen. One shipload turned back, but Karlsefni and the rest got to Vinland or at any rate close to it, then sailed north to Markland, probably Newfoundland or lower Labrador. There they met some of the inhabitants.

> They found five skraelings, of whom one was bearded, two were women, and two were children. The Norsemen caught

the boys, but the others escaped and sank into the ground. They took the two boys with them, taught them the language, and baptised them. They called their mother Vethilldi and their father Uvaege. They said that the skraelings were ruled by kings, of whom one was called Avalldania, and the other Valldidida. They stated that they had no houses; the people lived in caves or holes. They said there was a land on the other side, opposite their land, which was inhabited by people who wore white garments, and who carried poles before them to which pieces of cloth were attached, and they shouted loudly; people think that this must have been Hvitramannaland or Great Ireland.

The description at the end suggests a Christian ecclesiastical procession rather than anything recorded of native tribes. Irish monks wore white gowns.[6]

The *Eyrbyggja Saga*, written about 1250, tells how the ship of Björn the Broadwicker was swept away from Iceland by a sustained north-east wind and not seen again. Later, at some time after the year 1000, a merchant named Gudleif accidentally discovered the missing man. It happened when Gudleif's ship, sailing one summer round the west of Ireland on the way to Iceland, was caught by a gale and driven west and south-west. When a long time had passed at sea an extensive coastline spread out in front, and the merchant landed with his crew. They were immediately surrounded and captured by alien people whom they " deemed " to be talking Irish. After some anxious moments, however, a tall white-haired leader rode up and spoke in Norse. This was Björn, who questioned Gudleif about prominent citizens in Iceland. Gudleif accepted a ring to give to Björn's old love, set sail again when the weather was apt, and reached Ireland before winter. The country of Björn's exile is not named, but the reference to the language indicates that it was Great Ireland.[7]

These passages constitute a crux which has not been resolved.

They are all highly circumstantial ("deemed" to be speaking Irish is a vivid touch); they are carefully authenticated, with names and approximate dates; and, more to the point still, the *Landnamabok* paragraph about Ari Marsson is much earlier and much closer to the alleged events than the saga accounts of the Vinland voyages . . . which, nevertheless, are held to be substantially true. If the latter are accepted, then *a fortiori* the former should also be accepted. To allow Vinland and Helluland and Markland yet disallow White-Men's-Land is verging on special pleading, as Nansen recognised.[8]

In view of the *Landnamabok* reference to Hrafni of Limerick, it is likely that an Irish report hovers in the background. It is also likely that the name "Great Ireland" is formed on the analogy of "Magna Græcia," which denoted the overseas Greek settlements in Italy; hence, that it does point to an Irish colony. The distance is the most manifest difficulty. Six days' sail from what? Have we here a confused reminiscence of Pytheas's Thule, and is Great Ireland nothing but a blurred image of the Irish Icelandic community? But the passages quoted were written long after Iceland became familiar ground. The distinction between the two countries is clearly drawn, and the data given cannot apply to Iceland.

Several authors, accepting the authenticity of the words "from Ireland," have gone on (a trifle too eagerly) to reject the whole conception as spurious, because, if you sail west from Ireland, you cannot reach any land in so short a time. But even if the dubious phrase could be proved genuine, this easy way of evasion would not really be open. The Norse were wrong in any case about the width of the Atlantic. When they found themselves bearing round counter-clockwise along the northern route, they pictured the crescent of trans-oceanic lands as bending back toward Europe much more sharply than it does. In Vinland, the hot summer, berries, and wild corn apparently led them to imagine that they had reached the Fortunate Isles, where, according to Isidore of Seville, the corn was self-sown and the vines grew untended by human hand. This belief had to be squared with the knowledge that the Fortunate Isles of antiquity were supposed to lie more or less in the latitude of Morocco at a not incalculable distance; and in consequence Vinland was grotesquely misplaced, once at least actually being described by a Norse geographer as an extension of Africa. Given this compressed map, the idea of land six days' sail west from Ireland would not have seemed implausible. It is not a blunder that can legitimately be used to get rid of White-Men's-Land as a worthless fantasy. The same sort of argument could be applied to Adam of Bremen to prove the non-existence of Greenland, which Adam says can be reached from Norway in five days' sail past Iceland, or little more—a serious underestimate.[9]

At all events it has been claimed that White-Men's-Land was Nova Scotia or part of the United States; that this was the haven of the Irish who fled from the Icelandic settlements; and that occasional Vikings wandered over and saw the fugitives' descendants.[10] Irishmen in the late ninth century could have possessed ocean-going ships, built by themselves in imitation of the Norse, or bought or captured from them. Granted the primary supposition, it is conceivable that a few roamed on through Virginia and the West Indies, and that a few found their way back to Erin to tell the tale, which inspired the *Navigatio* and furnished its American matter.

It is a most alluring theory, but the Norse texts are very far from demonstrative. A further clue is needed, and such a clue exists in an author who tends understandably to be left out of account as an arctic expert, the Arab Idrisi. Working at the court of Roger of Sicily in the middle twelfth century, he compiled his *Description of the World* from a variety of sources and constructed a great silver map, unhappily lost. Besides his Sargasso testimony already quoted, he offers a list of Atlantic islands. Most of this is mythical, but it shows a shadowy acquaintance with Irish names if not Irish ideas; and in another part of the book he speaks of Ireland-the-Great, *Irlandah-al-Kabirah*, in terms that deserve attention, because here at least he restrains his oriental fancies and gives a bare statement alone.

> Between the extremity of Scotland and the extremity of Ireland, two days' sailing are reckoned . . .
> From the northern extremity of Scotland to Reslanda [Iceland], three days.
> From the extremity of Iceland to that of Ireland-the-Great, one day.[11]

These are not Arabian Nights extravagances but bald sailing notes, probably from a Scandinavian source, which put Great Ireland in a well defined relationship with real places. The transit from Scotland to Iceland is made too short, barely half of what it should be, but even if we double or triple Idrisi's times only one conclusion is feasible, and it brings no comfort to the partisans of America. " Great Ireland " and the synonymous " White-Men's-Land " are old appellations of Greenland, dating from a time before Eric's propagandist name was conferred or generally accepted. As a modern parallel we find cartographers of the early nineteenth century marking the southern continent as " Australia " and as " New Holland " and as " Ulimaroa," all three designating the same thing.[12] The identity of Greenland with this place rumoured in seafaring tradition under other names was perhaps not fully grasped, but it accommodates most of the statements. Idrisi's sentence indeed echoes another in the *Landnamabok:* that between the " Wastes of Greenland " and Kolbeins-ey, an islet near Iceland, the space is one day's sail.[13] So also with the mystifying " six days " in the *Landnamabok* narrative of Ari Marsson. Adam of Bremen, in the passage quoted, has the following:

> Besides Iceland, there are many other islands in the great ocean, of which Greenland is not the smallest; it lies farther away in the ocean. To this island it is said that one can sail

from the coast of the Normans [i.e. Norway] in from five to seven days . . .

It may be that the six days to White-Men's-Land were reckoned from Norway, and that the doubtful phrase "from Ireland" crept in as a mistaken gloss prompted by the Irish background.

If this identification is valid the Irish in Iceland did flee westward, but scarcely as far as North America. They stopped in Greenland. Ari Frode records indeed that Eric's followers, colonising the country themselves from 985 onward, discovered empty dwellings just as their forerunners in Iceland had done, not only in the milder south-western zone beyond Cape Farewell, but in the bitter wilderness lying closest to Iceland.[14] These however did not suggest former Irish clerical occupants but skraelings—aborigines. Perhaps refugee Irish monks or laymen "went native" with Eskimo women and fathered a tribe of nominally Christian half-castes, who lingered on for a century or two talking a pidgin-Gaelic, and then died out or were assimilated by their neighbours. Though the Eskimos have migrated, archæology indicates that a few were already in the right parts of Greenland at the right period.

While no solution is altogether satisfying, the Greenland hypothesis covers all the data at least as well as the American, with the added advantage of eliminating the long ocean voyage. Consider Ari Marsson. About 983 he is "driven across the sea" to White-Men's-Land or Great Ireland. That is exactly what happened to Gunnbjörn a lifetime earlier, when he stumbled on southern Greenland himself. The country "lies westward in the sea near Vinland." Greenland was the point of departure for the Vinland expeditions, and the bearing of Cape Farewell from either the British Isles or Scandinavia is more west than north. Ari is marooned and baptised; an Irish or Irish-descended priest could have administered the sacrament, or a layman could have done so in the absence of priests. He is recognised; why not by followers of Eric, exploring the coast from the colonies they planted soon afterwards?

Or take Thorfinn Karlsefni. He goes to Markland and is told by natives about another country " opposite " theirs where Christian-sounding processions are held, and this is assumed to be White-Men's-Land. The word " opposite " might, of course, look toward some other part of Canada, but it might equally well look toward Greenland.

As for the tale of Björn and Gudleif it is almost universally thought to be fiction, an invention inspired by the experience of Ari Marsson. It could, however, be taken seriously without prejudice to the belief that the scene is laid in some portion of Greenland not colonised by Eric, rather than in any portion of America. Björn is carried from Iceland by the north-east wind like other Vikings, and detained among the Gaelic-speaking near-Eskimos. Then Gudleif, passing along the Irish west coast on his way to Iceland, is borne away by the gale " west and south-west," arriving finally on the unknown shore where he meets Björn. His direction is the only real obstacle. But we are not told that the wind blew uninterruptedly all the way; after the first violent deviation from course Gudleif's direction is unspecified. Meteorologically the chances are that he would have found himself, after a while, in a steadier wind blowing his ship toward the north or north-east, and since this was the way he wanted to go, he would have taken advantage of it. Under the circumstances a landfall in Greenland would conform to the practical probabilities at least as closely as one in America.

3

These faint evidences of an Irish refugee colony, though they turn out to be of no help with the major problem, have a bearing on Brendan's legend. They hint at a hitherto unsuspected source besides Gunnbjörn for the Greenland matter in the *Life* and the *Navigatio:* for the whale, the walrus, the little dark people, and so on. Some of these details may be drawn, like the glimpses of Iceland, from reports brought back from that area by the monks, and indeed the old anchorite in the *Life* who warns Brendan of the great sea-cat is said (if anachronistically) to be the last survivor of a party of Irish. However, this line of argument fails to take us across to America, unless we attach importance to the fact that the anchorite gives Brendan directions for the next and concluding stage of his Voyage. White-Men's-Land is an elusive place, but it can be explained without pushing the ninth-century Irish or their mongrel progeny the whole length of the northern route to the New World.

Yet to reach Iceland incontestably, and Greenland quite possibly, was a feat in itself, and we who cover the entire route in comfort in a few hours owe these valiant precursors a debt of respect. To condemn the Irish as irresponsible fabulists without exhausting every chance of a better verdict would be to do less than justice to those who ventured so gallantly. If formal geography fails, formal geography is not the sole resource. In search of America looming through time beyond all islands as it looms to-day through space, I came to recognise the propriety and necessity of extending the search further, and delving beneath geography into its legendary substratum—the geographical apocrypha, so to speak—for the archetype of the Promised Land.

I faced in fact, among other things, Atlantis.

CHAPTER SIX

Atlantis and the Old Gods

WHEN I FLEW over the Viking route I had already scanned the immrama and the ancient geographies, and hit on no parallel to St. Brendan's continent. But besides pressing these to their unsatisfactory limit, I had set myself to ransack that other part of the Græco-Roman heritage of Christian Ireland. If it was not possible to break out of the cage in one way, it might be possible in another. From the classical world's mythology, if not from its serious geography, some antecedent American concept might emerge, whether, in the result, it cleared up the mystery or merely transferred it backwards. Yet I hardly foresaw the potent phantasms that did emerge, or the effect they had on my inquiries in America.

It is as a preface to those inquiries, to what I have to say about the far side, that the exploration of the remoter literary background now finds its place. For the European heirs of classical culture an Atlantic crossing is the translation of a spiritual and imaginative centrifugal movement into physical terms. That movement did occur in classical times; and perhaps it found its physical correlative even then.

2

Educated Greeks and Romans at the beginning of the Christian era saw the Earth as a mosaic of images derived from Greek folk-lore. The progress of science had damaged some of these images and corrected others, but the structure persisted, in poetry if nowhere else; nor did the academic geographers propose any substitutes for the hallowed conceptions which they cast doubt upon. Men who recognised that the Earth was far larger than their ancestors had supposed, and that some of the old cosmic fables could not be taken at face value, contented themselves with politely allegorising the fables and talking about " the known world " instead of " the world." They forbore to tamper with the scheme of the *orbis terrarum* which respected authors handed down from antiquity. The critical, sometimes hypercritical Strabo, who discussed circumnavigation fifteen centuries before Magellan, devoted several approving chapters to Homer as the first of geographers.

What prevailed, then, was an essentially literary map, into which the details supplied by scholars, traders, soldiers, diplomats and administrators were gradually fitted. Thus the map gained in exactitude and lost in romance, but it never radically altered. The inhabited land-mass or Oecumene was envisaged as a sort of gigantic disc, ragged at the edges. Natural boundaries divided it into three sections, namely Europe, Asia (meaning only the nearer parts of Asia), and Libya (meaning North Africa). Most of the greater rivers that rose in its elevated districts emptied into the Inner Sea or Mediterranean, and the Mediterranean itself was a kind of river, a tributary of Ocean having its confluence at the Straits of Gibraltar. The River of Ocean was the greatest of all. It flowed round the world-island, past Spain and Libya and Arabia, finally pouring, as some averred, into an arctic whirlpool. The Caspian Sea was an inlet from its eastern reaches; very few—Herodotus was an exception—understood that the Caspian's northern end was land-locked.[1]

Across the River of Ocean, in the westward arc of its huge circular sweep, lay . . . something. The prime fact in the growth of what may be called the Atlantic Myth is that no classical writer, however early, speaks dogmatically of Gaul or Spain or Morocco as the end of all land. Concerning what may exist beyond, opinions differ and fancies proliferate; but the belief in something there, beyond the Oecumene's immediate watery fringe, is constant.

Myth, in fact, is prior to several of the geographical ideas we have already reviewed. It was held by some in the Hellenic prime that there were hidden countries of the sunset not intended for ordinary mortals. Over the horizon lay a portal opening into Hades. There, also, lay the original Islands of the Blest or Fortunate Isles, those which were later made out to be Madeira and the Canaries, and the warm paradise of Elysium where games and music never ceased. To these carefree realms the heroes beloved of the gods had been translated at death or sometimes without death. Thus Hesiod, speaking of the warriors who fell gloriously at Thebes and Troy:

> They with soul untouched of sorrow dwell in the Islands of the Blest by deep eddying Ocean: happy heroes, for whom the bounteous earth beareth honey-sweet fruit fresh thrice a year.[2]

Thus Homer—Proteus speaking to Menelaus:

> The immortals will send you to the Elysian plain at the world's end, to join red-haired Rhadamanthus where living is made easiest for mankind, where no snow falls, no strong winds blow and there is never any rain, but day after day the West Wind's tuneful breeze comes in from Ocean to refresh its folk.[3]

A little was known also of the western gods. Ocean himself was a god, or rather a Titan, the Titans being the gods of a pre-Hellenic dispensation. There were about ten of them, notably Cronus and Hyperion, and Iapetus—the biblical Japheth— with his sons Prometheus and Atlas. Their chief was Cronus, whom the Romans called Saturn. Formerly worshipped with human sacrifice, he was portrayed holding a great sickle or scimitar, and sometimes equated with the Phœnician Moloch.

Cronus's own son Zeus, the sky-deity of the Hellenic peoples, had long since ousted his father and seized the cosmic government, delegating authority to his Olympian brethren. The Titans and their companions lived in exile, some underground and some at the limits of the world. The west had received the most powerful of them. Their war-leader Atlas, transformed into a mountain, towered over the Moroccan corner of Africa supporting the heavens on his shoulder. It was because of Atlas that the "Outer Sea" or neighbouring portion of the Ocean was called Atlantic. Cronus himself lived beyond it with many of his followers in a dark prison girdled with fog, though later and kinder myths moved him to sunnier regions and assigned him a consolation kingdom among the Blest. Ocean also concealed Kisthene where the Gorgons dwelt, and perhaps the Garden of the Hesperides. Both, as we saw, made their eventual appearance in the geographers identified with real islands, but both were far older than that identification.[4]

This picture of the cosmos may have been taken partly from the astrology of the Middle East. A Babylonian chart has been interpreted as showing a circular Earth with Babylon at the centre. The disc is ringed by the Earthly Ocean or Bitter River. Outside this are seven triangular islands spaced round the perimeter, with angles pointing away from the centre like the rays of a star, and outside again is the Heavenly Ocean inhabited by zodiacal deities. In the fourth or north-western island, according to the inscription, "semi-obscurity reigns"; in the fifth or northern "the sun is not seen"; in the seventh or eastern "the sun rises."[5]

Such notions were speculative enough, yet among the Greeks at any rate they were superimposed on knowledge as well as guesswork, a fact which makes them more interesting but also more difficult to assess. There were of course two Greek civilisations, the bronze-age and the classical, with a gap of darkness between. Classical myth and heroic legend looked back across the gap to the Ægean society of the period 1600–1150 B.C. This was a seafaring society with a wide range, and when the later classical civilisation translated the mythical cosmos into geography, the process was (to a certain extent) a retranslation and restoration, since the myths themselves were (to a certain extent) geographical and not purely imaginative in provenance.

The major centre of the bronze-age civilisation was Crete. Its predominant "Minoan" people, who apparently spoke a form of Greek, had suzerainty over many Ægean islands, and trade relations with Egypt and other countries. In spite of their naval dominance they were almost total strangers to war by land. The palace of Minos at Cnossus, excavated by Evans, reveals the brilliance of their art and technology; their warm baths, drainage, and adroit ritual bullfights have become familiar. From Cretan offshoots on the mainland of Greece developed the kindred Mycenean culture. Its political history is obscure, but somewhere about 1400 B.C., the mainlanders sacked Cnossus and extinguished Minoan power. Their own, however, endured for centuries longer.

Greek religion and Greek myth were rooted in this epoch. The tales of Theseus and the Minotaur, of Hercules and his labours, of Argo and Ilion and the House of Atreus, are all based on the affairs of these Ægean peoples, and are nearly all connected with sites known to Minoan and Mycenean archæology, such as Crete itself, Athens, Argos, Tiryns, Sparta.[6] Homer's Achæans who besiege Troy, though modernised in some respects, are warriors of the late Mycenean culture; and somewhere about 1200 B.C., warriors of that culture undoubtedly did besiege Troy. Homer may also preserve faint reminiscences of Minoan Crete, for example in his account of the Phæacians, those peaceable masters of the sea who receive Odysseus with warm baths, dancing, and the music of lyres; and the "immram" of Odysseus's wanderings may preserve garbled recollections of a Minoan knowledge wider than Homer's.[7]

And it is in this miscellany of bronze-age folk-lore, or rather in literature prompted by it, that we catch glimpses not only of

Atlantic islands and deities but of a line on the horizon that *could* be America.

Observe to begin with that Homer puts "red-haired Rhadamanthus," for no very apparent reason, on that far western Elysian plain. Rhadamanthus was the brother of Minos of Crete, and the conception is probably a Cretan one.[8] It has been inferred from the spread of Minoan influence to Sicily and Spain that the bronze-age Cretans travelled far, and that much of the voyaging later credited to the Phœnicians was really theirs;[9] thus the Atlantic home of Rhadamanthus may well be traceable to Cretan expeditions in that direction. But mainlanders of the related Mycenean culture made similar expeditions, and it is probable that they reached British waters and landed in the British Isles, or at least were in habitual contact with people who did. They learned that there was land outside the continent, land beyond the waves and the terrifying tides, and their knowledge must be reckoned with in the evaluation of myth.

Archæology yields up a little of the story. In the ancient East, especially in Egypt, there were many workshops for the manufacture of glazed faience beads—small, cheap, gaily-coloured. These beads and others made of glass were bought in bulk by the Ægean merchant adventurers for dealing with barbarians whom such trinkets delighted. They have been found along four principal trading routes: the route round the Black Sea, across the Caucasus, along the Caspian, up the Volga; the route up the Nile to East Africa; the route up the Danube to Hungary and Poland; and the route along the Mediterranean to the British Isles by way of Malta, Sicily, southern France, the Garonne and Brittany. That some tradition of this immense commerce lingered into classical times is clear from the discrepant versions of the Argonauts' legend, which take them outward to Colchis by the first route and homeward either by the same route or by something resembling one of the other three.

Faience beads unearthed in the graves of bronze-age Britain

are of several kinds and broadly dispersed, but a particular segmented design is rather common on Salisbury Plain. Possibly a Mycenean trading post was established on the Wiltshire Avon near Amesbury. This area was then the heart of a Wessex that had grown rich by exploiting its position on the roads by which the valuable metals of the British Isles were brought to the Continent. The power of the Wessex aristocracy may be judged from Stonehenge: the giant sarsens of the main circle, hauled from the Marlborough area and set up in the sixteenth century B.C., could only have been marshalled by an authority capable of organising hundreds of slaves over a space of years. But the implications of that circle, " Stonehenge IIIa," go much deeper. The sarsen ring is unique among northern megalithic monuments in being built of stones dressed over their entire surface. That fact alone would suggest a Mediterranean linkage; and suspicion moves toward certainty with the recognition that here alone in the bronze-age north is true architecture—architecture with Mycenean affinities—and that among the artifacts carved on the stones are a dagger of Mycenean type and several axes resembling the votive axes of Mediterranean religion. Stonehenge IIIa is not exactly a Mycenean structure, but it seems to have been inspired and perhaps designed by men from the Ægean. They, or some intermediate people strongly under their influence, rounded the Breton promontory and traded up the Avon with beads. Most striking of all the proofs is a set of dentated bone or ivory rings from Bush Barrow, a little to the north of Stonehenge. These are mounts for the shaft of a wand of office, a highly specialised object paralleled in one other known place and only one, a grave at Mycenae.[10]

The normal route of commerce cut across Gaul to the Bay of Biscay, and it is uncertain whether ships ever passed Gibraltar. But it has been claimed that early Greek emigrants founded colonies in Spain, that these colonies practised a cult of Hercules, and that the tangled narrative of that hero's tenth labour bears some relation to their history.[11] Hercules goes in quest of

Geryon's cattle by way of Gibraltar (Gibraltar and Ceuta are the
" Pillars " of Hercules) and captures the cattle on the island of
Erytheia, which is usually located just off Cadiz, but sometimes
in a vaguer distance. Its name means " red " and is probably an
allusion to sunset; those who care to do so may speculate about
the red earth and cattle of Devonshire . . . or the red men of
America. Afterwards Hercules comes back through Gaul and
Italy. A recurrent legend of his " companions " or descendants
scattered about the west may be a further echo of tentative early
explorations. We shall meet it again.[12]

What makes the amalgam of truth and fable so hard to separate is the fact that this bronze-age voyaging petered out. The
Ægean magnates were more interested in Asia Minor and the
Black Sea. Their route through the Hellespont and the Bos-
phorus remained open, and the saga of its first opening by the
gallant Jason flowered into popular romance, every Greek city
claiming to have contributed an Argonaut. The route to Gaul
and Britain lost its importance. New sources of metal were
discovered, Wessex declined, the British Isles faded into their
murk. Then the Ægean civilisation itself declined. When
Homer sang, Greece was recovering, but by then the western
seas were a preserve of aliens. For several centuries the Phœnician
and Carthaginian merchants monopolised the Atlantic and kept
all rivals away from the entrance to it.

An interruption, a cloud of ignorance, almost blotted out the
original Atlantic tradition. The tales that survived among the
renascent Greeks after 800 B.C. were unenlightening, and had
sometimes been transmitted circuitously through foreigners.
Nevertheless the constant belief—that the Ocean did conceal
something, that lands could be reached by way of it which were
not part of any familiar continent—had that factual substratum.
In scrutinising the shapes which the belief took, and the possible
American intimations, it is worth bearing in mind that the only
such lands for which there is solid evidence of knowledge among
the Mycenean Greeks (and hence among their Cretan mentors,

who were still flourishing when Stonehenge was built) are the British Isles.

3

Picking up the hint dropped by Strabo, let us look again at Homer, the most pervasively influential of all Greek authors. The *Odyssey* is the oldest Greek seafaring document; the boat-building scene in the fifth book is still of value to maritime historians.

Odysseus, its bronze-age hero, wanders widely enough, and one episode takes him into the Atlantic, the adventure described in the tenth and eleventh books when he goes to consult the shade of Teiresias at the doorway of Hades. He starts from Æaea, Circe's isle, and the enchantress gives him directions.

> Set up your mast, spread the white sail and sit down in the ship. The North Wind will blow her on her way; and when she has brought you across the River of Ocean, you will come to a wild coast and to Persephone's Grove, where the tall poplars grow and the willows that so quickly shed their seeds. Beach your boat there . . .

The reference to the North Wind is relevant only to the first part of the journey. Circe's island, to judge from other poets, was in the Adriatic.

Odysseus and his crew embark as instructed, and the ship speeds over the waves past Gibraltar.

> Thus she brought us to the deep-flowing River of Ocean and the frontiers of the world, where the fog-bound Cimmerians live in the City of Perpetual Mist. When the bright Sun climbs the sky and puts the stars to flight, no ray from him can penetrate to them, nor can he see them as he drops from heaven and sinks once more to earth. For dreadful

165

Night has spread her mantle over the heads of that unhappy folk.

Here Odysseus finds his way to the spot designated by Circe, and talks with the shades of the heroic dead. When the mob of ghosts at last frightens him into retreat . . .

> I made off quickly to my ship and told my men to embark and loose the hawsers. They climbed in at once and took their seats on the benches, and the current carried her down the River of Ocean, helped by our oars at first and later by a friendly breeze.

And so he passes " from the flowing waters of the River of Ocean into the wide spaces of the open sea," in other words the Mediterranean, and returns eastward.[13]

It is a meagre, elliptical account. Odysseus crosses the Ocean in a transverse direction against its supposed stream, reaches the land of the Cimmerians where the poplar-grove is, and comes back to Gibraltar with the stream. His Atlantic route must be roughly south to north on the way out and north to south on the way back. This implication—it is no more than an implication—is confirmed by the lines describing the Cimmerians, whose fogs and almost imperceptible days mark them as northerners. Geographers of later times place them in the Ukraine, but here such a location is impossible. If they are anywhere they are surely in the British Isles. Mediterranean visitors through all the centuries have spoken of London much as Homer speaks of the City of Perpetual Mist. The passage in which the Byzantine Procopius, Brendan's contemporary, reports with many particulars how the souls of the dead are imagined in north-west Gaul to be ferried over to Britain might be excusably ascribed to the persistence or recrudescence of ancestral beliefs.[14]

This voyage to the Grove of Persephone, together with the Elysian reference, is nearly all that we find in Homer about the Atlantic. Several authors ancient and modern have argued that other places which Odysseus touches upon must also be reached by going outside Gibraltar. Apart from the problematical Læstrygones, who seem to enjoy the midnight sun, there is virtually nothing in any episode to support such a construction. Two favourite candidates are Ogygia, the isle of Calypso where Odysseus is marooned, and Scherie, the country of the Phæacians, who greet him so hospitably and furnish him with a ship for the final stage of his homecoming to Ithaca. But no real case can be made out for either. After the loss of his original ship Odysseus drifts from the whirlpool of Charybdis to Ogygia clinging to the wreckage. This drifting occupies nine days, and since Charybdis is certainly in the Straits of Messina, Ogygia cannot be in the Atlantic. Greek commentators say it is Gozo. As for Scherie it lies north-east of Ogygia, and the consensus of classical opinion makes it Corfu.[15]

A certain mystery does, however, overhang the former of these two islands, and Ogygia, like Hercules, will turn up again.

4

So much for Homer. But now comes the outward leap we have been watching for: the leap of imagination beyond the girdling Ocean and isles of the Babylonian cosmos, to a land on the far side. This is executed by several Greeks, and the first and greatest is Plato, of whom J. Oliver Thomson declares that " in a sense he may be said to have invented America."[16] I refer of course to his myth of Atlantis; but not to those portions of the myth which are most often remembered.

The sketch given in the dialogues *Timœus* and *Critias* is the theme of studies by the hundred. According to Plato, when the Athenian lawgiver Solon was at Sais in Egypt, a priest remarked on the Greeks' ignorance of their own history, and told Solon that Egyptian records preserved the tale of an affair much to the Athenians' credit, of which they knew nothing.

Nine thousand years ago, he said, the world was trembling at the aggressions of the kings of Atlantis, a huge island in the Ocean west of Gibraltar, as large as Libya and Asia together. Atlantis was the domain of Poseidon and Atlas; its kings were descended from the sea-god himself. The Atlantean empire extended far into Europe, and included the Tyrrhenians and the Libyans. It also extended in the other direction, to a series of islands beyond Atlantis, by way of which it was possible to reach *the great continent encircling the Ocean*. Plato, following the Pythagoreans, thought the Earth was spherical, but in discussing Atlantis he does not directly say so. A reader anxious for coherence is driven to infer that he conceives more than half the globe as covered by land. His Ocean is not a river—that illusion has evaporated—but a gigantic lake containing the known Oecumene, with a westward bulge that used to contain Atlantis and the islands beyond it.

Atlantis had a pleasant climate, with two harvests a year, warm springs, and boundless mineral wealth. The kings made lavish use of various metals such as gold and copper and tin, decorating their buildings with golden statues, and inscribing their edicts on orichalc, a copper alloy (not solely Atlantean, as some assert; it is mentioned in the Homeric Hymns and elsewhere). They had the rare luxury of hot baths. In a fertile plain, the agricultural centre of the island, stood Poseidon's temple, a splendid circular precinct surrounded by concentric channels large enough for the docking of ships. This temple was the heart of Atlantis, and here the kings performed the bull sacrifice which was their chief ritual.

In a phase of moral degeneration and grasping militarism, the Atlantean armies surged forward to attack Greece and the eastern Mediterranean. Only the free-born citizens of Athens stood firm, and they alone managed to arrest the onslaught. At the moment of their triumph a terrific natural upheaval swept over the world. Everywhere earthquakes broke out, and Atlantis itself suffered most of all. In a single night it sank bodily beneath the waves, leaving shoals and shallows to impede navigation. Its empire crumbled away.

Such was the story which the Egyptian priest told Solon, and Solon passed on to the family of Critias, through whom seemingly it percolated to Plato. That Solon took an interest in an Atlantean legend of some kind appears from Plutarch's *Life* of him, but outside Plato there is no clear evidence as to what it was. Plato himself is certainly concocting a fiction, a mélange of Homeric reminiscences and Egyptian traditions about the Cretan sea-kings.[17] His Atlantis has features of resemblance to the country of the Phæacians in the *Odyssey*, which, as described, may be distantly Minoan in inspiration. The shoals and shallows left by the sunken land are the same phantom deterrents which the Carthaginians sowed broadcast about the Atlantic to discourage their business rivals. Reports of these were doubtless transmitted to Plato's Athens by way of the Greek towns in Sicily. Apart from the political moral which is the main point, we would be most unwise to take what Plato says seriously, and despite his prestige the Greeks themselves did not generally do so. Some of their authors dismiss Atlantis as fabulous, others speak of it in passing and non-committally, very few indeed argue positively in its favour. Yet the conception remains extraordinary, and invites guesses as to where it came from, if only for the purpose of interpreting the passage that matters here—the passage mentioning the islands beyond Atlantis, which might or might not be deducible from recorded myth, and the farther continent, which emphatically is not.

The location of Atlantis must be effected in time before it can be effected in space. Plato's period of nine thousand years is ridiculous. There has possibly been a mistake, at some stage, for nine hundred. Atlantis is made out to be a bronze-age realm of the Minoan-Mycenean era, about the sixteenth or fifteenth century B.C., the era which engendered so many other legends, and therefore may well have supplied material for Plato. If we are to hunt for an " actual Atlantis " as an ingredient of the myth

artificially combined with the others and inflated into pre-
dominance, the problem is to find a country within the orbit of
Cnossus and Mycenae which fulfils the minimal conditions.
We already have one.

In order to reach the " actual Atlantis " it must have been
necessary to get into the Ocean outside Gibraltar. The Mediterranean was too familiar for any of its islands to qualify, and they
were still palpably above water in Solon's time and Plato's. In
view of the Greeks' extreme vagueness regarding the west, the
precise direction may be an error, but Atlantis must have been
a country approached by way of the Outer Sea. Also it must
have suffered an inundation, and even if this was a mere local
catastrophe afterwards exaggerated, it must have been permanent
as far as it went. The last requirement rules out nearly all the
innumerable Deluge legends, which are sometimes quoted as
parallels, and guides attention toward north-west Europe. In
that area lie the effective possibilities. The Dogger Bank was
formerly inhabited land; stone implements have been dredged
up from it. The Straits of Dover were not breached till after
6000 B.C., and the water was gaining and appreciably altering
coastlines till after 2000 B.C., with local erosions later still: one
thinks of the Zuider Zee and Dunwich. Legends like those
relating to Lyonesse, and Ker-Is in Brittany, preserve folk-
memories of such changes. The Roman historian Ammianus
Marcellinus quotes a Greek who wrote in the first century B.C.
as finding such legends current among the Druids of Gaul.[18]

It seems plausible in the light of archæology that somewhere
behind Plato and his informants is the far-away Mycenean
image of Britain, and perhaps even a lost western saga corresponding to the eastern saga of Jason and the Argo. Bronze-age
Wessex was, as we saw, in touch with the Mycenean world in
the sixteenth century B.C., and temporarily important; it traded
in metals; Greek travellers must at least have heard of its grandiose
concentric temple, on a plain which was then the chief agricultural area of Britain and a Mycenean market. Inundations,

though small ones, occurred at the right time. Mount's Bay succumbed to the Channel a little after 1500 B.C., having hitherto been dry land and populated. It would have been surprising if in subsequent centuries no Greek had ever wondered about that immense island which nobody heard of any more, and if no stories had been devised to account for its disappearance from human ken, glorifying it in the process as medieval legend expanded an insignificant khanate into the mighty kingdom of Prester John.

Indeed some evidence exists of the way in which the Greek mind did weave fantasies round Britain. Thus Hecatæus of Abdera in the fourth century B.C.:

Opposite to the coast of Celtic Gaul there is an island in the Ocean, not smaller than Sicily, lying to the north—which is inhabited by the Hyperboreans, who are so named because they dwell beyond the North Wind. This island is of a happy temperature, rich in soil and fruitful in everything, yielding its produce twice in the year. . . . The inhabitants venerate Apollo more than any other god. . . .

In this island, there is a magnificent precinct of Apollo, and a remarkable temple, of a round form, adorned with many consecrated gifts. There is also a city, sacred to the same god, most of the inhabitants of which are harpers, who continually play upon their harps in the temple. . . . The Hyperboreans use a peculiar dialect, and have a remarkable attachment to the Greeks, especially to the Athenians and the Delians, deducing their friendship from remote periods. It is related that some Greeks formerly visited the Hyperboreans, with whom they left consecrated gifts of great value. . . .

The supreme authority in that city and the sacred precinct is vested in those who are called Boreades, being the descendants of Boreas, and their governments have been uninterruptedly transmitted in this line.[19]

Thus far Hecatæus, with some curious astronomical details not to our purpose. This Britain which looms so queerly through the fog, with its round temple, its double harvest, its ancient Hellenic contacts, and its heaven-descended rulers, has obvious Atlantean affinities.

To say that Britain " is " Plato's Atlantis would be an over-simplification with little meaning. It would imply that his statements about the vanished empire are of value for British history, a very perilous proposition. Dim hearsay of bronze-age Britain may have been worked up by his literary genius into a haunting myth; that is all. But the problem of the islands beyond Atlantis, and the farther continent, is still there. If Minoan or Mycenean knowledge is the ultimate source, what are we to make of these geographical statements? They are wholly gratuitous, with no bearing on Plato's moral aim . . . and they are right, or more right than wrong. Given the British orientation, the passage conveys a plain hint at the northern route. A voyager *can* go from Britain by way of islands beyond—the Orkneys, Shetlands, Faeroes, Iceland, Greenland, or a selection of these—to the New World.

5

Plato's words must on no account be overloaded. He is clear as to the existence of continental land beyond the Atlantic. But he seems to think of it as only a segment of a solid ring encircling the whole Ocean—the opposite bank, so to speak, replacing the Heavenly Ocean of the Babylonians. He is clear also as to the existence of an island-chain leading to this opposite land. But he gives no real indication as to where the islands are. They are simply said to have been accessible from an Atlantis of such colossal dimensions that its subject archipelago might be almost anywhere. The hypothesis of a confused knowledge of Britain offers a clue, and the geography may once have been more explicit, but by the time it finds its way into the philosopher's dialogues it is verging on the incomprehensible.

Much the same would apply to Theopompus of Chios, one of Plato's younger contemporaries. His work is lost, but a fragment quoted by the Roman Aelian tells of a legendary visit paid to King Midas by Silenus, companion of the Satyrs and the god Dionysus, in the course of which Silenus gave Midas a great deal of unusual information.

Amongst many other things, Silenus told Midas that Europe, Asia and Africa were islands surrounded by the Ocean; that there was but one continent only, which was beyond this world, and that as to magnitude it was infinite: that in it were bred, besides other very great creatures, men twice as big as those here, and they lived double our age: that many great cities are there, and peculiar manners of life; and that they have laws wholly different from those amongst us: that there are two cities far greater than the rest, nothing like to each other; one named Machimus, warlike, the other Eusebes, pious: that the pious people live in peace, abounding in wealth. . . . They live, as he said, free from sickness, and die laughing, and with great pleasure. . . .

The inhabitants of the city Machimus are very warlike, continually armed and fighting. . . . They die sometimes of sickness, but this happens very rarely, for most commonly they are killed in the wars by stone or wood, for they are invulnerable to steel. They have vast plenty of gold and silver, insomuch that gold is of less value with them than iron with us.

He said that they once designed a voyage to these our islands, and sailed upon the Ocean, being in number a thousand myriads of men, till they came to the Hyperboreans; but understanding that they were the happiest men among us, they contemned us as persons that led a mean inglorious life, and therefore thought it not worth their going farther.

He added what is yet more wonderful, that there are men living amongst them called Meropes, who inhabit many great cities; and that at the farthest end of their country there is a place named Arrostus (from whence there is no return) which resembles a gulf. . . . That there are two rivers in this place, one of pleasure, one of grief; and that along each river grow trees of the bigness of a plane tree. Those which grow up by the River of Grief bear fruit of this nature; if any one eat of them, he shall spend all the rest of his life in tears and grief, and so die. The other trees which grow by the River of Pleasure are of a contrary nature; for who tastes thereof shall be eased from all his former desires: if he loved anything, he shall quite forget it; and in a short time shall become younger, and live again his former years; he shall cast off old age, becoming first a young man, then a child, lastly, an infant, and so die.

This, if any man think the Chian worthy credit, he may believe. To me he appears an egregious romancer as well in this as in other things.[20]

As Aelian implies in his postscript, it is hard to know what to say about such a rigmarole. An arguable view is that the source is an early satyr-play—a type of comedy in which Silenus normally figured—and that Thespis, the founder of Greek drama, wrote it partly in ridicule of Solon and his talk of Atlantis. Plutarch records that the lawgiver and the dramatist quarrelled, Solon accusing Thespis of corrupting the minds of the citizenry with extravagant fictions. A skit on Solon's own extravagant fictions might have been Thespis's retort; and an actor could manage a crude word-play on the names " Solon " and " Silenus." [21]

Granted this parody element, whatever its precise target, there must still have been a more literal assertion to parody. The existence of the trans-Oceanic continent, and of a way from one land-mass to the other, is in fact affirmed here just as in

Plato, and one would judge that such a belief must have
held by somebody. In the Machimites' abortive expedi
from world to world the terminus of the path at our own en
is made out to be the country of the Hyperboreans. If the
Hyperboreans of Theopompus are the same as those of Hecatæus,
in other words Britons, this passage is most interesting, being
a direct hint at the northern route. Whether they are or not,
they are certainly northerners; and Ptolemy, the greatest ancient
geographer of all, calls the ocean north-west of Britain the
Hyperborean Sea.[22]

I have found nothing else in mythology to connect Silenus
and his low Satyr companions with the Ocean or with land
across it. Yet seemingly a connection existed. Pausanias, in his
Description of Greece, mentions a stone on the Acropolis where
Silenus was alleged to have sat, and this relic inspires a curious
paragraph.

The oldest of the Satyrs they call Sileni. Wishing to know
better than most people who the Satyrs are I have inquired
from many. about this very point. Euphemus the Carian
said that on a voyage to Italy he was driven out of his course
by winds and was carried into the Outer Sea, beyond the
course of seamen. He affirmed that there were many unin-
habited islands, while in others lived wild men. The sailors
did not wish to put in at the latter, because, having put in
before, they had some experience of the inhabitants, but on
this occasion they had no choice in the matter. The islands
were called Satyrides by the sailors, and the inhabitants were
red haired, and had upon their flanks tails not much smaller
than those of horses. As soon as they caught sight of their
visitors, they ran down to the ship without uttering a cry
and assaulted the women in the ship. At last the sailors in
fear cast a foreign woman on to the island. Her the Satyrs
outraged not only in the usual way, but also in a most
shocking manner.[23]

Pausanias merely piles the unexplained on the unexplained. It is just conceivable that Euphemus accidentally reached the West Indies: Lafitau, an early authority, speaks of the Caribs as putting on horses' tails, smearing their heads red, and behaving nastily. Yet this interpretation seems almost precluded by the sailors' having been there before. On the other hand the suspicious circumstance of Euphemus being carried all the way out of the Mediterranean by an east wind is, curiously enough, credible. That did happen to a Greek named Colæus. But Silenus's notion of America is not illuminated by this grotesque report, which, in any case, has nothing to say of any mainland beyond the Satyrides.[24]

6

Although Plato and Theopompus may both be drawing on a stock of ideas remotely associated with Britain, neither makes the plain statement that the route to the farther continent is by way of Britain and islands beyond. Plutarch, however, about A.D. 75, does make the plain statement. He bases it partly on beliefs current among the Celts of the British Isles, beliefs which can be traced among the Celtic Irish. Furthermore, he gives details that raise the possibility of a crossing, in a much more specific and discussible form.

The passage occurs in an imaginary dialogue on " The Face in the Moon," which is mainly a piece of poetic but sensible astronomical debate, and includes some lively speculation as to whether the Moon has people on it. One of the participants is Sextius Sylla, a Carthaginian cited elsewhere by Plutarch as an antiquarian adviser of his. Sylla promises to recount a myth about the Moon and the destiny of the soul, and after many conversational setbacks he does. He attributes the substance of it to a stranger he met in Carthage, who learned it while sojourning in a western isle; and the stage-setting introduction is what concerns us.

Sylla explains that parties of pilgrims—Carthaginians perhap but he never quite elucidates—set out at long intervals on religious migration.

I will first, if you see no objection, name the poet, beginning in Homer's words—
<blockquote>Far o'er the brine an isle Ogygian lies—</blockquote>
distant from Britain five days' sail to the west. There are three other islands, equidistant from Ogygia and from one another, in the general direction of the sun's summer setting. The natives have a story that in one of these Cronus has been confined by Zeus, but that he, having a son for gaoler, is left sovereign lord of those islands and of the sea, which they call the Gulf of Cronus.

To the great continent by which the Ocean is fringed is a voyage of about five thousand stades, made in row-boats, from Ogygia, of less from the other islands, the sea being slow of passage and full of mud because of the number of streams which the great mainland discharges, forming alluvial tracts and making the sea heavy like land, whence an opinion prevailed that it is actually frozen. The coasts of the mainland are inhabited by Greeks living round a bay as large as the Maeotic, with its mouth nearly opposite that of the Caspian Sea. These Greeks speak of themselves as continental, and of those who inhabit our land as islanders, because it is washed all round by the sea. They think that in after time those who came with Hercules and were left behind by him, mingled with the subjects of Cronus.

Every thirtieth year, Sylla continues, when Saturn is in Taurus, men chosen by lot are sent forth in a flotilla of well-provisioned ships.

They put out, and naturally do not all fare alike; but those who come safely out of the perils of the sea land first on the outlying islands, which are inhabited by Greeks, and day after day, for thirty days, see the sun hidden for less than one hour. This is the night, with a darkness which is slight and of a twilight hue, and has a light over it from the west. There they spend ninety days . . . after which they pass on, now with help from the winds. . . .

The natural beauty of the isle (of Cronus) is wonderful and the mildness of the environing air. . . . Cronus himself sleeps within a deep cave resting on rock which looks like gold, this sleep being devised for him by Zeus in place of chains. Birds fly in at the topmost part of the rock, and bear him ambrosia, and the whole island is pervaded by the fragrance shed from the rock.[25]

Cronus, adds Sylla, is attended by spirits who were his comrades when he was king over gods and men. They interpret his dreams, which reflect the plans of Zeus. The stranger who told this tale spent thirty years there, studying astronomy and other sciences, and then joined the next expedition on its return.

Plutarch's myth is a composite like Plato's, and again we have the task of deciding what to take seriously. It is not literally true, but is it pure fiction or fiction based on fact?

While the name Ogygia is borrowed from Homer, this island cannot be Calypso's. The Greek-speaking descendants of Hercules's followers are reminiscent of his tenth labour, the westward quest for Geryon's cattle, and the commemoration of that bronze-age adventure by similar pseudo-pedigrees, in Gaul and other countries. Cronus and Hercules were both worshipped at Tartessus, the ancient trade centre on the Spanish Atlantic coast.[26] However, the description of Cronus in his cavern is a more notable matter. This takes up the theme of his western banishment, but with a fullness unknown in previous literature, though allusions elsewhere to darkness and a frozen Cronian Sea convey the same impression of a somewhat high latitude.[27] Plutarch

makes contemporary British Celts—" the natives "—rc
for some of the information, and here at all events he
what he says, because in another dialogue, *The Silence of Or*
he quotes a government agent named Demetrius as reporting tr
same thing, also from the lips of Britons.

> There is, they said, an island where Cronus is imprisoned
> with Briareus keeping guard over him as he sleeps; for, as
> they put it, sleep is the bond forged for Cronus. They add
> that around him are many deities, his henchmen and
> attendants.

The phrase about the bond of sleep is conclusive, and much of
Plutarch's text in the " Moon " dialogue is doubtless a fuller
version of what Demetrius told him.[28]

The god called Cronus resembles the Celtic hero Arthur,
who also lies in a cave with his henchmen round him. He has
an affinity too with the sleeping giant in the *Life of St. Machutus*.[29]
But he cannot be either of these. In the first case certainly, in
the second probably, legend has grafted an ancient theme on to
a new character centuries after Plutarch's time. One could wish
to identify the god equated with the father of Zeus. Unfortunately there is no agreement as to what the name " Cronus "
signifies. It sounds like *corone*, a crow or raven, and the Titan
is said to have been portrayed with the bird as his familiar.
Now as we have seen, the name of the Celtic voyager Bran
actually means The Raven, and it has been suggested that Bran
and Cronus, far back in the dawn of European mythology, were
the same.[30] Right or wrong, this theory does show how a
confusion might have arisen. The conversation is easy to
reconstitute.

DEMETRIUS: You say that " Bran " went to a western island
and lived there. I don't know that name.
What does it mean?
BRITON (through interpreter): *Corone*.

RIUS: Ah yes. Thank you. (Aside to interpreter.)
Obviously a misunderstanding of " Cronus."
How interesting to find them holding the same
view of his whereabouts as Hesiod and Pindar!

Much the same process could have taken place in the other
direction.

At any rate Plutarch gives us a mythical motif which is
explicitly taken from the Celts, and of which variants can be
recognised in Wales and Ireland. This linkage makes the
context all the more deserving of study. Here is a set of sailing
directions, almost a sketch-map, which has some sort of connection with St. Brendan's people. Can we decipher it?

Plutarch makes the decipherment more difficult than he
might, because he goes over the ground twice, with different
particulars. The first task is to fix the starting-point. Ogygia
and the other islands lie west from Britain, but which part of
Britain? The choice is practically forced by the brief summer
night experienced on the way. Since a voyage defined
as westerly rather than northerly leads to a place where the
night is very short, the point of departure must surely be in
Scotland.

While the initial five days' sailing extends to no possible
landfall, this error in itself does not justify immediately dropping
the whole inquiry. It is of a piece with the similar under-
statements in Adam of Bremen, Ari Frode and Idrisi, for distances
measured into the same quarter. With all of them the terminus
of the measurement is, or appears to be, Greenland; and southern
Greenland, the temperate strip from Cape Farewell to Godthaab,
is by no means a bad candidate for Plutarch's Ogygia. Cape
Farewell is nearly due west of Cape Wrath. The question is
whether it is worth provisionally granting the possibility of a
Celtic map compressed in the same way as the Norse and Arabic
maps, in order to get the pilgrims over this first obstacle. The
plausibility of the rest of their pilgrimage is a sufficient answer.

They reach Ogygia and some "outlying" satellites (say Greenland and its coastal islets) about midsummer, obsc the brief night, and stay for three or four months. In autum they row five thousand stadia, about five hundred miles or a trifle more, to the coast of the continent past drifting ice and debris: this is the crossing of Davis Strait from Frederikshaab to Labrador. They coast round into a "bay as large as the Maeotic": Belle Isle Strait leading into the Gulf of St. Lawrence might well suggest the Strait of Kerch leading into Maeotis, i.e. the Sea of Azov.

As for the three islands that lie closer to the continent than Ogygia, they are described as equidistant from Ogygia and also from one another. This arrangement is difficult to picture, since, if all three are farther west, the geometry is impossible. The probable meaning is that they form a rough equilateral triangle, and that it takes much the same time to go from Ogygia to any one of them by the route specified. They are also described as lying in the general direction of the summer sunset, a bearing which the context allows to be reckoned from Ogygia or from Britain or perhaps even from Greece, where the dialogue takes place. All the conditions are adequately satisfied by the larger bits of land in the central part of the Gulf of St. Lawrence. Plutarch's informant could have been thinking of western Newfoundland and any two of the principal inner islands, Cape Breton, Grindstone and Anticosti. The Gulf nowadays is far from mild in winter, but there is evidence that the climate has deteriorated; and it still has a hot summer and enough pleasant spells to excuse the idyllic sketch.

This myth has not received much attention from writers on geography, doubtless because the book that embodies it is not avowedly geographical. Kepler, treading in the footsteps of the famous Ortelius, analysed the passage and arrived at something like the interpretation proposed, bringing in Greenland, Labrador and the Gulf, though he was handicapped by the uncertainties of his own period. Raingeard, the modern French editor of the ue, refers without disrespect to what he calls " the American ...othesis," but prudently avoids the issue it raises.³¹

Again the *Navigatio* problem: is it guesswork or knowledge? At least four things are in Plutarch's favour. In the first place, he indicates correctly that in late autumn there are icy seas far to the west of Britain, and not merely to the north—a good guess if it is no more, since in those days nothing had been learnt of the Gulf Stream's warming effect, and there was no obvious reason why all parts of the Atlantic in the same latitude should not be equally free from ice. (We are reminded of Brendan's berg.) Secondly, he is right as to the distance, five hundred miles or slightly more, from Ogygia-Greenland to the farther continent. Thirdly, he says the pilgrims are helped, when passing to the bay where the Greeks are supposed to live, by a following wind; and here too he is right, since the prevailing wind out of Baffin Bay carries boats along parallel to the Labrador coast toward Belle Isle Strait. Fourthly, and most surprisingly, he is right within a degree as to the bay's whereabouts. He says its mouth is nearly opposite that of the Caspian, evidently meaning (so Raingeard construes the phrase) that it lies in the same latitude. Now the forty-seventh parallel passes through the main outlet of the Gulf of St. Lawrence between Newfoundland and Cape Breton Island; and it also grazes the north end of the Caspian, that portion of the inland sea which most Greeks imagined to be a channel or mouth opening into the circumambient Ocean.³²

As with the *Navigatio*, to attribute so much to chance is to stretch the probabilities. If twenty classical authors had tried to delineate a route to the other continent, and nineteen of them had been hopelessly wrong, a few acceptable touches in the twentieth text would mean nothing. But there are not twenty texts, there is only one text. Plutarch stands alone, and Plutarch is right, or fully as close to being right as many classical geographers are when describing places much nearer to home. His account is more intelligible than, say, Pliny's account of the

African coast and islands.[33] If this accuracy is due to kno
and not to luck, then we shall ask what knowledge, and
obtained, and from whom? If an explorer mapped the Gulf
St. Lawrence in or before the first century A.D., why did no
news of the exploit leak through to anybody except Plutarch
and his circle? Why is Ptolemy's *Geography* silent about the
kingdom of Cronus?

It is the profusion of clues, not the scarcity, that bewilders.
The allusion to Hercules is interesting in itself. But so also is the
association of Sylla's stranger with Carthage. So also, especially,
is the citation of informants in Britain, not only because it looks
ahead to the later Celts, but because it so clearly recalls those
Britons who told Pytheas about Thule, and must therefore have
crossed the sea or heard the reports of men who had.

Again an eye seems to be straining into the mist beyond the
British Isles, and again we cannot determine whose eye it is.

7

A clue, however, to the Promised Land of the *Navigatio* can be
tracked down by pursuing the Platonic trail in another direction.

At Pergamum in Asia Minor during the Hellenistic age, the
royal library came under the charge of a certain Crates, Crates
of Mallus, a person of enough distinction to be sent on a diplo-
matic mission to Rome in 165 B.C. He became engrossed in the
old riddle of the adventures of Odysseus, and tried to chart them
by using Plato's conception of a round Earth and, in a general
way, his conception of land outside the Oecumene. The result
was a flash of insight. Crates designed a globe (it is not established whether he actually made one) with an Equatorial Ocean
going round it in a wide band, and a similar strip of water
encircling it by way of the poles, intersecting the Equatorial at
two opposite places. This arrangement gave four island-
continents divided by sea. One was the Oecumene itself, comprising the linked masses of Europe, Asia and Libya. On its

Orb of Crates

southern edge, said Crates, lived some of the Ethiopians, and across the Equatorial Ocean from these were the rest of the Ethiopians, in a southern continent of " Antoikoi "—dwellers-on-the-far-side. The land-mass corresponding to the Oecumene in the other part of the northern hemisphere, " North America " as we might say, was the land of the Perioikoi or dwellers-round; while to the south of this, diametrically opposite to ourselves in the fourth continent, lived the Antipodeans.

This audacious flight of imagination attracted less notice than it deserved. Strabo gave it a glance but rejected it. Then, strangely, it was rediscovered and put forward as a simple state-ment of fact by Macrobius, in a commentary on a philosophical work by Cicero, about A.D. 400. Martianus Capella, the same who rearranged the Hesperides, took it up soon after. The medieval scholars who kept alive belief in a spherical Earth usually relied on Macrobius, or Capella, or both. Bede favoured this theory, and from the ninth century onward it was more widely accepted such eminent scholars as Giraldus Cambrensis and Robert Grosseteste had the same notion of the globe as Crates, and according to one authority the Imperial Orb of the Holy Roman Emperors, with its intersecting bands, represented the Earth conceived in this manner.

Here at last, as a Platonic derivative, we have the *Navigatio* idea of an island-continent across the Atlantic, in writings current before the *Navigatio* was composed. Moreover, it was almost certainly known to somebody concerned in the growth of Brendan's legend. The prologue to a German version portrays him scornfully burning a book which refers to the Antipodes, and being forced to go on sea-pilgrimage as a penance for his arrogance. In all likelihood the offending book is Macrobius's or Capella's.[34]

Thus we have a possible explanation for the " North America" of the *Navigatio*. It is the Perioikean Land. We have no explanation yet for its Paradisal character, but this too can be traced among the more recondite items of the Platonic heritage; specifically, in the work of the eccentric Cosmas, a contemporary of St. Brendan himself.

Cosmas " Indicopleustes " was perhaps an Egyptian. He was trained as a merchant, and practised that occupation successfully, travelling through India and rounding Cape Guardafui. In Ethiopia he was welcomed at court during the year 525 and pursued antiquarian research in his spare time. Later he entered an Alexandrian monastery. From 535 onward he was busy with a book which, after much rewriting in response to readers' criticisms, he cast in its final form about 547: a book entitled *Christian Topography*.

It is a mainly retrograde production, which jettisons centuries of science. Yet it has individuality, and makes its own peculiar mark. Whenever Cosmas is talking of what he knows, he is good; embalmed in his generally absurd discussion are many paragraphs of direct and conscientious description, and he has ery few tall tales. He improves on most of his predecessors in at least one respect by illustrating his text with little pictures and maps. Moreover he is not, as some have imagined, a mere spokesman of dark-age obscurantism and clerical authority. On the contrary he is wildly original, with few disciples and almost no influence, himself alone. One sees him as the self-made man become a self-educated crank, a type more familiar in modern times and among the English-speaking peoples—a forerunner of such lovable figures as Ignatius Donnelly, the backwoods senator who wrote on Atlantis, the formation of the Earth, and Bacon's authorship of Shakespeare.

Cosmas's aim is to sweep aside the impieties of pagan cosmography in favour of a purely scriptural system, and as the Bible has nothing very precise to offer, he is driven to draw astonishing inferences from his chosen texts. His key passage is a verse which implies that the tabernacle set up by Moses in the desert was meant to be (like King Arthur's Round Table) " an image of the mighty world." He interprets this literally, presenting his readers with a box-universe, a kind of enormous trunk, twice as long as it is broad. A flat Earth fills the whole bottom of the box. The sun is a ball of fire circling about inside; it cannot go underneath at night, because there is no " underneath "; it hides behind a huge northern mountain. Far above our heads is the lid, with angels like flies on a ceiling pushing stars round it.

Cosmas, of course, has no use for Plato's globe. But he does adopt Plato's Ocean-girdling continent. He adopts it explicitly, acknowledging his source, and his further claim that the Greek philosopher stole it from Moses need not detain us. The Oecumene in the bottom of the box-universe is surrounded by water, which in turn is surrounded by a rectangular frame of land in contact with the sides of the box; if you were to cross it in any direction, you would come to the foot of an outer cliff thousands of miles high. The frame-land was the home of humanity before the Flood. All its inhabitants were drowned except Noah and his household, and the Ark drifted inward over an empty and sub-

merged Asia to haven on Ararat, after which the water subsi⸱
It is now the frame-land's turn to be empty, Cosmas explain
and the Ocean cuts us off from it.[35]

When Cosmas considers the Earthly Paradise where Adam
started his career, logic compels him to put it in the antediluvian
realm, and Genesis ii. 8 leads him to put it eastward, in the
portion of the frame beyond the Pacific. To explain the four
Paradisal rivers in verses 10–14 of the same chapter, he says
that a spring from which they all rise is at the Earth's eastern
margin, and that after their separation they " cleave a passage
through the Ocean " and reappear—perhaps by way of caves—
inside the Oecumene. Tigris (Hiddekel) and Euphrates emerge
among us as the rivers known under those names, Gihon becomes
the Nile, Pison becomes either the Ganges or the Indus. Cosmas's
trans-Oceanic Eden is probably no more than a consequence of
his exegesis, but it is barely possible that he took a hint from some
Chinese or Japanese legend which he heard on his travels. Islands
of the Blest are mentioned in oriental tales not unlike their
European counterparts.[36]

8

In the *Navigatio*, it will be remembered, though not in the *Life*,
Brendan's Land of Promise is explicitly Paradise. Let us try to
imagine the author pondering on the plan of his work.

" The climax of St. Brendan's Voyage has to be his discovery
of the Earthly Paradise after all those years of searching. But
where is the Earthly Paradise? It certainly isn't in Mesopotamia
or anywhere like that; ask the Arabs. The only useful hint
seems to be Cosmas's, that it lies eastward across the sea beyond
Asia, quite separate from the continents we know.

" But wait a moment. Cosmas believed in a flat Earth, and
that's all nonsense. Macrobius gives its true shape—spherical—
and puts this Perioikean island-continent of his round the other
side from us. That is what you would really come to if you

eastward across the sea from Asia. So then, Cosmas's radise must be there. But you could also get to the Perioikean Land by going westward across the sea from Europe. That's it! If I take Brendan right over the Atlantic, I can get him into Eden by the back way. And the pagan ideas of Elysium ... well, of course, they don't mean the same thing and I'd never trust them in themselves ... but they do more or less fit."

In two other cases, very distinguished cases, something like this train of thought did unquestionably occur. Dante locates the Earthly Paradise on top of the Mount of Purgatory, in an island at the antipodes of Jerusalem, and he makes Ulysses come within sight of the Mount on his last voyage by sailing south-westward from Gibraltar. Columbus himself, when he discovered the Orinoco, identified it with Gihon and surmised that Paradise lay up-country in South America.[37] This guess of Columbus recalls the great river of the *Navigatio*, which looked like the Ohio; but Brendan's Ohio turns out most unexpectedly to stand a much better chance of being the upper Euphrates.

When the author had arrived at this notion, he would still have had the problem of hitching the Paradisal land on to the rest of his map, and deciding how to conduct Brendan across to it. He may (despite the difficulty over Greek) have read Plutarch and the other classical writers. He may only have had access to the same fund of legend which they used and elaborated, knowing in a vague way of the hints at a trans-Atlantic mainland, and of the Elysian associations of Cronus or whatever Celtic god Plutarch bestowed his name upon. But coupled with these was that idea of a " Hyperborean " route across Ocean from the British Isles, and the Irish author may have heard of it indirectly or from Celtic tradition, whether he read the classical texts or not. In his narrative, at all events, he does follow in the steps of his predecessors. He takes Brendan along the northern route, westward from the Faeroes—a course much the same in effect as that indicated by Plutarch. He gives no Ogygian details, but he does block the path with a barrier of darkness and fog, which is perhaps genuinely suggested by rumours of the New foundland Banks, but is part in any case of the classical Atlantic mythos with antecedents as far back as Himilco.

My own discovery of Cosmas persuaded me that what had seemed to be my main search was now, rather abruptly, over. The geographical apocrypha of the myth-makers, philosophers and theologians had provided a solution. The sun-drenched vision of North America in the *Navigatio* could be fully explained as a bold feat of imagination, fusing different versions of the idea of a Trans-Oceanic Continent into a memorable synthesis. As such, it did credit to the author, and was worthy of the talent he displayed elsewhere. But the question whether it was a happy guess only, or an authentic reflection of some actual if distant contact with the New World, would depend on the assessment of the sources. Granted at last that it was not necessary to postulate Irish voyages to the North American mainland. But Macrobius, Plutarch and the rest . . . were *they* purely speculative, or were they communicating beliefs derived from real voyages, though not Irish ones? What was the nature of that outward leap from the Oecumene?

Furthermore the *Navigatio* itself still had a loose end, and this too had to be kept in mind. I mean the " West Indian " matter, the apparent glimpses of the Bahamas with the neighbouring sea, and Jamaica. These places are not brought into relationship with the Land of Promise, to which in fact the West Indies are so close; indeed they are not brought into relationship with the map at all, though everything else is. It might be argued that Brendan is supposed to have sailed round Macrobius's Equatorial Ocean, and that the islands are not West Indian but Asiatic or Pacific. I doubt, however, if the descriptions could be fitted so well to any other locality. In *Mael Duin*, where we do find what may conceivably be a traveller's tale of an atoll in the Indian Ocean—the island has a wall of water (suggesting a fringing reef with breakers) and trees with large edible nuts

...uggesting coco-nut palms)—the particulars are not in the least like those in the *Navigatio*.

The flat island, the grape island and the transparent sea are not part of the author's image of North America, and cannot be inferred from Macrobius or the Greeks. Yet it is out of keeping that this solitary part of his story should be unfounded fantasy. Everything else has turned out to be traceable to sources in books or seafaring, some virtually certain, all at the very least arguable; one would hesitate to dismiss the " West Indian " portion as the exception, the single baseless fabric, all the more as it happens to be so challengingly like the real thing in half a dozen respects.

We catch sight here of a separate cluster of ideas, which falls into position alongside similar items in the classical context. Indefinite allusions to an opposite continent need not mean anything. But the hints at a northern route to it, Plutarch's account of this route, the details applicable to the Davis Strait area and the Gulf of St. Lawrence—these are perplexing; and the *Navigatio* West Indian matter is perplexing in the same sense. The authors do not supply a convincing delineation of the American mainland, but they do supply snapshots (as it were) of the nearer approaches to it, the termini of the subsequent voyages of the Norse and Columbus.

The Platonic literature yields a further paragraph of the same type. It is in a commentary on the *Timæus* composed by the philosopher Proclus between 432 and 440 A.D.[38] Although he interpreted much of Plato as allegory, he was one of the few scholars of antiquity who believed in Atlantis, and he wrote of it in these terms:

> That such and so great an island once existed, is evident from what is said by certain historians respecting what pertains to the external sea. For according to them, there were seven islands in that sea, in their times, sacred to Proserpine, and also three others of an immense extent, one of which was sacred to Pluto, another to Ammon, and the middle (or

second) of these to Neptune, the magnitude of which w.
thousand stadia. They also add, that the inhabitants of .
preserved the remembrance from their ancestors, of the
Atlantic island which existed there, and was truly prodigiously
great; which for many periods had dominion over all the
islands in the Atlantic sea, and was itself likewise sacred to
Neptune. These things, therefore, Marcellus writes in his
Ethiopic History.[39]

This is an enigma like some of those in the *Navigatio*. Apart
from the religious excrescences, Proclus's paragraph would not
be far wrong . . . if only we could admit that his islands were
the Antilles, the main chain of the West Indies. Seven is a fair
round number for the principal Lesser Antilles: the islands
intended could be Guadeloupe, Dominica, Martinique, St.
Lucia, Barbados, St. Vincent and Grenada. The three greater
members of the chain are Cuba, Haiti and Porto Rico, all big by
Mediterranean standards; Haiti, the middle one, is approximately a thousand stadia—i.e. a hundred miles or a little over—
from side to side. In addition, the Spanish discoverers of the
Indies learned that the natives of this area had an unusual Deluge
legend. Instead of saying, like most nations, that the flood-water
subsided, they said it stayed where it was, in possession of the
ground it had swallowed. Many of the Antilles in fact had
formerly been joined into a single mass, but a disaster in ancient
times had split it into fragments with sea between. Such a
tradition was recorded among the Caribs and among the tribes
of Haiti itself, the very island to which Proclus's assertion would
seem to point.[40]

It is impossible to tell how old Proclus's information actually
is. His references to previous writers fail to settle the question.
He may be copying it all from the lost work of Marcellus, or
he may be fitting together a mosaic of quotations, or he may be
eking out shorter and less definite statements with ideas suggested
by recent speculations . . . or by recent discoveries. Proclus is

.tunately not a geographer, or interested specially in ɔgraphy. It remains a fact that he describes, toward the year .40, a western archipelago not described in any surviving earlier text, and that he manages somehow to register a quadruple hit.

Finally, as we now have two texts (Proclus and the *Navigatio*) which may be construed as possibly showing a knowledge of the West Indies, there is an excuse for giving just a nod of attention, after all, to Pausanias's Satyr yarn with its quasi-Carib touches.

The classical items are fragmentary, and I must stress again that such things would not deserve much notice if they were outweighed by a body of material dealing with land across the Atlantic altogether wrongly. But they are not so outweighed. Every classical author who ventures on the subject, even the silly Theopompus, contrives to score somehow, as the *Navigatio* author does. (The satirist Lucian wrote a Gulliver-like *True Story* which is a sort of exception, but it is frankly extravaganza, not to be considered seriously as "right" or "wrong.") Can we follow the clues these authors give, perhaps not to the certainty of a pre-Norse discovery of America, but to a delimitation of time and circumstance which will at least indicate how and when it might have been made? And can the West Indian matter in the *Navigatio* be thereby accounted for?

To these questions my own American explorations were closely related, as I shall now explain.

Part Three

ON THE OTHER SIDE

CHAPTER SEVEN

A Megalithic Bridge?

WHEN I FIRST caught myself sliding Atlantis-drawn toward the hypothesis of a crossing by way of Britain before 1400 B.C., I stared at it for a while and decided that it wouldn't do. But fortunately or unfortunately it refused to be consigned to the background. I had already been sent a packet of printed matter from the United States about some ruins at North Salem, in New Hampshire; a brochure had informed me that these were supposed to be the remains of an Irish monastery, built by fugitives from Iceland. Not deeply impressed, I had filed the brochure for future study without taking much notice. But Atlantis was scarcely out of the way when North Salem was thrust back on my attention by an article in the *Saturday Evening Post* (8th August, 1959). The writer, Evan Hill, referred to the site as an unsolved mystery, with the Irish theory as only one suggestion among several, and no longer an especially popular suggestion. He added that the ruins were under scrutiny by Mr. Frank Glynn, the President of the Connecticut Archæological Society, and that Mr. Glynn, following up a hint offered by T. C. Lethbridge in England, had begun investigating possible parallels with . . . of all places . . . bronze-age Malta. North Salem was turning out to be reminiscent of the megalithic and Minoan-influenced culture of the Mediterranean island.

The coincidence was a shock. On literary grounds I had arrived at the notion, unprecedented as far as I knew, of a discovery of America during the second millennium B.C. by a

195

te in the sphere of Ægean civilisation. And within a month
so of my formulating that notion and shelving it, here was the
same notion being put forward at the other end of the northern
route, on archæological grounds!

I re-read the article and examined the photographs of the
ruins. They showed blocks of rough stone assembled into walls
and huts. Nothing much could be learnt from these, but the
text was more informative. The recorded history of the North
Salem site, in outline, was that between 1835 and '55 it had
belonged to a local farmer called Jonathan Pattee. After a
lengthy derelict phase it had been acquired in 1936 by William
B. Goodwin, an antiquarian. The Irish monk theory, which
depended mainly on an extremist interpretation of Great Ireland,
was his. He had fenced in the ruins, excavated with regrettable
carelessness, and refused to let anybody in except supporters of
his own dogma. On his death in 1950 he had left the property
to an interested friend; and to-day, according to the article, it
was being run by a small syndicate as a tourist attraction under
the name of Mystery Hill.

I wrote to Frank Glynn, and we exchanged several letters.
He told me that his reaction to the Maltese idea had been very
much like my own to the implications of Atlantis. It sounded
fantastic, and he had not even tried it till months after receiving
it. Now, however, the case was altered. He was doubtful what
to think about the nature of any bronze-age communication
between the Old and New Worlds, but the parallels were in
favour of its occurrence. I explained to him that I hoped soon
to visit America in an effort to sort out certain things I had been
reading and meditating upon. The ruins at North Salem (Glynn
used the geographical name for the site, not the public-relations
name) would be put on my itinerary.

Before the tour I consulted one or two people better qualified
than myself to offer opinions. Among the curraghs and mountains of Kerry I remembered to introduce the *Post* article in my
conversation with Dr. Reidy, the Dean of Tralee. He smiled at

the mention of archæological evidence for a pre-Norse discov‑
Archæological evidence, he remarked, had been cropping up ‑
America for fifty years, but none of it had survived criticism.
He bent over the pictures of the ruins. No, he said, there was
nothing in them to remind him of Ireland. But apart from
that . . . ?

Later, when the day of my departure was closer, I went to
the University of London Institute of Archæology to interview
Professor John Evans, who had been kind enough to grant me
a few minutes of his time. My purpose was simplification. In
the hope of hitting on a test for the Malta theory, I wanted to
find out whether the Maltese megalithic sites had any special
characteristics which an untrained eye might recognise in another
context. Few could be more competent to tell me than Professor
Evans. I talked to him in an office where the chief item of furni‑
ture was a large table covered with labelled and classified speci‑
mens—tiny heaps of earth, handfuls of stone or pottery chips,
I am really not sure what: the display was so lavish I could not
take it in. Such order inspired confidence. A dramatist wishing
to present an archæologist in a play would have hesitated to put
such an object as that table in his stage directions. It was too
professional, too good to be true.

Professor Evans read through some of Glynn's notes. I
enlarged on them, and raised the possibility of Minoan or
Mycenean expeditions to bronze-age Britain and beyond. As
to these he was a trifle damping. It was not at all clear, he said,
that anyone from the Ægean had actually gone as far as Britain;
the indubitable traces of trade, the probable traces of artistic
influence, could be explained by contact through intermediaries.
If it was a question of searching for ocean-going peoples during
the second millennium B.C., his own money would be on the
north-west Iberians. But to prove any connection with the
Old World over such a distance would require, not merely
parallels, but parallels of a highly specialised kind in combination.

" Yes, that's more or less my point," I said, and asked him

.t to look out for at North Salem. Whereupon (a remarkable
..ng in an expert of any sort) he gave me a prompt, simple and
practical answer.

"First," he suggested, running his finger over a plan of a
Maltese site, "look for a cloverleaf formation—walls curving
round to make near-circles that join up. And you might try
the 'porthole' characteristic—square windows cut through big
slabs of stone—though that is not so distinctive."

Cloverleaves and portholes. With these in mind I went my
way, passed over the northern seas as related, and in due course
reached Vinland.

Malcolm Pearson, the owner of the North Salem site, met me
at Boston Airport on a fierce June morning. We drove straight
there. The neighbourhood was quiet and rural, with winding
lanes and fragrant woods not conforming at all to standard conceptions of the United States, so that on getting out at the base
of the hill I began to have an appropriately odd feeling of un-
reality. This wore thin later as America reasserted itself with its
native bird-calls and scampering chipmunks, but the first impression of that secluded shade defeating the hot sky was never
quite lost.

Beside the car park stood a large wooden hut containing an
office, a souvenir stall, and a lunch counter. Here I saw tourists
being placed in the charge of youthful guides employed by
Richard Elston, the manager. Mrs. Elston was responsible for
the souvenirs and her husband for the more academic aspects,
in the shape of a row of diagrams, photographs and press cuttings.
These, I noticed, were impartially chosen, and included an article
by a Harvard archæologist denying that the site had any claim
to antiquity at all. At the end of the room there was a world
map with coloured pins stuck in it to show where visitors had
come from; the United Kingdom was already represented, and
an arctic pin inexplicably denoted somebody on an ice-floe in
the Beaufort Sea.

Mr. Elston led the way through the woods toward Goo▮ wire enclosure and along the boardwalks deployed among ruins themselves, with handrails in tricky spots. He pointed o▮ every detail, drawing my attention to many things he regarded as " unusual "—a favourite word of his—and to the somewhat conjectural signboards he had had put up. But he made no attempt to restrict me to a conducted tour or to force any views on me. In common with the other custodians he displayed a perfectly open-minded attitude, and gave me plenty of time, after the first rapid circuit, to look round for myself at leisure.

There is no accepted name for this site; if it acquires archæological status it will probably be called simply " North Salem." On several plans the central group of ruins inside the fence is designated as " Pattee's Caves " after the former owner, who built his house on top of one of the stone structures. It was burnt down, but there are still traces of his improvements in the stonework below, including chips of mortar. Apart from this modern patching all the stones are held in position by their own weight and skilful arrangement. Understandably a great many were carried off during the post-Pattee phase of neglect, and employed for road construction. To judge from early photographs the ruins must formerly have been far less open and more cavernous, and inequalities in the weathering of some of the blocks give hints at the way the plunderers dragged and toppled them.

The ruins in the enclosure cover about an acre, rising in steps up the east side of the hill. This is the more sheltered side, away from the nearest river (the Spicket, a tributary of the Merrimack). Most of the coniferous growth that shuts the place in is recent, and there may once have been a wide prospect eastward. The typical structure is an artificial cave or chamber built up from stones of various sizes, most of them rough, or only dressed very crudely. Normally the chamber is roofed over with a heavy flat slab or slabs laid across. The skill of the builders is not evinced in formation or design but in stability—in the careful packing and the wise use of the natural rock face, which breaks rough shallow soil. Some of the chambers are dwarfish, more than two or three feet high, and the loftiest ceiling anywhere is not much above six.

It is debatable whether any significance attaches to the marks on some of the bigger stones. Elston and Glynn have gone over them for carvings comparable to the axes and dagger at Stonehenge, but found nothing conclusive. On one outward-facing surface it is just possible to make out a head with a huge chin and a pair of horns, but this could be accidental. Otherwise, such marks as exist have, for the most part, a strictly utilitarian air. Several stones have rectangular sockets cut in them, and a single isolated and horizontal slab has been pierced through close to its edge by two holes drilled from opposite faces. These holes converge badly, at an angle, and the upper hole is rough inside, as if the tool that made it was primitive.

There are two small wells at different levels, which may be modern, though a cache of quartz crystals at the bottom of one of them has excited some speculation. More obviously interesting are the drainpipes that descend the hill-side in a smooth gradient. These are well constructed and lined with stone; one is forty feet long, another sixty feet. There are also several gutters or ostensible gutters, which, however, fail to convince as effectively as the drains.

Low walls wind in and out among the ruins and spread over the hill-side, forming incipient fields and half-hearted avenues that never quite take shape. Big flat slabs set edgeways are recurring components of them; these slabs are fitted into slots with a rubble backing, a laborious arrangement not at all characteristic of New England farming, and detectable in some cases to a surprising depth in the soil. The North Salem walls keep on starting and stopping all the way up, and over the top of the hill, which is a bumpy wooded plateau. Across it to the west the ground falls away steeply to the river, breaking completely at one level to make a miniature cliff and ledge.

My discovery of these latter features was delayed. On the

first ascent through the woods and ruins Elston was looking at the time for Frank Glynn, the archæologist, and in the upper part of the enclosure we found him. He proved to be a short, gentle-voiced, courteous man with a moustache. Mr. Glynn is as much of an amateur as Goodwin (he is assistant postmaster at Clinton, Connecticut), but he is blessed with a sense of humour and an ability to theorise without slipping into dogmatism or distortion. When he sighted us he called out jocularly, "How are the Irish monks?"—a thing which I am sure the zealot Goodwin would not have done. After some conversation they introduced me in detail to the most remarkable portion of the main site, a group of structures near the top which powerfully suggests ritual purposes.

A high, artificially drained ramp or stage, banked up and walled, faces eastward. The perpendicular bisector of the straight front edge of the stage, running in that direction with only a slight deviation from the compass, traverses two objects. In a kind of orchestra pit immediately before and below the stage, an enormous flat stone weighing four tons rests on squat legs like a table-top. (When it was first examined its upper surface was level with the ground; the legs were exposed afterwards by soil removal.) The stone is shaped like the profile of a bell, the straight edge or base being parallel to the edge of the stage. A deep artificial groove follows its outline completely round, a few inches inwards from the rim. This could be a trough for liquid, like the gravy channels of Victorian meat dishes, and the effect is strengthened by what appears to be a drainage gutter running from the groove to the straight edge some distance off centre. Inevitably this forbidding table-top has been associated with blood and sacrifice, perhaps human sacrifice, and has been explained as an altar stone (see opposite p. 208).

The aforesaid bisector, passing east over the altar stone from its base to its curving farther rim, goes on over a mound of rocks and earth which that rim touches. Inside the mound is a chamber called, from its shape, the " Y-cavern "; the bisector runs down

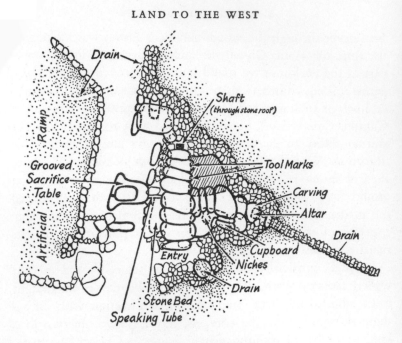

Sketch plan of North Salem
(supposed ritual area only)

the upright of the " Y " to the far end. Strictly speaking it is a " T " rather than a " Y," since the arms are practically in a straight line and form a single cross-stroke going from north to south.

This chamber has two entrances. One is at the south end of the cross-stroke, and it was by this that I went into it myself. On my left a couple of yards along was a ledge of rock wide enough to hold a small human body lying with knees drawn up. Near the ceiling a little shaft led horizontally to the outer air through eight feet of piled rocks. Farther along again, the northern arm of the cross-stroke shelved upward, and light streamed in down a vertical chimney. I turned east into the upright of the " Y " or " T," twenty-three feet long and sloping downhill. Its corbelled roof, the only one at North Salem, rose

202

six and a half feet above the floor, and here I could walk comfortably if cautiously. On the right was a niche, a sort of cupboard, and on the left was what appeared to be a narrow seat. In the left wall near the tapering lower end of the passage was a stone with a carving on it—at least it looked like a carving: a design in a few flowing strokes (possibly made by a series of overlapping punches) which some, I gathered, interpreted as a sketch of a deer. Opposite this was the other entrance, admitted to be fairly modern owing to marks of destruction not paralleled at the upper one.

Several things need to be said about this chamber. First, as to the small shaft above the ledge. It comes out of the mound under the altar stone, and it is highly resonant and can be used as a speaking-tube. Second, as to the chimney. If you light a fire under it, the whole chamber becomes a hot-house; if you block it, the smoke pours out of the mound through the speaking-tube; and at the top of the chimney there is a shutter contrivance indicating that under some circumstances it was meant to be blocked. Third, as to the lower end. This narrows, but to an orifice, not a cul-de-sac. The sixty-foot drain extends from the orifice downhill, a permanent safeguard against flooding. When this was discovered it was sealed up with rocks as if the site had been deliberately abandoned.

Such are the stone edifices at North Salem. They are not merely ruins but the ruins of ruins, catastrophically reduced during the last hundred years by the spoliations of road-makers and the erratic spade-play of Goodwin. However, enough is left to be provocative and bewildering. The comments of a distinguished teacher of architecture, Vincent Fagan of Notre Dame University, are worth quoting: " The big things are too little, the little things so big. There was, at one and the same time, gigantic confusion and childish disorder—deep cunning and rude naïveté. There was explosive disarray held together by the fine thread of a great weaver."

Richard Elston has asked a long series of visitors for their own

.npressions and theories. Formerly he kept a suggestion book, and one entry in it says, " Indians, drunk." But an epithet that recurs in discussion if not in writing is " megalithic." Person after person has been reminded of the massive structures that rose over Europe between 3000 and 1200 B.C., not indeed the advanced architecture of bronze-age Mycenæ, but the cruder work of the Maltese, Iberians and others. This reaction is easy to understand, yet so far it has not been translated into verifiable terms. Supposed clues such as obtuse angles and cubit measurements have failed to lead anywhere. Megaliths perhaps, but waif megaliths, without clues to their family.

Moreover, what about the inhabitants? No burials have been found, nor any unquestionable human remains. According to a nearby landowner, skulls used to be dug up on the ledge the other side of the hill, but no such skull has been produced. Of course the site may have been a temple or cult-centre without any stable population. More disheartening than the absence of burials is the absence or acute shortage of artifacts. The fruits of Goodwin's excavations, of a more systematic dig in 1955, and of Glynn's own activities, are still scarcely better than negligible. Shards and chips of plain brick-like pottery, occasionally bearing what seem to be grain impressions and bands of paint, are scattered here and there; Goodwin unearthed some smoke-marked pieces at the downhill outlet of the long drain from the Y-chamber. These at present have no story to tell, and the searchers have done little more otherwise than clear away a layer of refuse left by Jonathan Pattee.

It is on the lack of relics, a negative but strong argument, that professional archæologists have based their refusal to spend much time on North Salem. They say that nothing found on the site need be earlier than Pattee's occupancy. A single tree-stump is admitted to have grown in such a position that the adjacent stonework cannot be dated later than 1769, but this exception is not allowed to cancel what is held to be the predominant effect: that the whole assemblage of walls and ramps and rock chambers is a kind of " folly " built by Pattee himself, owing to insanity or extreme eccentricity, or else for some rather obscure illegal purpose.

This theory must be accorded a fair hearing before the more romantic ones can be entertained. A few of the local people accept it, but most do not. The present Pattee generation asserts the more usual view, that old Jonathan only added to the site by converting bits of it for his own use. Charges of mental aberration and criminality are quite unsubstantiated; he seems to have been a solid and reputable citizen. Furthermore, some very grave difficulties arise, the first of them from the sheer magnitude of the job. Sceptics talk airily about the help Pattee could have got from his " large family," but research has pretty well disposed of this family. The farmer had several daughters, but only two sons, one of whom died in infancy, so that the effective able-bodied household comprised no more than two men. He would have had to hire numerous labourers, and a lunatic project on such a scale would have been remarked upon and remembered. There would be no doubt in the district, or among his descendants, as to how the buildings got there. But there is doubt, and the earliest printed reference to them does not mention any current belief in Pattee's responsibility for them—it treats them as mystifying.

Another difficulty is the surface appearance of the stones. Glynn showed me patches of weathering that hinted at millennia of exposure, and assured me credibly enough that even colonial stonework, let alone post-colonial, never has that antique look.

And in any case, if the ruins are the self-made monument of a crazy farmer, what sort of craze are we to imagine? What was this allegedly unbalanced man trying to do? It is hard to see what purpose he could have had in mind for any of the structures. It is harder to see why, or how, he laboriously anticipated archæological finds in distant countries, not made during his lifetime. Instances are the speaking-tube, the stone drain-pipes, the orientation, all paralleled on Old World megalithic sites. The altar stone is another crux. Its manufacture would have involved an alarming amount of work, and, in the world of a Yankee farmer, entirely senseless work. Colonial Americans used comparable articles for grape-pressing and soap-making, but none of the same pattern or anything like the same bulk.

Some day a long-lost diary or letter may still reveal, after all, that Pattee was the culprit. That theory has not been disproved. However, it has emphatically not been proved. Pattee is simply one candidate, a far from satisfactory candidate, and the field is wide open for conjecture.

Other guesses that demand no sensational migrations are that North Salem was put up by aboriginal Indians (whether drunk or sober), or by Eskimos. An Indian occupation is plausible, and the pottery scraps are in its favour, but neither race has erected anything similar anywhere at all close. Goodwin's Irish monk theory is now recognised to be even weaker. It was founded on the American identification of Great Ireland, which, as we have seen, Idrisi refutes. Goodwin collected data on several other unexplained structures in New England and threw his findings together into a big, lavishly illustrated book, unhappily disfigured by the personal feuding which readers tend to take as a mark of the crank. After so much devoted effort, one might wish him to have been right. But he was wrong. Nothing about North Salem conveys any hint of Christianity. The special features of a Celtic monastic settlement—distinctive crosses, distinctive graveyard, boundary ditch, round tower—are nowhere to be seen.

We may revert, then, to the megalithic idea and see what can be made of that. It is not strictly necessary to go to Europe for megaliths: they are found in Central and South America; but none exist between North Salem and Mexico to trace out an overland path of influence, and an isolated sea colonisation across thousands of miles by the non-seafaring Mexicans would be intrinsically stranger than an intrusion from bronze-age Europe.

If Europeans, who? Inquiry only seems to add to the chi_ series of negations. North Salem was not built by the mo_ civilised Ægean peoples. It was not built by Phœnicians, whose entry into the Atlantic was much later than the megalithic period.[1] The stone drains have set some visitors thinking of Skara Brae, an Orkney Neolithic hamlet which also had them, but they have not thought to very much purpose. As for the Malta theory that caught my own attention, the speaking-tube is paralleled in a Maltese oracle shrine, and there are other resemblances. But when I looked for Professor Evans's portholes and cloverleaf walls, I found neither. Glynn conceded that the cloverleaves, if any, were incomplete, and inspection of the plan bore him out. Though he told me that he still considered the theory interesting, and referred to a site at Hal Tarxien, I felt that he was veering away. Malta had been valuable as a hint, a pointer, a stimulant, but perhaps not much more. He mentioned Spain and Portugal, and remembering Professor Evans I put in a word of encouragement. Beyond doubt the ancient Iberians did possess ocean-going ships, and did go to the British Isles; there are signs indeed of a major migration, the objective substratum of some of the Irish settlement legends.

A trustworthy dating of the North Salem site would be a long step forward. The last time I saw Frank Glynn he was wielding a shovel in a small trench far up the hill-side, in quest of charcoal for radiocarbon study.

"They had a fire here all right," he said, holding up a minute black speck. "But I haven't got enough. Anyhow, it's likely to be contaminated."

With remarks like this in my ears, I could hit on no illuminating reply to the custodians' queries. What opinions had I formed? Well, it wasn't Irish monks . . . and it wasn't Indians . . . and it surely wasn't Pattee . . . but I had no real idea who it was. I felt sad at having so little to offer in return for so much hospitality and helpfulness, but, at the time, nothing more was honestly possible.

2

alem seemed to lead back to the myths and legends and
er significations they might have: to Atlantis, to the
ard banishment of Cronus, to the labours of Hercules,
ps also to the fabulous chronicles of ancient Ireland. If
ted into any process of exploration that could be glimpsed
n the European end, its character pointed to a bronze-age
covery which might be called, for want of a better name,
e Platonic.

Plato's island route from Atlantis to the far side would make
better sense if we could identify his Atlanteans with a real nation.
All we can say, however, is that his imaginative brew does look
as if it included bronze-age British ingredients, and that this item
about the farther continent is intelligible in British terms. It is
paralleled by the Britons' report to Pytheas concerning Thule,
and its applicability to the northern route is shared by Theopompus's tale with its " Americans " ferried over to the country
of the Hyperboreans, who are undoubtedly northerners and,
according to Hecatæus, British, while the Hyperborean Ocean in
Ptolemy is the sea north-west of the British Isles.

If there is anything in the theory that Theopompus borrowed
from a satire on Solon, the northern trans-Oceanic route was
probably part of the Atlantis legend as Solon told it, before
Plato took it up. This deduction would transfer it two centuries
further back, and into the safer hands of the great legislator.
The idea may well be drawn ultimately from Minoan or
Mycenean contacts with Britain about the time of the building
of Stonehenge, and from stories current among the Britons.

In the *Odyssey* passage already summarised, Odysseus's crossing of the Ocean is associated with the legend of a northern
Cimmerian nation which at least *could* be somewhere in the British
Isles. Homer's brief reference (*Iliad*, viii. 477) to Cronus's place
of banishment, which puts the lost Titan in a distant Tartarus

North Salem ruins: the " altar stone "

North Salem ruins: space adjacent to " altar stone ".
The speaking-tube from inside the mound opposite
comes out close to the pole

La Venta: Olmec stele with profile of " Uncle Sam "
near base (see Chapter Eight)

where the sun is not seen, may be interpreted as glancing the same way. Hesiod (*Theogony*, 729–48) situates Cronus in clouds and gloom, explicitly beyond Atlas. These earliest accounts of the Titan's exile, like the hints at an icebound Cronian Sea, put him in the north-westerly rather than the south-westerly quadrant. His residence in the Fortunate Isles is a poetic afterthought; a phrase alluding to it in Hesiod's *Works and Days* is interpolated.

Belief in a British trans-Oceanic route as far back as the Greek Heroic Age could have been due at least partly to guesswork on immram lines, to an imaginative extrapolation of the Hebrides and Orkneys. Some weight must be given to the potentialities of the argument from bird migration. Shrewd observers might always have drawn the inference that the birds were not flying into a void, without actually checking it for themselves. Yet Plato's opposite continent, which is definitely not part of the old cosmology, and just as definitely irrelevant to his own myth, does seem to call for a fuller explanation. Also the British knowledge of Thule implies something more than inference, and while its provenance may be later than the Bronze Age, it is not necessarily so: the Arthurian legends of Lyonesse and the magical transportation of Stonehenge indicate that bronze-age traditions persisted among the British peoples, not merely till the fourth century B.C., but well into the Christian era.[2]

3

Antique elements like the god Cronus and the companions of Hercules reappear in Plutarch's " Moon " myth, and so do Britons. But if he is to be regarded as grounding his fiction on any rumour of fact, Atlantean imaginings are not enough. His sudden array of geographical detail, after centuries of meagre scraps, cannot be the outcome of any faint lingering Mycenean tradition. It necessitates something further. Also, confusingly, it supplies a much more definite hunt for North Salem.

Take one of Plutarch's details only, the assertion about the latitude of the bay. It was not an obvious thing for him to hit on. The general tenor of his story would suggest that Cronus's kingdom ought to lie in the Ogygian sub-arctic, and the same inference would follow from the literary allusions elsewhere to the Cronian Sea. Once he had mentally committed his pilgrims to coasting along the opposite continent, he had moved away from the logic of the myth, and there was no inherent motive for locating the outlet of the bay on one parallel rather than another. However, for some non-mythical reason, the place he chose was correct within a degree or so. The main opening of the Gulf of St. Lawrence actually is in the same latitude as the so-called opening or misapprehended north end of the Caspian.

This exactitude is not merely alien to the spirit of the previous texts, but out of accord with them also, one would say, in a chronological sense. Any supposed " Plutarchian " discovery of America must be later than the " Platonic." A correct observation of latitude could not have been made when there was nobody who knew how to make it, and the astronomy of the Bronze Age, even in Crete, was probably not equal to such an assignment. Measurement of the kind required is believed to have begun, among Europeans at any rate, in the fourth century B.C., and the first person specifically credited with performing it is no other than Pytheas, who deduced the latitude of Marseilles from the shadow of a gnomon. If he was not the actual inventor of the method, his feat was novel enough to rate a special mention.[3] Hence, if Plutarch's myth has any authenticity in it, some at least of his material would seem to have been drawn from a much less distant past then Plato's, or from a non-classical civilisation. The latitude alone would not be decisive—it might be a stab in the dark, or a clever construction from directions and distances—but its geographical precision is all of a piece with other particulars. Plutarch's mapping of the farther Atlantic has no earlier counterpart, and implies a fresh source. Moreover (for what the fact is worth) he quotes his contemporary Sylla having met someone who actually made the Atlantic crossing The whole setting of the tale is recent, not ancient.

Even if the passage is wholly fanciful, even if its touches of accuracy are mere lucky shots, its character might well set a reader looking for elucidatory facts in the stretch of years between Plato and Plutarch—between 347 B.C., when the former died, and approximately A.D. 75, when the latter composed the dialogue. Two theories commend themselves. It may be that America was discovered or rediscovered in that period by some neglected explorer of the northern route. Or it may be that Plutarch tapped a new source of information or misinformation, not accessible to his predecessors, and not generally accessible to the scholars of his own time.

The obstacles in the path of the first theory are manifest. Plutarch never makes it clear who his pilgrims are, and it is unlikely in the last degree that anything so obscure as his myth is our sole record of an important expedition, carried out in the limelight of Roman civilisation, but not noticed by a single geographer. Yet Proclus too, with his apparent Antilles, deserves to be recalled here; so does Pausanias; and Crates may not have spun the Perioikean Land entirely out of his own dreams. We must in fairness ask whether an Atlantic passage might have been accomplished, doubtless not under the Cæsars, but in the tumultuous age just before the establishment of the Pax Romana, when it could have been overlooked.

Plutarch's travelling stranger is said to have "discovered certain sacred parchments which were buried at Carthage when the old city was destroyed;" and there are one or two other Carthaginian references. The African port and its vast maritime traffic sank into eclipse in 146 B.C. when the Romans overran and erased it. But could the myth be a tangled reminiscence of some Punic discovery in the two-hundred-odd years subsequent to Plato?

No serious doubt has ever been cast on the spacious extent of

.thaginian sailing, and the possibility that it extended to
.merica has hovered for centuries in the background of geographical speculation. Richard Hakluyt took it for granted
that Hanno, the Punic captain who explored the African coastline,
had found his way to the New World, and Southey gave a brief
airing to a similar theory in the notes to a poem.[4] By far the
most interesting hint after the " Moon " dialogue itself is the
paragraph in Diodorus quoted on page 132 about the large island
far out west from Morocco, and the Carthaginians' plan to keep
it as a refuge in case of disaster to their own city. The other
allusion to the island, wrongly fathered on Aristotle, is sometimes
quoted as placing it sixty days' sail off, but that exciting figure,
I am afraid, must have crept in through misunderstanding; the
usual identification with Madeira is compatible with both texts.
What seems never to have emerged is whether, when the disaster
came, the refuge was used. The last scene of the tragedy is
missing.

Any flight which took place need not have been deferred till
the very last instant. For a full human lifetime before the end
Carthage was in retreat and decline, and far-sighted Carthaginians
might well have judged the prospect hopeless and emigrated,
escaping from a Mediterranean transformed into a Roman lake
to seek for new homes beyond Gibraltar. Such a diaspora would
fit in with potentialities recognised at the time, as Diodorus
attests. We might picture the dispossessed Africans plying to
their Madeira haven, spreading through the Azores (whence the
Corvo hoard), and drifting outward from Sierra Leone along the
Equatorial Current; while others, steering for Britain, hear the
same reports Pytheas heard and probe along the northern route,
unconsciously sowing legends among the islanders. The picture
is not invalidated, as so many conjectures are bound to be in this
field, by the argument from silence. The normal Punic reticence,
the fall of Carthage, the intention of flight without return, the
likelihood that very few such emigrants ever would have returned,
all these things suggest that this is a way in which a discovery of

America could have been achieved without leaving more than wisps of hearsay in the Old World: Plutarch's dim vision of the northern route, perhaps a rumour of the Antilles in Proclus, perhaps also a hint in the globe of Crates.

Having stated this theory as forcefully as I can, I must go on to register my total dissent from it.

Evidence that the Carthaginians got to Madeira and the Azores is not evidence that they got any farther, and if they did, their exploits would still be of no help in the exegesis of Plutarch. When we turn northward, we find no proof that they even visited Britain. They reached Brittany, and their trade went beyond, but it need not have been direct. That these sunburnt business-men, who were strictly and rather horribly practical, should have gone roaming through Hyperborean fog when they had the whole tropical realm before them, is a most far-fetched supposition. It may none the less be true, and the future findings of archæology are impossible to forecast. But its lack of cogency is an incentive toward the second theory: that Plutarch, in his myth, is using a special and semi-private source.

Here the prospect looks brighter at once, because he indicates himself that he is. He is drawing on statements revealed in his dialogue on Oracles to have been collected among the outlying Britons by the civil servant Demetrius, whom he presents as a sober investigator to be treated respectfully. And so we are driven back to Britain again. But this information, as a matter of history, would not have been directly available to Greeks in Plato's time, and in Plutarch's it was already slipping out of reach. Plato was dead before Pytheas renewed contact with Britain after the millennial break, and for many more years Pytheas himself had almost no imitators. Apart from Julius Cæsar's hurried incursions, the Græco-Roman society only penetrated Britain on an appreciable scale in A.D. 43 with the Roman conquest. One of the first aims of Imperial policy was the stamping out of the Druids, whose Order was the main repository of British scholarship and mythology. In 61 the invasion of Anglesey suppressed the Druids' last stronghold. Roman civilisation and education were imposed throughout the province, and within a few decades the door which had been opened upon the native mind for sympathetic inquirers like Demetrius was resolutely shut again.

Plutarch, therefore, may well be giving us a genuine fragment of Celtic British lore caught on the wing by one lucky southerner just before its disappearance. This view is the more attractive because of the parallel (that recurrent parallel) with the Thule report. In Britain over a long period there were men with definite notions of islands beyond their own. To judge from the "Moon" dialogue these notions reached out a very long way beyond, and, more puzzling still, were fuller for the far side of the Atlantic than for the near side. Demetrius's acquaintances apparently spoke to him of sailing westward from Britain, but did not tell him which part of Britain, and unless he misunderstood them they were badly astray as to the length of the sail. But after that their narrative was more circumstantial and more accurate, introducing the short Greenland summer night, the correctly measured Davis Strait, the floating ice and debris, the wind on the Labrador coast, the correctly located Gulf, and the islands.[5]

This distortion is queer on any hypothesis advanced up to now, even the unsatisfying hypothesis of pure fiction. What are we to think, moreover, of Cronus (or the god here called so) and his cave of detention? The myth is valuable for its connection and continuity with later Celtic matter, but like the other details it concerns the far side, and one wonders whether it embodies or disguises anything factual. Cronus's prison, on the face of it, has to be in the central Gulf of St. Lawrence: on Anticosti, or Grindstone, or Cape Breton, or some western promontory of Newfoundland. Since the Cretan cavern which mythology averred to be the birthplace of Zeus turned out on examination to be an ancient cult-centre littered with votive offerings,[6] it may be that some fact of religious practice does underlie the tale of Cronus. Little is known at present of the archæology of the Gulf region. Anticosti—formerly the private estate of Menier, the chocolate magnate—has never been thoroughly explored. Grindstone, the principal island of the Magdalen group, has high cliffs and caves, " dark red and lined with emerald moss in spots," but erosion is so rapid that the aspect of the place two thousand years ago must have been very different.[7]

There are, however, two points of interest, one being of quite extraordinary interest. The Micmac Indians, an Algonquin tribe living in Nova Scotia, have many legends of a divine hero named Glooskap who taught them useful arts in the distant past. At the end of his residence among them he went away, and in one version he is said to have vanished into a cave in Cape Breton Island, where he still is. This cave is characterised by a " roaring sound " and " an entrance that closes down smaller and smaller as one approaches until it is only a tiny hole." The explanation seems to be that it is at the base of a cliff on the precipitous north-west coast, and a high tide almost closes the entrance, or did close it at some past time when the conformation was different. The Indians say that a party once explored it without seeing anything unusual; but you never know.[8]

Plutarch's description of the prison raises a more intriguing issue, the nature of which will perhaps have grown clear already.

Cronus himself sleeps within a deep cave resting on rock which looks like gold, this sleep being devised for him by Zeus in place of chains. Birds fly in at the topmost part of the rock, and bear him ambrosia, and the whole island is pervaded by the fragrance shed from the rock as out of a well. The Spirits of whom we hear serve and care for Cronus, having been his comrades in the time when he was really king over gods and men. Many are the utterances which they give forth of their own prophetic power, but the greatest and those about the greatest issues they announce when they return as dreams of Cronus; for the things which Zeus pre-meditates, Cronus dreams.

This passage gives five essential elements: the cave itself; the god asleep on a rock bed inside; a shaft or chimney above; "fragrance" overspreading the neighbourhood ("the whole island" is surely hyperbolic) from aromatic substances introduced into the cave; and oracular utterances by the occupant. All of these particulars, as I suddenly realised after a time-lag of several weeks, agree felicitously with the Y-chamber at North Salem.

It is a cave, if an artificial one. It contains a rock ledge big enough to lie on. It has a chimney, and the smoke from a fire inside the chamber can be forced out vigorously through the small shaft by blocking this chimney. The small shaft itself is an excellent speaking-tube for transmitting the voice of anyone —a priest-interpreter, for example—standing by the rock bed. Plutarch does not make any allusion here to the most notorious features of the Cronus cult, human sacrifice and the god's ugly sickle; but North Salem has its altar stone just by the Y-chamber, and the clearest part of the curvilinear scrawl inside the chamber might be meant for an outstretched forearm with a long sickle in the hand.

Since the American site is on the mainland, hundreds of miles away from the Gulf, it is scarcely probable even on the most sanguine reading that North Salem is the place intended. But it might be a relic or outpost of some lost "Cronian" culture. It might be modelled on a larger and more important sanctuary, with priests or seers impersonating the god, which existed once on an island in the Gulf and was construed by the British Celts in their way and by Demetrius in his. The coincidence, at all events, is too striking to pass by. There is only this one descrip-tion in all classical literature of a sacred place on the other side of the Atlantic, and North Salem, otherwise unexplained, answers to it in half a dozen respects.

As to who the Cronians might have been, where they might have come from, and what territory exactly they might have occupied, nothing can be affirmed at the moment. Plutarch makes a large number of the Titan's subjects live along the coast of the bay, and off-hand I do not see why we should not believe him, especially when we recall the kindlier Gulf climate of that era. But he gives no help in accounting for the pioneer settlers. The tendency of our clues so far is perhaps to indicate that the original Cronians (if they existed at all) were bronze-age European megalith-builders, and that their emigration was the historical fact behind the myth of their god's exile.

Plutarch distinguishes two strata of population, Cronus's original subjects and the Greek companions of Hercules, long since intermarried; and he says the Cronian pilgrimages are launched when the planet Saturn, Cronus's star, is in the constellation Taurus, the Bull. Now Hercules came to the far west to capture cattle; and the " Red Island " where the cattle lived was supposed to be off Tartessus; and that district had two famous temples, one of Cronus and one of Hercules, whom the Phœnicians worshipped as Moloch and Melkart.[9] Some connection between the Titan and the deified hero must have been in Plutarch's mind. But rather than pursue phantasms like these, let us look at his myth from another angle. North Salem, if there is anything in it, is another factor that tells in the Britons' favour. They did not guess, they knew. But as we have no good ground for postulating convenient Carthaginians, how did they know?

I revert here to that unpromising person Theopompus, and to a thing he says on the alleged authority of Silenus. While he does not speak of anybody as going across from Europe to the opposite continent, he does speak of the Machimites' expedition as coming over from it to the country of the Hyperboreans, i.e. perhaps Britain. With all his absurdity he opens up a new line of thought. Being conscious of the technological short-comings of Red Indians, we normally assume that any trans-

217

Atlantic contact must have taken the form of a " discovery of America," a transit from the Old World to the New. This assumption has led to difficulties. But perhaps it is not justified. Perhaps voyagers could have come the other way.

While maintaining a careful agnosticism as to origins,[10] let us suppose North Salem to be the work of a " Cronian " nation of some antiquity flourishing in the Gulf area and New England, a nation which, even if its ancestry was European, diverged in its culture. Let us conceive our Cronians, not as very numerous or as highly adept in such activities as building (otherwise they would have left more conspicuous traces), but as skilful, scientifically capable, and above all venturesome at sea. Finally, let us picture them as skirting the Atlantic in both directions, exploring the West Indies, and passing at various times by way of Greenland to the British Isles but no farther—an extent of sailing no more improbable than the odysseys of the Pacific peoples, or the Norse. I am not offering this *jeu d'esprit* as a serious conjecture; not yet, anyhow. My point is that even such a fantasy has a cautionary value, and should serve as a warning against the reckless multiplication of early " discoveries of America." For it covers nearly all the data better than imaginary "discoveries" can. It also resolves the paradox—and when all allowances have been made, it still is a paradox—that these nebulous ideas of the New World occur in classical authors without an atom of evidence that anyone went over to visit it from the Old.

If " Cronians " came across to Britain at intervals, it is comprehensible that the more learned Britons—bards, priests, eventually Celtic Druids—should have gleaned something from them about the seas, the islands, the farther continent, and the religion practised there, whether the god was the true Cronus exported or a foreigner similar to him. If the visits ceased while Britain was still more or less isolated from Europe, as it long was (*penitus toto divisos orbe Britannos* even in Virgil), it is comprehensible that only stray scraps of what the Britons had heard should ever have trickled through to the Greeks and Romans. The course of events is easy to reconstruct. Cronian sailors' yarns of America and of their own crossings via the Faeroes, Orkneys and so forth, circulating in bronze-age Wessex, are passed along the trade lanes to the Ægean world, and emerge at last embedded in Greek mythology: hence the passages in Plato and Theopompus, hence also perhaps the Homeric and Hesiodic image of Cronus's banishment, hence also perhaps the Perioikean Land of Crates. Cronian stories of Iceland and the midnight sun, current in the Britain of the fourth century B.C., are retailed to Pytheas. A rough Cronian map, or verbal equivalent of a map, is preserved by Druids as part of their lore, and some account of this is transmitted to Demetrius and by him to Plutarch. A Cronian version of the West Indian archipelago also drifts round to Britain, and finds its way, through the surviving academic Druids of Gaul, into the texts of Proclus and conceivably Pausanias.

The virtual extirpation of British Druidism, and the Romanisation of the British educated class, would have extinguished most of these traditions. The Druidism that persisted in Ireland, however, carried on the teachings of the defunct British schools, and the hypothesis of a Cronian deposit would give the Irish voyage-literature a new and interesting dimension. Bran the Raven is Cronus in his enchanted retreat across the waves, and the immram notion of the medley of Atlantic isles is in part a vestige of Cronian sea-lore. As for the *Navigatio* itself, its tenth-century author still retains a valid conception of the northern route, and he reads Macrobius and the rest—as nobody outside Ireland does—in the light of an ancestral conviction, however blurred, that there is *something there*. His evocation of the Perioikean Land is an intelligent act corresponding to historical realities, not a meaningless exercise in copying.

Thus the Cronian theory, whoever we presume the Cronians to have been, is simpler and more fruitful than any combination of invented " discoveries " could be; and after all, somebody must have built North Salem. It solves every problem ... with a single exception. The exception is that part of the *Navigatio* dealing with the flat island, the grape island and the transparent sea—the " Bahaman " and " Jamaican " matter. That remains hanging as before, an obstinately loose end. It cannot be derived from the classical texts or from any probable source behind them; Proclus's West Indies, indeed, are precisely and ironically the wrong West Indies. In view of the snapshot details, and the Christian community on the flat island, a pagan tradition fully a thousand years old is not a satisfactory explanation here.

To bring order out of confusion, something else is needed. North Salem has injected a fresh ingredient, and while North Salem itself may be a mare's-nest, the hint which it supplies is worth following up. Can we get any more enlightenment from America? Are there any more facts that might suggest the presence of unknown people there, whether from this side or the other; facts indicative of a discovery fitting in with some of the literature, or facts converting the Cronian notion from a mere debating point into a theory to be considered? If such facts exist, do they help to resolve the last riddles of the *Navigatio*?

I pass on to my search for the answers: to the breaking out of the cage, the reversal of the problem. The scene now changes, the stage revolves.

CHAPTER EIGHT

Serpent and Sea-Foam

FACING CENTRAL PARK, a Teddy Roosevelt of heroic proportions bestrode a mighty horse. Behind him rose the façade
of the American Museum of Natural History. I went up the
sunlit steps into the main hall, where aphorisms of the rough-
riding and hard-reading President admonished me from a
series of plaques, till I half expected to find the adjective " bully "
somewhere. A floor plan directed me through dark galleries
(where one might have hesitated whether to be pleased or
regretful that air-conditioning had not yet moved in) to the room
housing relics of the early cultures of Meso-America, from the
Mexican plateau to the Isthmus of Panama.

In a case devoted to El Salvador I hit on the first examples of
what I had come there to see. Faces stared at me from dumpy
thousand-year-old pots about six inches high, rather like Toby
jugs. They were forbidding little faces with hooked noses, and
they had fairly abundant fringe beards underneath. Close to
these pots were some figurines with a strong family resemblance
to them. Afterwards, in the South American room, I examined
an even older pottery jar from Trujillo in the coastal zone of
Peru near Ecuador. It was a handsome piece of " Chimu " ware
in two colours, red and cream. The outside of it, opposite the
handle, was decorated with a male face, and the face had a long
beard trimmed to a point.

But the peoples of Meso-America and Peru, before the
Spanish came, did not grow such beards.

Four days later I stood in another museum, the Museo Nacional de Antropologia in Mexico City, crowded into its corner of the Palacio a few yards from the cathedral. Smaller, more cramped, less elaborately endowed, it still had much to show me. A clay Fire-God of the prehistoric Olmecs on the Gulf coast squatted cross-legged like Buddha with a huge brazier on his head, and a pointed beard on his chin. A burly "wrestler" from Vera Cruz sat in much the same posture, also visibly bearded. A clay gentleman from Tres Zapotes wearing a kind of Phrygian cap recalled Napoleon III, chiefly because the beard was right. I knew that I had by no means exhausted the supply of such paradoxical art-objects from the centuries before Columbus. Thor Heyerdahl has published photographs of several more in connection with his Kon-Tiki theory, and drawn attention to pictures of the same sort in Mexican manuscripts. The late G. C. Vaillant, writing of a heavily bearded pottery head from Rio Balsas, Guerrero, frankly called it a mystery.[1]

The indigenous races, I repeat, have never grown beards of any size. Plentiful hair on the jaws is supposed to be an attribute of Old World stock. Who then were the models?

These beards on ancient faces in America sometimes go with an idiosyncrasy of feature hinting at alien ancestry. The characteristics always or nearly always appear in isolated individuals, not groups. Most Mexican collections include a few figures that display them, but only a few, sharply distinguished from their neighbours; they are never common enough to suggest that a hirsute race or tribe lived in those parts. In the Museo Nacional I noticed a row of dancers from Monte Alban in Oaxaca, all of them smooth-faced but one. The most striking instance of such a freak is on a basalt stele at La Venta in the Tabasco swamps where Mexico narrows down toward Guatemala. This exhibits the profile of a majestic elder with a copious flowing beard, aquiline nose, and fantastic head-dress. The face has a European look, and is in glaring contrast to the other human representations on the site, which are Mongoloid or quasi-Negroid; the archæologists who discovered the stele christened the figure "Uncle Sam," a nickname which nobody would apply to an American Indian (see opposite p. 209).[2]

Bearded sculptures and ceramics like these, many of them dating not merely from before Columbus but from long before the Norse voyages, raise a problem which is sometimes admitted but seldom properly confronted. Moreover, it is embroiled with larger issues. For one thing, the beards are not confined to Mexico or even to Central America; there are also the Chimu jars from Peru, like my New York specimen. For another, they are related somehow to a native myth, legend, or tradition—great caution is requisite in deciding on the best word or words —which once asserted that these countries had been visited in the distant past by white, bearded men from across the ocean.

2

In April 1519 Hernando Cortés landed at Vera Cruz with five hundred Spanish followers and ten cannon. He proposed to conquer Mexico, and in defiance of all probability he did. Most of the provinces that mattered were controlled by the Aztecs, a civilised and warlike race obedient to their Emperor Montezuma II. Yet the rash invasion met with only weak and unorganised resistance. The Emperor sent out not generals but ambassadors, who came to the Spanish camp offering weird gifts and incomprehensible honours. As Cortés led his force through the mountains on to the central plateau, disaffected vassal chieftains told him a little of what was going on in the councils of their masters. Montezuma, it seemed, fancied that the intruder was a god, and feared to oppose him.

With rising confidence the Spaniards approached the brackish lake that surrounded the island-capital Tenochtitlan, afterwards to grow into Mexico City. They marched up an undefended causeway into the opulent streets, and Cortés went to his first audience with Montezuma. His ignorance of the Aztecs'

Nahuatl language, and the consequent necessity of relying on native interpreters, made it hard to follow the explanations precisely; but he soon perceived the outline of the illusion which had delivered an empire into his hands.

Over the eastern ocean, the Aztecs thought, lay a country called Aztlan, a " place of clouds and mists." They had a notion that they themselves had come from there, and certainly they had moved into Mexico from a previous homeland not so very long before. But they inherited from their Mexican predecessors a sacred tradition about another inhabitant of that region beyond the sea, the god Quetzalcoatl. Once upon a time, in human shape, he had sailed across from his cloudy eastern paradise, disembarking on the Gulf coast and toiling to civilise the tribes till his enemies expelled him. He had gone away, but was expected to return in triumph from the same quarter.

Montezuma had two principal reasons for supposing Cortés to be the returning god. The first was that the Aztecs, in common with other advanced nations in Mexico, had a complex calendar with astrological significance, and this laid down that the second advent would happen in a year numbered in a particular way: a " One Reed." Years rotated in cycles of fifty-two, rather as if you were to number them from a pack of cards and speak of an " Ace of Spades " year, a " Two of Spades," and so forth. During the last cycle there had been frightening omens, and 1519, by an amazing coincidence, was the fatal One Reed year. When the foreign ships neared the coast, Aztec scouts were already watching for them.

The second reason for Montezuma's belief was that Quetzalcoatl, when he came in his human guise, had not looked like an American Indian. Tradition insisted that he was a white man with a beard, and so were the lesser demigods who had sailed in with him and aided him in his mission of enlightenment.

Such was the myth which Cortés exploited for his own ends. Spanish friars who accompanied the conquerors during the next few decades took a more intelligent interest. Questioning Aztec

Bearded Olmec head from Tres Zapotes, Vera Cruz

Bearded pottery head from Rio
Balsas, Guerrero, Mexico

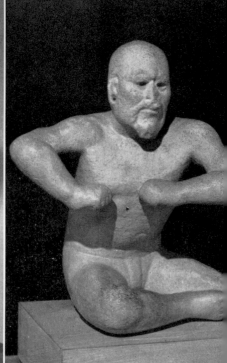

Above, left: Bearded Olmec Fire-God
Above, right: Bearded Olmec
"wrestler". *Left:* Bearded Chimu
pottery-jar figure from Northern Peru
Several of these have been found. They
are all very much alike and bear some
resemblance to a conventional type of
Central American figure, which in
turn seems to derive from the
Olmec Fire-God

scholars, they learned that Quetzalcoatl had condemned the human sacrifice customary in Mexican religion; that he had taught the people to venerate the cross and observe chastity; that existing ritual included a kind of baptism, a kind of confession, a kind of eucharist. They inferred that a Christian missionary had reached Mexico ahead of them, very far ahead indeed, and they guessed that the bearded man identified with Quetzalcoatl was the Apostle Thomas, who was said in Christian legend to have evangelised an indefinite " India." [3]

Many further particulars that might have been recorded while Aztec culture survived did in fact perish through Spanish destructiveness and indifference. Research, however, has disinterred at least some remnants, and supplied some details of the cult into which Cortés so neatly and catastrophically fitted.

Quetzalcoatl in his divine nature was quite unlike his benevolent earthly avatar.[4] The Aztecs adopted him from an earlier people, the Toltecs, who had dominated the plateau before their own entry as conquerors from the north. These Toltecs in their day had created great architecture and imposed a measure of cultural unity, and Quetzalcoatl, the local god of a still earlier people, had swelled under Toltec auspices into a complicated and prominent deity, reaching his apogee about A.D. 950.

His name meant " Quetzal-Feathered Serpent." The quetzal, *trogon splendens*, is a small bird with a fuzzy black top, gorgeous green and red plumage, and prodigiously long black tail-feathers; the American Museum of Natural History has a stuffed specimen. It is not native to the Mexican plateau but to the southern isthmus near the Guatemalan border, and among the ancient Mexicans its rarity made it more or less proverbial. The prefix " quetzal " implied that a thing was precious. Hence the god was the " Precious " or " Pre-Eminent " Serpent.

In religious art his aspect varied. Sometimes he was symbolised by a plumed snake with nothing anthropomorphic about it. Sometimes, on the other hand, his earthly mission was recognised by a semi-human portrayal ... but very much "semi."

He might be given a scraggy beard, but the beard was liable to be suspended below a red crested beak protruding from a face of a ghastly yellow. He wore a butterfly-shaped jewel on his neck; a red, white and black feather mantle; gold stockings and gold sandals. His sacred insignia, which Montezuma presented to Cortés, included a mask with turquoise mosaic on it and features formed by a convoluted snake.

Quetzalcoatl's cult was practised at Cholula and Teotihuacan, and in distinctive circular temples elsewhere. It included, despite his alleged doctrines, the annual sacrifice of a youth representing him. But his attributes were chaotic. In his earthly manifestation he was a " culture-hero " teaching morality and useful arts, but as Serpent God he had little connection with such affairs. Primarily he was a wind-god, derivatively he had a good many other functions. Since the wind brought clouds and rain, he was an agricultural fertility-spirit, and since fertility applied to other living things besides crops, he was invoked by barren women who wished to increase and multiply. By some obscure extension of this idea (less obscure, perhaps, in an age of big business) the god of increase and multiplication was also the god of thieves. Furthermore he was the planet Venus, and when it was inferred from the planet's position that his astrological influence was weak, victims were slaughtered to revive him.

In the Mexican pantheon, when Cortés arrived, he had an odd status which presupposed the inverted theology of the Aztecs.[5] According to this the deities were not, on the whole, good or harmonious, but sinister and wrathful. In order to keep the world going it was held necessary to propitiate them with huge quantities of their favourite food, human hearts and blood. The chief god or demon was Tezcatlipoca, the " Smoking Mirror " (a notable evocation of the type of nightmare-imagery which is at once meaningless and horrific). For him and his associates the altars flowed endlessly: when a temple was dedicated by Montezuma's predecessor, twenty thousand victims were killed. Under such circumstances fresh material was always in demand. Wars were waged with no other motive than the capture of prisoners for sacrifice, and the warrior, not the priest, was supreme in the State. Thus all the gods were kept nourished; yet the gods were far from being at peace among themselves. Tezcatlipoca and Quetzalcoatl were eternal enemies, perhaps because of past conflict between their devotees. In Montezuma's reign Tezcatlipoca was in the ascendant, but the belief that Cortés was Quetzalcoatl, resuming a manlike guise to reclaim his own, confronted the Emperor with an appalling dilemma. Which would win, which god should he back? He gave way to the Spanish because he thought Quetzalcoatl was the destined victor. The priests of Tezcatlipoca thought otherwise, and clamoured for war, but the Emperor's policy prevailed till it was too late.

Such was the Pre-Eminent Serpent. As for his strangely discordant earthly mission, Cortés's information was not in error. It actually was believed in central Mexico that Quetzalcoatl had come over the Gulf hundreds of years before, presumably from the place of mist and cloud called Aztlan, the paradisal ancestral home of Montezuma's own people. "Aztlan" has been variously spelt and translated. It may mean simply " place of the Aztecs," a dead-end conclusion, since there is no reason to suppose that the ruling race of Mexico were in fact immigrants from overseas; the Alaskan crossings by which America was populated from Asia happened far too long ago to be relevant. Another interpretation is " place of herons." Another is " place of water." This is more interesting, since the plumed-serpent symbol in American art does tend to have watery associations, and the name of Jamaica carries the same suggestion. However, speculative writers have also enlarged on the resemblance between "Aztlan" and "Atlantis" or "Atlantic," the object being to trace Mexican and classical legend to a common source.[6]

At any rate the terrestrial Quetzalcoatl came from the sea, from the Gulf of Mexico. He came in the form of a grave and handsome man, white-skinned, dark-haired, with a full black beard and a white robe marked with red crosses, attended by helpers like himself. He made his headquarters at Tollan or Tula, fifty miles north of Mexico City. There for some years he reigned, simultaneously king, priest, and prophet, instructing the tribes in agriculture and architecture, in metallurgy and the calendar. Besides forbidding human sacrifice in favour of innocent offerings of fruit and flowers, he taught fasting and the adoration of the cross, which he called the Tree of Life. He was celibate himself, and he founded celibate communities. Banished, however, through the plots of his rival Tezcatlipoca, he moved to Cholula and lived there for twenty years. But finding that his teachings were ineffectual, and still hounded by his implacable foe, he made his way down to the coast in the Tabasco area. The accounts of his vanishing were discrepant. According to one version he immolated himself on a pyre, from which his heart soared into the sky and became Venus. According to another the waves opened to let him pass. According to yet another he embarked on a " raft made of snakeskins," hoisted his own mantle as a sail, and dwindled away over the horizon. But one thing was sure: he would return. He would return in the One Reed year, and reassert his rights. Hence Montezuma's capitulation. The Aztec Emperor feared that if he angered Quetzalcoatl-Cortés the wind would drop, no clouds would come, and life would perish. The only course was to appease him, and hope, at best, that he would presently go away of his own accord.[7]

Parts of the legend are undoubtedly historical in a sense, but not in a very useful sense, because the divine missionary became confused at some stage with a real Toltec monarch called Topiltzin, who was a priest of the Serpent God and assumed his name. Quetzalcoatl-Topiltzin's reign at Tula in the tenth century A.D. was a period of prosperity, memorable for the first smelting of metals, for new developments in the arts, and for improvements in the calendar. About 978, however, he was forced out by a revolution, and fled south in the Tabasco direction. The events of his career were grafted on to the biography of the god whose name he had taken.[8]

As for the main corpus of the legend, its background can be pieced together to some extent from non-literary evidences. It grew, partly, round the cult-centres. At Tula, Quetzalcoatl's sacred precinct is still impressive in ruin. At Cholula, sixty miles south-east of Mexico City, his pyramid temple is the largest thing of its kind on earth: it is 250 feet high, its base is over 1400 feet square, and its flat top is an acre in extent. The matter of the crosses which so impressed the friars is more contentious. There is not, of course, anything specially Christian about the cross as such; the question is how the known Mexican examples should be construed. The Yucatan rain-god had a cruciform emblem. A large inscribed cross discovered at Palenque in the isthmus, and assigned to the seventh century, has two standing figures beside it like the supporters of a coat of arms, and a long-tailed bird above. In Oaxaca Cathedral there is a plain wooden one said to have been brought to the town in the sixth century by a stranger approaching from the west end of the valley—that is, along the road from the central plateau. These seem uninformative. But others are in a different class.

A Mexican manuscript known as the Codex Magliabecchiano XIII. 3 contains pictures of gods which undoubtedly derive from pre-Spanish originals, and in three of them—two portraying Quetzalcoatl in contrasted aspects—the divine figure holds a shield-like object with a kind of Maltese cross on it, combined with circles in such a way as to recall Ireland. In another compilation, the Codex Fejervary-Mayer, there is a large cross which is supposed to symbolise the world-diagram of Mexican cosmology, based on the compass-points. It is artistically related to the Palenque specimen, since on each of its broad arms it bears a conventionalised drawing of a tree with a standing human on either side and a bird on top. The arms themselves spread out, Maltese fashion, from a square hub which is filled by another drawing, and in the quadrants between the arms there are long loops or petals. This complicated design does not amount to a ring-cross in the style of the great standing crosses of Ireland, but the artist's practice in crowding it with pictures, as the Irish sculptors did, is noteworthy.[9]

3

These bearded white men equated with the god and his followers —did they, historically, exist, and if so where did they come from?

The carvings and ceramics *prima facie* suggest living models, and they are far too old to have been copied from Spaniards. But quite apart from these, Quetzalcoatl himself, as a developed god, clearly carried his own internal evidence of an evolution too peculiar to gloss over casually. He was, after all, self-contradictory. In his earthly guise as the white teacher or prophet, he had tried to stop human sacrifice. That was the firm and stubborn tradition. Yet it went utterly against the grain of Mexican religion; it was so alien as to be almost incomprehensible in Mexican terms; and the friars' hopeful inference to a Christian missionary was by no means absurd. There was indeed a still deeper discrepancy. Quetzalcoatl as prophet condemned not only his divine colleagues but himself. The trend toward human sacrifice on a giant scale, and toward the use of warfare to take prisoners for that purpose, dated from the seventh century, and the cult of the Pre-Eminent Serpent had followed the trend as faithfully as any other. When the conquistadors reached the capital they found a temple where he was adored with a cannibalistic ritual that gave him full rank in the Mexican Olympus. An undercurrent of disquiet at the inconsistency could perhaps be detected, but the two conceptions did endure, monstrously, side by side.[10]

Quetzalcoatl by 1519 was in any case a composite, a portmanteau divinity. But to judge from this outright antinomy in his nature, he was not merely a well-known god who happened to have attracted a medley of myth and cultus, but a true theological hybrid with a double origin far back in the old tribal Mexico. In some network of valleys or villages there had once presumably been a tale of a culture-hero, a white prophet or demigod from the sea, who had come to the folk and taught them wisely. In some other network of valleys or villages, people of different stock and language had presumably practised the barbaric religion of a Pre-Eminent Serpent. Then, in the partial Toltec fusion, the two had been for some reason combined, and the Prophet was said ever afterwards to have been an avatar of the Serpent God.

Thus at least the case may be reconstructed. It is certain at any rate that the Prophet cannot possibly be deduced from the Serpent. He is unlike, and he is un-Mexican, and it is hard to see how he was ever thought of.

One must appreciate first that he is only part of a much bigger problem. The white, bearded, robed culture-hero who appears out of the east or the sea with his companions, and goes away promising to return, is not confined to Mexico. He is the most persistent figure in the pre-Columbian mythology of America, with a vitality of his own. And when, in the course of dissecting Quetzalcoatl, we pursue the fortunes of his historical Toltec priest-king Topiltzin, we begin to perceive the shape of that autonomy. Topiltzin, overthrown at Tula, was driven away south-eastward, but not finally crushed. A Toltec faction under his leadership marched down to the isthmus, and some pushed on into Yucatan. This land was inhabited by the Maya, a civilised people on the wane, who had lived for some centuries in isolation from central Mexico. The émigré Toltecs made new homes among them and introduced their king's deity, whose name was translated as "Kukulcan" and whose rites were practised at Chichen Itza. But the peaceable Maya never greatly cared for the Serpent God, whom they tended to regard as a savage interloper too fond of blood. He failed to become popular with them, and by the sixteenth century his cult was almost extinct.

Spanish missionaries, however, carrying out such researches as they could among the decadent remnants of the nation, discovered a surprising fact. The Maya had their own prophet or culture-hero like Quetzalcoatl . . . only he was not Quetzalcoatl. The advent of the Serpent in the tenth century under Toltec sponsorship was called, somewhat slightingly, the Lesser Arrival; the advent of the hero himself, Itzamna, was called the Greater Arrival and assigned to a much earlier period. A venerable man with a Roman nose, Itzamna had entered the Yucatan peninsula from the east—from the Caribbean—and gone about with his followers teaching medicine and the art of writing, which was his invention. Some said he had made the world. The details of his departure were obscure, but, like Quetzalcoatl's, it was understood not to have been permanent. White, bearded men from the realm of sunrise had always been expected to come again.[11]

So here is the Prophet specifically distinguished from the Serpent, a distinction confirming the suspicion that their fusion in central Mexico was a misguided blending of independent concepts. Kindred figures appear more fleetingly elsewhere in Meso-America, sometimes with the added motif of an eventual retirement by the divine visitor into a cave. But we can go beyond Meso-America altogether. The Muyscas of Colombia used to give a circumstantial account of a very similar prophet called Bochica, who strode out of the llanos of Venezuela and made his way to Sogamosa, north-east of Bogota. Certain marks on the ground at Uboqui were asserted to be his footprints, and near Coto a hill was pointed out from which he had addressed the people. He too had a cruciform emblem. Bochica's sphere of operations was in the northern Andes, but east of the Andes the Indians had tales of another prophet, namely Zume.[12]

More surprising still were the Peruvian legends. The ancient cultures of Peru extended over a broad region stretching from what is now the border zone of Ecuador to what is now the Bolivian plateau, one of the most important of them being the "Tiahuanaco," which spread from the neighbourhood of Lake Titicaca somewhere about A.D. 500. The famous Incas were late-comers from Cuzco who unified Peru by conquest, mainly in the last century before the Spanish invasion. When Pizarro landed in 1532 with his two hundred or so adventurers, he had the same experience as Cortés: Inca resistance was half-hearted, because of an apprehension that the Europeans were bearded white demigods whose return from over the sea had long been anticipated. Again the belief paralysed opposition, again an empire succumbed to a prodigious bluff. As in Mexico, the theology of the crisis was far from simple. The Incas worshipped the sun, and had a developed pantheon and an elaborate religion attaching all sorts of significances to stars and holy places and relics and ancestors. The tendency, however, was henotheistic. Above all other divinities stood a Creator, who, though associated with the official solar cult, was not himself the sun. His name was Viracocha, and the ways of this god to men were the foundation of the Incas' confusion and the Spaniards' success.

"Viracocha" is an honorific and means "Lord," but it seems to be composed of two elements, one of them denoting a large body of water and the other, literally, "grease"; the most plausible interpretation is "Sea-Foam." The Sea-Foam God was probably the chief deity at Tiahuanaco, the megalithic structure near Lake Titicaca from which archæologists have taken their label for the culture that grew up there and later radiated outward. Viracocha, however, was not only worshipped at Tiahuanaco but credited with its actual building, having come there many ages ago in the shape of a bearded, robed and tonsured white man with companions or minor "viracochas" resembling himself. After a civilising mission among the primitive tribes he had gone down to the Pacific and away over the waves. But he was destined to come back—according to one prophecy, in a spirit of vengeance. At the news of Pizarro's expedition the Peruvians surmised that they had " viracochas " to deal with, and acted (or failed to act) accordingly, hesitating and trying to interpret the strangers' behaviour till all was lost.[13]

That is still not the end. Outside the fields of higher American civilisation we catch sight of minor culture-heroes not unlike the imposing sages of Mexico and Peru. Paraguay had its own version of Zume, and far off to the north beyond the Gulf of Mexico, there are distinct analogies in the tales of Hiawatha and Glooskap.[14]

It is a pity that much of the fundamental work on these topics was done by D. G. Brinton, who wrote at a time when it was standard practice to explain almost everything as a sun-myth. This theory is now pretty well discredited, partly through a *reductio ad absurdum*. The arguments purporting to prove the mythical character of various people were long since shown to apply equally well, or better, to real celebrities such as Napoleon and Lincoln. Brinton's own case met with a bad setback when archæology exploded his claim that Quetzalcoatl's Tollan or Tula was nothing but a fabulous paradise, and his attempts to vaporise the strangers themselves have a sadly old-fashioned air, especially in view of the repeated discoveries of apparent portrayals of them. Thor Heyerdahl, whose thesis about these legends is part of his theory of migrations to Polynesia, has criticised the solar notion unanswerably.[15] Heyerdahl goes to the opposite extreme. According to him, all the legends grew from historical tradition. A long while ago there was a white race in America, a race of advanced attainments and quasi-European appearance, possibly descended from Old World ancestors drifting across on the Equatorial Current. These people—proud, intermarried, ethnically distinct—meandered slowly southward from Mexico as " culture-bearers," and about A.D. 400 some of them sailed from Peru to the South Sea Islands on rafts. Quetzalcoatl and the rest, if not literal individuals, are symbolic of the wandering race, and their doings have a substratum of fact. Polynesian genealogies go back to white demi-gods supposedly coming from the east, and the Polynesian divine name Kon-Tiki is derived from Con-Ticci-Viracocha, which is given as a fuller title of the Peruvian deity.

On the main issue, the reality of the white men or at least some of them, Heyerdahl argues ably and with a forceful array of evidence. By and large the tide is flowing his way. Un-questionably sun-myths are out of date; and in the last decade or two we find one specialist conceding that Hiawatha is half-historical, another allowing that the culture-heroes of South America may possibly have been actual people.[16] The potency of the basic idea among the Aztecs and Incas is sufficiently evinced by its effect on their conduct, since it drove them to surrender their formidable empires to handfuls of Europeans whom they could have overwhelmed on the beach. It must have had its roots in vivid experiences of some kind, not in dreams; and these experiences must certainly be referred to the remote past. Contact with unrecorded Spaniards before the conquistadors cannot be the solution. Nobody imagined that the previous advent of Quetzalcoatl or Viracocha had occurred within living memory.

But a more positive and more interesting argument against any solely mythical view is that while these white beings are always described similarly, the attached mythologies differ. The divergence is clearest among the Maya, whose culture-hero Itzamna was so carefully distinguished from the Pre-Eminent Serpent, but much the same considerations apply everywhere else. Viracocha as god is not, like the Serpent, an inchoate demonic factotum in undignified feud with an even nastier rival, but a sovereign deity much more nobly and serenely conceived. Bochica is identified with a nebulous male power married to the rain-goddess, and Zume seems to be primarily a wizard, with no celestial status. Throughout thousands of miles of territory the story of the white visitors is substantially constant, while the theology is variable. Each nation, having adopted the story, welds it on to its own cosmic system, but the antecedents of the story itself remain hidden. It has no necessary link with the religious themes, nor can it be explained in merely imaginative terms, astrological ones for example. A point made by Heyerdahl in his attack on the solar hypothesis is that whereas Viracocha departs westward, Quetzalcoatl departs eastward. Theories founded on the compass, or on the properties and motions of heavenly bodies, simply will not work. Quetzalcoatl's connection with the planet Venus, which might appear to be in favour, is actually adverse: he is connected with Venus as Evening Star and therefore, theologically, with the west,[17] yet the white prophet who bears his name comes from the Atlantic and goes back to it. An attempt has been made to deduce his whiteness from the Mexicans' mystical allocation of colours to compass-points, but white was the western colour, the eastern being red.[18]

We are driven back on the silent testimony of the art-objects. Since American Indians not only described bearded men but made images of bearded men, they must have seen bearded men. A light-bringing divinity might well be pale-skinned; that would not perhaps be so queer a thing for a red race to invent; but abundant hair on the face, in three or four realistic styles, would be a very queer thing indeed for an almost beardless race to invent. Further, the singularity of the sculptures and portraits is in full harmony with the legends. The impression conveyed is not of an ethnic stock, but of a small minority of extraordinary foreigners who supplied models and left traditions behind them. If that reading of the data is sound, a personage like the earthly Quetzalcoatl may have been a representative figure, the Bearded White Man in archetype and apotheosis; or he may have been a single, literal, historical human being, deified by the folk among whom he came. Within living memory Mexican villagers in a secluded district were caught paying divine honours to Montezuma.[19]

In a few cases where modern anthropology has been able to anatomise the creation of a divine figure comparable to the

American heroes, the figure has turned out to derive from real human beings and not from mythopoeic imagination. That at least is a fact. Captain Cook's deification is well known, and a delightful episode was reported not long ago from the island of Tanna in the New Hebrides. The Tanna people, after a phase of disjointed contact with white men and their ill-understood material civilisation, were found during the 1940's to be worshipping a white god named John Frum. Their ritual was imitative of actions watched but not comprehended, such as talking over the radio, by which the whites were supposed to obtain their envied possessions magically. Over the past couple of decades the Tannese have set up crosses, model radio masts, model aircraft, and a scarlet-coated image of John Frum himself, who will come back from his residence in the east bringing them boundless wealth—" cargo," as they call it—and inaugurate a golden age. Meanwhile some of his followers are staying in Tanna at the bottom of a volcano.[20] The ubiquitous white culture hero of America looks very like a John Frum gigantically magnified by longer development and the rise of more elaborate native societies.

To sum up, it is quite logical to conclude provisionally that the story of the white visitors must go back to real people, whether their homeland was in the Old World or in some corner of the New. Difficulties begin when we try to reconstruct what they did. The attempt leads straight to a deadlock. Without real people, the legends and art-objects are inexplicable. But what group could have walked about for centuries as a unit impressing the natives so consistently and indelibly over such a huge area?

This last question is fatal, I regretfully think, to the efforts of Irish writers to clear up the imbroglio by simply equating Quetzalcoatl with St. Brendan or some other Celtic sea-pilgrim. They have failed to reckon with his South American counterparts, and with the complexity and especially the chronology of the problem.[21] Their notion is not so grossly inadequate as it seems, for a reason which will emerge, but it cannot account for everything. Heyerdahl has at least faced the question and not shrunk from the consequences of his own answer, when he presents his cohesive body of culture-bearers as having migrated by stages from Mexico to Bolivia and thence to Polynesia, inspiring all the legends *en route*. But his grandiose marches and successive halts, allegedly going on for twenty or thirty generations, are not easy to accept.

4

My own visit to Mexico was undertaken with the deadlock already in mind, and the first hint at a solution darted at me out of a conversation in transit, one of those unpredictable dividends which you can only collect by going to investigate for yourself.

With the growth of civil aviation it has become an open secret that air travel is much more erratic and incalculable than anybody would judge from the advertisements. In common with several other outward-bound passengers I spent an unexpected day at the Seaway Hotel in Idlewild Airport, waiting at the airline's expense for a specially chartered plane to replace another which had developed engine trouble. The Seaway Hotel, for some reason, is a favourite with honeymooners even if they are not flying anywhere, and it was a fitting accident that our party included such a couple—a magnificent brunette with a husband undeservedly in partial eclipse, as young Americans often are. In the evening, when we were finally supposed to leave, we were transported by bus to the airline office, told that the aircraft was still not ready, and whisked off again to dinner at a second hotel. Having checked my hand-luggage, I went to the dining-room and found eleven of the party already seated at a long table. It had six chairs on each side, with one more at the head and one at the foot, fourteen altogether. All six were occupied on one side, and five on the other, only the end chair next to the head being vacant. I sat down in this, but had

238

scarcely done so when the honeymooners arrived, in anxious conference with a waiter. To force them to the only remaining empty chairs, at opposite ends of the table, was unthinkable; I surrendered my place and went down to the solitary vacancy at the foot.

My move gave me a new neighbour, an older man who at first struck me as reserved. However, I asked him whether he knew Mexico well, and put a query to him about the safety of the drinking water. This was not an essay in small talk, I genuinely wanted to know. Luck, or providence, or telepathy, had put me next to the right passenger. He was Dr. Manuel O. Zariquiey, of the International Medical Section of Eastman Kodak, and he took me meticulously over the properties of Mexican water, its effect in combination with rarefied air, and the chemical correctives, adding as a footnote that when first in Mexico and unduly cautious he had used Coca-Cola to clean his teeth, the mixture with toothpaste producing an unusual flavour.

Then he made a remark which showed, to my surprise and immediate absorption, that his major non-professional interest was the study of American archæology and anthropology. There had in fact been some question of his joining the Kon-Tiki expedition, though the course taken by Heyerdahl's plans had, in the end, stopped him from going. He was still following Heyerdahl's research, but was no longer as much of a disciple as he had been formerly. We discussed the mysterious bearded men. I pressed him on a crucial point about which Heyerdahl and others have written somewhat ambiguously: whether aboriginal tribes had been found anywhere in America with full enough beards to account for the portraiture and legends. No, he replied, none. He had come across Venezuelans with scanty beards, but not full ones, and in any case they were out-of-the-way and primitive folk. The things I had mentioned were unfathomable. Somebody had advanced a theory that the beards in the portraits were a sign of honour. He was reminded, himself, of ancient Middle Eastern sculptures, and thought there might well have been a sprinkling of untraced aliens, but Heyerdahl's idea of a compact migratory group failed to satisfy him. It was too neat.

During that protracted meal (while, a few hundred yards off, mechanics were presumably grooming our understudy airliner) the Doctor gave me some fascinating glimpses of the obscurer corners of Latin America. Among other matters he recalled a legend about a lake, which he had heard from a tribal story-teller in the Venezuelan backwoods. At the bottom of this lake, said the Indian, was a sunken village, which had vanished long ago because of the misconduct of a native princess with a white man. And this white man was no other than Christopher Columbus. The Genoese was still there, under the water in Venezuela.

" You know," said Dr. Zariquiey, " he made it so convincing that I felt like getting a diving outfit and going down to see."

Columbus was never anywhere near the lake. But the Indian story-teller " made it so convincing . . ." It dawned on me after some reflection that others might have been similarly convinced before, in similar cases.

Let me put it like this. Characters in a story may be real people, but because the story locates them in a certain place it does not follow in the least that they were ever there. That is a principle immeasurably antedating the novels of Scott. Alexander the Great was a real person; but Arabic fantasy is not to be trusted when it takes him dragon-slaying in the Canary Isles. Arthur was probably a real person; but the Italian legend which brings him to Sicily is no proof that he so much as left Britain. The Hindu epic *Mahabharata* makes " Yavanas " or Greeks participate in a battle near Delhi before the Trojan War. Likewise, Dr. Zariquiey's folk-tale transplants a European—in native eyes, the most memorable of all Europeans—from his true context to the country where the tale took shape. Might we not account for many of the pre-Columbian legends in the same way?

Somewhere the starting impulse is given and somewhere the theme is launched on its long career: the Saga of the Wonderful White Men. Then comes the diffusion. That such a saga could have spread widely, with geographical tricks akin to the Venezuelan; that the supposed visitors could have turned into local culture-heroes, undergone identification with various gods, and become associated with famous events and buildings [22]; that in areas of superior culture the saga could have grown snowball-wise, drawing in historical happenings such as the downfall of King Topiltzin, and perhaps even annexing snippets of Christianity from later contacts—all these potentialities are patent. We can admit the weight of the evidence from legend without granting Heyerdahl's conclusion. A bearded race *may* have trudged through the Americas for hundreds of years without losing its character, but, on the other hand, it may not. It may only have touched on a single coastline, just long enough to overawe the inhabitants and set the saga in motion.

When pondering origins, in fact, it is wisest to begin with the least romantic and most economical suggestion, and ask whether a saga could have arisen simply from a report of the Norse, either transmitted southward from tribe to tribe or inspired by some unchronicled probe of sea-rovers beyond Vinland. This idea was put to me by the Dean of Tralee, who, as I at length realised, had been sagaciously thinking along the same lines for years. However, Norse voyages occurring about the year 1000 cannot provide the answer. Even apart from the art-objects, many of which are much earlier than that, the legends themselves must be held to be antecedent, at least in their birth if not in their elaboration. Topiltzin, for instance, definitely belongs to the middle tenth century, and the basic story of Quetzalcoatl must be even older than the grafted Topiltzin element.

Moreover, the propagation of a saga implies contact, and by medieval times the American world was irreparably disjointed. Mexico and Peru diverged in the prehistoric past, and there are

241

few signs of subsequent influence either way. To unearth an epoch of intercommunication we must delve back to what is known as the formative era, the last pre-Christian millennium. In the early Christian centuries the zones became distinguished and stabilised, folk-movements were reduced in scope, and inter-zonal trade (if indeed there had ever been any) shrank to insignificance. A conjectured migration from Central America to northern Peru between A.D. 100 and 300 would have been a last flicker.[23] The dissemination of a Saga of the Wonderful White Men fits more easily into the formative era, long before the Norse, than into any later one.

All this is speculative, but clearly it is not a scientific procedure to lunge indiscriminately at the legends here, there, and everywhere in search of lurking truth. Whether the white men, if any, did actually perambulate a large area or a small area, the root of the problem must be sought where there is something tangible to go on, and some prospect of working back to the fountain-head if the diffusion theory should prove to be best. These requirements point imperatively to Mexico. The Peruvians had no written history, in fact no writing. They recorded some strictly utilitarian information by a code system of knots, but their tale of Viracocha was an oral tradition, only committed to paper by friars and colonists after the conquest. The Aztecs, however, did set things down in pictures and symbols. Spanish clerics, horrified at their dreadful gods, burned many of the manuscripts as satanic, but the quantity of Mexican history salvaged was not beneath contempt. It was capable, furthermore, of being checked archæologically, a process which is still going on. If we want something tangible, Mexico is the place.

My talk with the invaluable Dr. Zariquiey did at last end. Our aircraft received us, and a few hours later the latticed lights of Mexico City spread out below.

5

From Montezuma's capital a modern highway runs north, over a miniature pass and on to a stretch of dried-up lake bed, level, brown, windswept and dusty. The flatness extends so far that the encircling mountains are curiously lowered by distance. Thirty miles from the city, without any obvious reason for being there in particular rather than somewhere else on the plain, are the hallowed buildings of Teotihuacan. The name means "Place of the Making of the Gods," and it is one of the irritating freaks of American prehistory that the first portion of that name so strongly and pointlessly resembles the Greek *theos*. Teotihuacan is the work of an unknown people, possibly under influences from the Gulf coast, who attained the zenith of their peaceable civilisation abut A.D. 300 and quarried all the stone —do not ask me how—without metal tools.

I came there in quest of the Serpent God. My taxi-driver steered in and out through the complexities of the "ceremonial area," and set me down in a car park near the foot of the largest structure, the Pyramid of the Sun. Contorted and damaged by foolish would-be reconstruction, this now rises in five tiers to a height of 215 feet, with a base over 700 feet square. Its flat summit was once the floor of a temple, but no trace of that remains. The present surface is not so rugged as that of the Great Pyramid in Egypt, and since the altitude is much less while the base is about the same size, the gradient is not so steep.

Turning the corner of the pyramid nearest the car park, I approached the stairs leading up its brown face. The souvenir hawkers hovered and darted, offering tiny statues for sale. Such objects in Mexico are of two sorts: those which are frankly copies of articles dug up on the site, and those which purport to be the real thing, sometimes authenticated by a fake excavation pit. However, the Latin American is preferable to the Arab in that he will take " no " for an answer. I disengaged myself and started the arduous ascent, mounting slowly and somewhat giddily above the hawkers, and the bushes, and the scrubbed tourists from the United States debating whether to go all the way up. Circumnavigating the top terrace in a hot murderous wind which forced me to squash my hat into my camera-case, I took a photograph of the smaller Pyramid of the Moon in the middle distance. Then I battled round to gaze in the opposite direction at the temple of Quetzalcoatl himself, which is another stepped pyramid inside a great quadrangular enclosure, the " citadel." Like much else at Teotihuacan it is inscrutable. In the absence of calendric inscriptions it cannot be exactly dated. Dragon-like stone heads, and wavy decorative lines which may or may not represent water, symbolise the god; and violent surges of air and dust are perpetual reminders of his role as a wind-god.[24]

But whether I looked at the temple from the Pyramid of the Sun or at close quarters, I saw only the Serpent, not the Prophet. This place was irrelevant to the topic of the white men, and so big and so alien as to reduce my past fancies about deified Irish monks to the plane of triviality.

Back in Mexico City, that abode of phenomenal women and sedulously nurtured historical continuity, I made an appointment with the archæologist Joaquin Meade. Señor Meade had written to me at generous length a year or so previously as a result of a news item. He said he had excavated a number of sites of the Huaxtec people in eastern Mexico, and had tentatively concluded that there might (monks or no monks) be something in the theory of an Irish contact, which appealed to him personally because of his own Irish blood. The correct English of his letter, and of others that followed it, encouraged me to hope that my own linguistic nullity would not strangle conversation, and when the time came I awaited him in the hotel lobby with interest and no anxiety.

When you meet somebody hitherto known solely through the written or printed word, some readjustment almost always ensues. The personal impression may finally be important, or it may not. In this case it was. Sr. Meade turned out to be taller than most Mexicans, grey-haired, with a slight hesitancy in movement betraying an eye trouble which I discovered to be severe. He was in fact carrying on through a complication of illnesses with conspicuous courage and good humour; I was disposed, as anyone would have been disposed, to view him with admiration and consequent trust. We had an exceedingly late Mexican dinner on a top floor overlooking the Zocalo, which was the Aztecs' place of assembly and is still a principal square of the town. Sr. Meade's talk flowed graciously on without acquiring an obvious direction, yet during that altogether unsystematic evening I somehow absorbed a lecture on Mexican antiquities which enabled me to sort out my reading into immeasurably better shape.

Such sorting out is needed if you are going to study Mexico. You have to begin by picturing the Olmecs of Vera Cruz and Tabasco flourishing in the last pre-Christian centuries and fading away about A.D. 300; also the Maya of Guatemala and Yucatan, inventors of the calendar. On the foundations laid by these pioneers, several " Classic " cultures grew up in the early centuries of the Christian era: the mixed Zapotec culture in the south, the cryptic Teotihuacan, the less famous Huaxtec; then the civilisation of the Toltec master-builders with their city of Tula, rising slowly after the sixth century to supremacy in the tenth, and learning from the rest; last, the gaudy imperialism of the conquering Aztecs.

But Sr. Meade maintained that there was something elusive in all this. The process, as he saw it, was not progressive. An initial impulse of unknown origin faltered and was partially dissipated, and the Aztecs at the end were less civilised than some of their forerunners. The secret was hidden, the thread for the moment lost. That thread could perhaps be dimly discerned in the evolution or synthesis of Quetzalcoatl himself. As Serpent God he was probably Huaxtec; as Prophet he came from somewhere else; as a composite deity and culture-hero he passed to the Toltecs and from them to the Aztecs, successive overlords of the plateau, like a token.

Sr. Meade thought Quetzalcoatl very mystifying, and his own individualistic and effective research had driven him to ask questions without any pretence of being able to answer them. It appeared that he owned a ranch, and had traced a number of sites round about by the enviable method of sifting the public archives for sixteenth-century land grants. These sometimes referred to ruins as landmarks, and when they did so he went and searched on the spot, often successfully. He had not dug up any bearded heads, but naturally he knew of those at La Venta and elsewhere. Some, he said, were extremely ancient, and dated back to the last centuries B.C. Whatever visit or immigration it was that had inspired them, it had occurred as early as that. The problematical contact of Mexicans with Christian Irish was, on the face of it, a separate topic. He had been led to treat the idea with respect through disinterring some late Huaxtec pottery decorated with Maltese crosses like the rudimentary Celtic crosses; and he had noticed also that Quetzalcoatl was sometimes drawn carrying an object like a bishop's crook, and that a head-dress worn by the Aztec emperors resembled a mitre. He gave me a copy of his monograph *La Huasteca* in which I found drawings and photographs of these things, and an appendix reviewing some of the evidence for Irish voyages.

Despite the Aztecs' exercise of the victor's prerogative in falsifying history, Sr. Meade assured me that a cautious use could be made of their chief chronicler, the alarmingly named Ixtlilxochitl—who, as I happened to know, had been borne out by archæology in at least one controversial matter, the historic role of the town of Tula. He was a nobleman of the conquest period who compiled two works on the legends and traditions of Mexico, which I had studied already in a French edition. One of the first steps I took after my talk with Sr. Meade was to turn up my notes on these and give them some further thought. I now felt justified in searching here seriously for a hint.

While Ixtlilxochitl (the " x " is pronounced " sh ") has survived the more ruthless hatchet-blows of criticism, he cannot be reckoned as a scholarly historian. His correlation of native and European chronology is uncertain, and his two books give somewhat different time-schemes. The dating in any case is artificial and semi-mythical, assigning equal and improbably long reigns to a whole series of Toltec kings from the sixth century onward.[25] Nevertheless the sequence of peoples is not absurdly misrepresented, and as Sr. Meade said, Ixtlilxochitl's blend of myth and legend and historical fact does repay scrutiny.

He divides the history of the world into four ages, each presided over by an astrological power called a " Sun." The first or Sun-of-Waters age ended with a general deluge, the second or Sun-of-Earth with an earthquake. In the latter epoch Mexico was inhabited by giants, some of whom survived the disaster. In the third or Sun-of-Air age the Olmecs and another race, the Xicalancas, came from the eastern sea in canoes and settled between Puebla and Cholula. They were enslaved by the remnant of the giants, but rose against their oppressors and wiped them out. A phase of Olmec prosperity followed . . . and here the Aztec historian begins to write what is arguably semi-historical. During that prosperity, " a man whom some called Quetzalcoatl and others Huemac " arrived among the Olmecs, taught them in the way we already know, and sailed off. It was foretold that in a One Reed year he would return and his doctrine would be accepted. Soon afterwards the Sun-of-Air age drew to a close with tempests, which overthrew a tower at Cholula; the present pyramid in the same town was built on the ruins. But many people had perished and the Olmecs were eclipsed. The present age is ruled by the Sun-of-Fire and will end with a conflagration.

Even here, where Quetzalcoatl's theological trappings are

few and his human life is the sole theme, the authentic tradition about him cannot be safely reconstituted from the text. His alternative name "Huemac," for instance, betrays confusion, since Huemac appears also as a legendary Toltec sage who cannot have been the same person. Yet Ixtlilxochitl's dates are interesting. He says that Quetzalcoatl came about the time of Christ, and he also says, in his other book where everything is put sixty years or so later, that the Cholula tower fell in A.D. 299. Either the divine prophet was in Mexico for much longer than a mortal lifetime, or the transitional phase of storms, beginning soon after his departure, went on for two hundred years. Neither explanation is encouraging, but of course neither date matters much in any case. What does matter is that the general period assigned for these happenings is plausible, and fits archæologically. Quetzalcoatl is made to visit the Olmecs between, say, 50 B.C. and A.D. 300, during their prosperity. That prosperity in fact began earlier and may have ended a little later, but the target, more or less, is hit: Ixtlilxochitl, allotting the prophet to the Olmec era, gives at least some concurrent indication that he knows what he is talking about. Perhaps then we have a clue here to the centre of narrative diffusion. Perhaps the mission of Quetzalcoatl is a reminiscence of actual events in Olmec Mexico, from which area the saga spread.

When I took leave of Sr. Meade I was beginning to weigh that possibility, but was still convinced of the necessity for suspending judgment and assembling more facts, about Viracocha, for example. I had booked my flight to Peru and Bolivia. "After Mexico," Sr. Meade remarked, "you will find things smaller there." It was a forecast that startled me, yet it was to prove true in a figurative as well as a literal sense.

6

But even apart from the imponderables of Peru, there were other Mexican matters to be taken into account. These brought me to a street near the waste space in front of the capital's railway terminus, and induced me, despite the allurements of the railway, to brave a turbulent booking-office and buy a bus ticket to Oaxaca. I had to see what lay south.

The bus left in the early morning. When I took my place aboard, an expansive Indian grandmother followed behind and sat down next to me, only to be dislodged, after a courteous altercation, by a small man. It transpired that she had read something on her ticket as the seat number when in fact it was not. She padded equably away, the intended occupant sat beside me instead, and I discovered that a Mexican bus could be quite comfortable. This one was also powerful and road-worthy, and it needed to be. Secure in the protection of Our Lady of Guadalupe, whose picture hung above the windscreen, the driver hurled his vehicle merrily up the long tortuous ascent past Popocatapetl and through the recesses of the hills, missing the cliffs and chasms by inches. The other passengers rode with equanimity, munching sandwiches or dozing, and gradually I too became inured. When it was time to watch for Cholula, and Quetzalcoatl's pyramid, my attention was no longer dizzily distracted every few seconds.

In due course the town drifted into sight. Cholula is unique in seeming to consist entirely of churches. They are sprinkled over the plateau at every angle like cake decorations, most of them built in the relentlessly repeated colonial style, with two towers at one end and a low dome at the other. The local joke is that there is a church for every day of the year, but the true number, I believe, is thirty-seven. Few other buildings are to be seen. The explanation is that Cholula was once the nucleus of a thickly populated district, but the people moved to Puebla and left their ecclesiastical establishment stranded.

The pyramid itself was a long way off, but visible enough, indeed unmistakable—bigger than anything at Teotihuacan or for that matter at Gizeh. I had once compared Glastonbury Tor to a Mexican pyramid; now, having seen Mexican pyramids,

I felt inclined to return the compliment or at least reverse the comparison. This pyramid at Cholula, overgrown with grass and shrubs, insistently recalled Glastonbury Tor, even to the inevitable church on top. Not much is known about it. The interior chambers have fascinated archæologists, but nothing could be seen of them from the main highway.

On and on southward the bus careered. An enormous vista of upland and mountain ranges spread out ahead and then rapidly closed in again; the road wound through valleys, with sparsely wooded slopes on each side. Tall cactus plants were becoming common, some consisting of a solitary vertical stem, others like candelabras. At intervals there was another partial opening-out of the country, but always the brownish-greenish mountains pressed back. In a more fertile stretch, farms shot past with momentary visions of goats and donkeys and Indian or mestizo peasants. Again the road climbed, again the vegetation grew thinner. Instead of cacti, the characteristic tree was now a scrawny palm with a bare stem and a mop-like head. But after a while the bus entered a more gracious landscape with coniferous forest on the hills, huge swift panoramas, and well-cultivated valleys. I noticed, at first without comprehension, the cactus fences: the yard of a farmhouse would often be enclosed, not by the clumsy work of men's hands, but by a row of single-stem cacti planted side by side, so close together that no human being or large animal could squeeze through.

And so in the cool of evening to Oaxaca, the city of the Zapotecs, in its long broad valley a mile above sea-level; the city of pale-green stone, or so at least it is conventionally described, though to me the green looked so pale as hardly to count. But whatever its colour it was an attractive town, with a fine hotel and a genuinely helpful service to tourists. I immediately faced a decision. There were two important sites in the neighbourhood, Monte Alban and Mitla, and I could not easily visit both and the museum also, because the long Idlewild delay was still having repercussions on my time-table. Monte Alban, being older, was the obvious choice, but a more or less accidental cause determined me in favour of Mitla, and I had no reason to be sorry, since most of what concerned me at the senior site had been transferred to the museum and was on view there. (I did catch a glimpse of Monte Alban after all when flying back to Mexico City.)

My morning was taken up with Oaxaca itself. I strolled round the cathedral and discovered a side chapel with a plain, dark, aged-looking wooden cross over its altar, the upright above the arms being very short, and the right arm slightly damaged. This might have been the cross alleged to date from before Columbus, but I could learn nothing about it. After paying my respects to the civic patroness, the Virgin of La Soledad (one of those pyramidal Madonnas, in robes of black and gold), I tackled the museum. It was arranged round a court, like most large buildings in Mexico, and the actual galleries had a somewhat gloomy air which I was now prepared for. Monte Alban was represented by dozens of photographs and a superb treasure hoard from one of its tombs. Here again I singled out a few human figures with beards, little squatting men wearing showy head-dresses and dating from the last period of the site, about the ninth or tenth century A.D.

Then came a sudden insight, and a further justification of my journey, as I would probably never have achieved it if I had not seen a fair number of these articles in the space of a few days. I am not indulging in retrospective fancy; the words are there in my note-book a few lines below a sketch. " Bearded faces could have been copied from bearded faces. . . . It is only the originals that require models." The art-objects in fact could be regarded in the same way as the stories. Somewhere, no doubt, bearded men had been seen and portrayed, but once the portraits existed they could have been copied without limit anywhere in America, with no need for local specimens. Indeed I already had some reason to think that such copying had occurred. These Monte Alban figures were not realistic but stylised, variations on a template. To study them was not to feel for an instant that the artists must have had bearded sitters in front of them. I was on the trail of another simplification paralleling the simplification offered by the Saga idea.

That afternoon I joined a trio of American tourists for the drive out to Mitla, along the valley to the east. Mitla is popularly spoken of as " the place where it never rains," but I heard that when an archæologist gave a lecture there with that title, it did rain. We, at any rate, explored the site under clouds so heavy and moist that we felt no confidence in the nickname. Aided by our bilingual and knowledgeable driver, we stumbled down from the walled enclosure into the stuffy interior of a Zapotec royal tomb. The Mitla tombs are cruciform, but probably for structural, not religious reasons: a chamber formed by two intersecting passages can be roofed over with single slabs un-supported by pillars, whereas a square chamber of equal area cannot, unless it is very small. Much the same applies to the Y-chamber at North Salem. Outside, we were invited to notice the repeated multiples of thirteen—thirteen courses of bricks and so forth. They might have galvanised a student of Welsh folk-lore, in which thirteen is a magic number, but this too would have been a false alarm, since the thirteens can be deduced from the calendric obsessions of ancient Meso-America. We were also shown a fat column with a superstition attaching to it, that if you threw your arms round it as far as they would stretch, the space left between your fingers was a measure of your remaining lifetime. This notion clearly penalised everybody with long arms. The tourists preferred not to try; I did try, and being eight inches taller than any of them, ascertained that my expectation was brief indeed.

We filed into the dingy museum at the entrance to the ruins. This time I had a more definite conception of what I was looking for, and sure enough the pattern recurred. Scattered up and down on the shelves, exceptional as always, were stylised male statuettes with tufts or fringes on their chins, essentially like the ones from Monte Alban, and (as I now began to observe) with a common resemblance in design, though not in realism, to the clay Fire-God I had seen in Mexico City. They could undoubtedly be explained as copies, or as copies of copies. . . . And so perhaps could those Salvadorian Toby jugs in New York —the comparative lateness of their date, as of the Zapotec items, was altogether in keeping with such a theory—and perhaps even some of the peripheral types, such as the Chimu jar from Peru which I had examined in the same place.

Ixtlilxochitl's history, with its allusion to the Olmecs of the Gulf coast, had given a hint at the centre of narrative diffusion. Where was the centre of artistic diffusion, the area where real portraits from living models might have set off a chain reaction of imitation? I returned from Mitla to Oaxaca and from Oaxaca to Mexico City conscious of possessing another clue, but well aware that it was a provisional clue. Tiahuanaco, the scene of the divine Viracocha's activities, might confirm my insight or modify it. Quetzalcoatl was substantiated to some extent by archæology. Among the Mexican faces were some at least which must surely have been taken from real bearded men. But was Viracocha substantiated in the same way? Did comparable portraits exist in Bolivia or highland Peru, and if they did, what became of my theory of copying?

On, then, to Tiahuanaco.

CHAPTER NINE

The Beard and the Cross

FLYING TO BOLIVIA is an easy way to increase your tally of countries visited. After taking leave, at Mexico City Airport, of Sr. Meade and his pretty daughter who had driven us there; after boarding an American airliner that left almost on schedule; after sighting the Pacific and confusedly telling a fellow-passenger it was the Gulf of Mexico—after these preliminaries, I found that the plane halted at every single republic. Guatemala, Salvador, Honduras, Nicaragua, Costa Rica . . . during the actual journey they struck me as noticeably different from each other, unexpectedly so, but in retrospect it is hard to remember which was which. They close ranks and compose a montage-picture of defunct volcanoes, forbidding masses of green, circular hollows full of stagnant water, and limitless lakes: the whole series culminating in the anti-climax of a long hot stop-over in the small hours at Panama Airport, with inky blackness all round, and no consolation but the discovery of a paperback edition of *Doctor Zhivago*, a novel which I might not otherwise have got to for years.

The next day, having added Colombia and Ecuador to the list, and having made my entry into the southern hemisphere, I watched the coast of Peru slipping past below. Beside the ocean ran a broad strip of pallid sandy wilderness, dotted here and there with crescent-shaped dunes. Roads ran through it without self-evident meaning, and occasionally a river or a clutter of houses broke the monotony, but the prevalent effect from above was of a dead-level waste. The weather was clear and the air transparent. However, the plane descended into Lima through dense cloud, and on the ground it was clammy and overcast, a singular conclusion to thousands of miles of sunshine. A night stop was necessary; the airline had made hotel reservations. The following morning we passengers dutifully checked out, boarded a bus, and arrived at the airport. The plane soared up above the clouds on its course for La Paz, and the Andes streamed backward on the left for an hour or two . . . then suddenly we noticed that one of the propellers was idle, and a few minutes later the Andes were streaming backward on the right. The captain's lugubrious voice over the intercom confirmed our forebodings. Number Three Engine was " losing oil " and could not be relied on to hoist us over the pass to Bolivia. We were returning to Lima, not to leave again till early next morning. Soon after lunch we were all back ignominiously checking in at the same hotel.

Equipped with what purported to be a map, I set out that afternoon to see some more of Lima and look in at the archæological museum, which, however, I never found. I still do not know what is in it: something, perhaps, that makes nonsense of this whole book. At two in the morning my room telephone summoned me to the bus. Again we all took our places in the airliner, again we flew for a while, again the captain told us that Number Three Engine was losing oil and we were returning to Lima. A grim grey dawn was breaking as we dismounted there for the third time. We sat in a glass-fronted gallery watching the mechanics tinker; then climbed aboard for a fresh attempt and saw the Andes stream backward on the left; then perceived with sinking hearts that they were not streaming backward on the left any more, but on the right. Number Three Engine, the captain explained, was losing oil. Again we dived into the cloud-stratum, again we touched down at that accursed airport. But this time deliverance was in sight, since they had given up trying to mend Number Three Engine, and were trundling out a new plane for us.

The appointed hour brought the take-off. Yet again we approached the fatal pass. Would it, would it . . .? The peaks on the left crept nearer but did not vanish, others came looming up on the right, and then, Viracocha be praised! we were above the Andes.

They spread out in interminable contours of green and brown, with a snow-line close to the top. Our attention was directed to Misti, a gaunt volcano, and then to that long-anticipated marvel Lake Titicaca, two and a half miles above sea-level. The enchanted expanse lay bluish under the mountain sun, overlooked by ramparts of snow towering to twenty-one thousand feet. Titicaca, I thought, had a quality in common with Popocatapetl and Cotopaxi—it was so utterly a place of romance that I could not really believe that this was it. No, it must be another lake of the same name.

Ahead stretched the highland extremity of old Peru, to-day politically distinct. The aircraft crossed the frontier and the wide plateau between the ranges. Bolivia's Altiplano looks like a desert, but is not; it supports a fair-sized population. La Paz itself is almost literally down a hole, and quite invisible as you circle to land.

After a scrimmage in the customs shed, I shared a cab with a sales representative of Imperial Chemical Industries. Night was falling or rather tumbling with a velocity wholly new to me, but on the long downward spiral into the crepuscular hollow which was the capital of Bolivia, I saw enough to realise that this was the most alien country yet, most of the inhabitants being manifestly and undisguisedly Indian. Daylight revealed other things. Bolivia is poor and, according to some, ill-governed, with a grossly inflated currency. Though its white population is a minority and not an especially large minority, I observed that the people portrayed in advertisements were almost invariably white. Whatever spending-money there was clearly did not belong to the Indians. In such a community the prospects were not hopeful for any consciousness of the aboriginal past, and my apprehensions were strengthened by a tourist brochure referring to Tiahuanaco as "Inca," a howler which I knew the Indians had laughed at when the Spaniards perpetrated it ages ago. La Paz might pride itself on its noble setting and its fine modern buildings and boulevards—Latin American capitals are no longer deficient in such respects—but it lacked the sense of continuity which I had seen fostered in Mexico. I was soon expecting Bolivia to prove, from my immediate point of view, negative. So perhaps it did. But there are negatives and negatives.

2

My excursion to Tiahuanaco entailed hiring a taxi with a two-man crew consisting of a guide who spoke some English but, as I rapidly discovered, understood very little, and an agreeable driver who grinned at me without ever disclosing whether he could do either. The car climbed up out of La Paz and cruised along the road over the plateau. Lorries, at intervals, came pounding the other way, always jammed with astounding numbers of Indians, and always kicking such clouds of dust behind them that the air was opaque for many times their own length. My driver paused at a village with a venerable colonial church and a big market-place, which, the guide explained, was the original site of La Paz. Gay cloths and streamers were attached to upright poles for the imminent feast of St. John the Baptist, and groups of Indian men and women in the market-place were rehearsing for it, in other words snake-dancing and rock'n'rolling to the music of itinerant trumpeters.

The taxi negotiated a gentle pass with a panorama of peaks to the eastward, and approached Lake Titicaca between two lines of hills. But it never got within sight of the lake, because Tiahuanaco came first. I was gazing up the highway ahead to the roofs of a village, when I became aware, abruptly and most undramatically, that there were a few grey stones sticking up on the left and that in short . . . this was it. Sr. Meade's prediction was fulfilled. Stonehenge, notoriously, looks small in the distance but overwhelming at close quarters; Tiahuanaco, the Stonehenge of South America, looked small in the distance and went on looking small.

Perhaps Mexico had spoilt me, and perhaps the grandeur of the country was too severe on the works of men, but that liar the camera bore a share of the blame for my disappointment. What I saw was an oblong walled enclosure chequered with excavation pits. It covered several acres and could therefore be described as large, but because of the space rather than the architecture. The eye took in stairs and a few monolithic sculptures and a gateway with carving on the top. I knew—and tried to allow for the fact—that some of the monoliths, including the tallest, had been carted off to a museum in La Paz. However, I had seen pictures of that gateway with its complicated designs, posed so as to resemble a Stonehenge trilithon; and the shock of finding that it was really a sort of landscape-gardener's whimsy, not nearly high enough to walk through, was considerable. So also with the stiff, square, conventionalised human figures carved out of monoliths—that is, the ones that still remained on the site. I had imagined something like British Columbian totem-poles or Easter Island colossi. Instead, blockish little fellows gazed back at me who, if made of wood, might almost have been stowed away in a Cadillac as souvenirs.

Well, this was Tiahuanaco nevertheless, and its ancient founders had at least managed to surround their creation with an aura of mystery, which my guide did nothing to dissipate. Some writers, I gathered (not from him), had made it an Atlantean site, some had made it a quarter of a million years old. Even Posnansky, an archæologist of repute, had talked imprudently of Phœnicians.

All agree that Tiahuanaco was a place of importance in its day, but hardly of such revolutionary importance as these theories would imply. It was one of the foci in the cultural growth of old Peru. The chronology of that growth is dubious, but there seems to have been a long florescent era from roughly 300 B.C. to roughly A.D. 500, marked by the development of textiles and ceramics and metallurgy; and an Early Tiahuanaco culture arose during this era alongside other cultures such as the Moche in the north. The actual ruins are the remains of a group of edifices built during the first Christian millennium, perhaps about the middle, at the heart of a Classic Tiahuanaco culture which spread out and modified others. However, it withered, and was dead before the Incas were heard of.

The place has not revealed its precise nature to archæologists. It must have been a shrine for some kind of religious ceremonial, and its art has an impersonal, formal air, even the statues conveying no suggestion of individual portraiture. In its disjointed structure there are affinities, but rather remote affinities, to Celtic menhirs and stepped pyramids. The carved inscriptions on the gateway (sometimes called the Sun Gate) and on scattered stones are partly geometrical, partly representative. One conspicuous quasi-human form is supposed to be Viracocha as deity. There are condor and puma motifs, weeping eyes, an equal-armed cross, concentric rings—all found, I believe, in other areas under the Tiahuanaco influence, and all very obscure in their significance. Many objects besides monoliths are no longer on the site but in museums. Praise is due to the artists and builders for their skill, energy and patience, but not for any special magnitude or marvellousness of achievement. Tiahuanaco is only mysterious, not extraordinary.[1]

It is possible that the Incas were descended from an offshoot of the Tiahuanaco nation. They were a gifted tribe originally ruling in the town of Cuzco and a few square miles round it. During the couple of centuries before Pizarro arrived they conquered all Peru and welded it into an empire. As a ruling warrior-caste, they sought like the Aztecs to associate themselves with the whole past history of their territories, and devised historical myths accordingly. Hence the Peruvian past filtered through to the Spanish, as in Mexico, contaminated by the policies and falsifications of the victors. Still the legend of Viracocha was potent, and enough independent tradition survived for it to be notorious that Tiahuanaco, with which his name was connected, was not really Inca handiwork.

Combining my observation and reading after inspecting the place, I was able to review the southern version of the multiform aboriginal gospel a great deal more fully and critically than hitherto. I give it here, as compiled from various sources. The discrepancies, all things considered, are remarkably slight.[2]

Viracocha was the chief god and made the world. In the beginning all was dark, yet not dead, for under the black heavens a primitive human race contrived to exist. Alongside these groping savages Viracocha set down some giants whom he had carved out of stone and brought to life. But his creatures failed to satisfy him. Some of the giants he turned back into stone at Tiahuanaco; the rest he drowned, all but two, in a deluge, together with most of the night-dwellers.

Then he took human shape to restore mankind. He came— from the south, as some said—to Lake Titicaca, founding his first headquarters on the principal island. From this island he sent the sun, moon and stars whirling into the upper air, and in the new light the aboriginal remnant saw him: a white man of middle age and impressive bearing, slightly but not exceptionally above average stature, with grey tonsured hair, a long beard, a white robe girdled at the waist and almost brushing the ground, a staff in one hand and a book-like object in the other. He had a number of white and bearded companions, men like himself. There were no women among them.

Crossing over from the island to Tiahuanaco, he began to create fresh human beings and animals out of clay. He also built the stone edifices there, and put up walls and dug irrigation canals. His supernatural powers moulded the landscape, and set the waters flowing where only bare rock had been before.

Meanwhile his followers were instructing the clay-born race and the flood survivors together. Viracocha called the people his sons and daughters, counselled them wisely in a spirit of universal love, and sent them out with his blessing to populate different countries.

But now there is a break in the story, and a sinister element creeps into it. Apparently some of the god's attendants had remained on Titicaca Island governing and educating a tribe of "long-ears," so called because they perforated their lobes and stretched them with weighted ear-rings. All was not well among the lake-people. One of Viracocha's companions was murdered, and his corpse drifted on a raft to Cachamarca near the south end of the lake, whereupon the land divided making a channel which is still there, the bed of the Desaguadero River. Worse was to follow. Another of Viracocha's companions became rebellious and had to be dismissed. He embarked on his own raft and floated off along the newly-formed Desaguadero, uttering vows of vengeance. In the end the whites on the island seem to have been disowned by their master. They cohabited with native women, and their mestizo progeny drove them out.

A time came when Viracocha himself, at Tiahuanaco with the main body, was ready to extend his work. First he dispatched all but two of his followers eastward to various designated spots, where they presided over the supernatural birth of more human beings. The last two he kept with him for a little while longer, but finally sent one of them south-west and the other north-west, on missions of the same type. As for himself he roamed about Peru braving the enmity of his forgetful creatures, who often greeted him with insults and violence. At Yamquesupa his divine retribution destroyed the village. At the lake of Carapaco he was seized and bound, but the thongs dissolved and he glided off over the lake on his outspread mantle. Some of the people did stay loyal, however, and to one friendly chief he left his staff as a keepsake. It changed to gold.

At last he took the road over the mountains to Cuzco, creating men as he went, healing the sick, enlightening the tribes. At Cacha he was attacked yet again, but a celestial fire drove off the assailants, and the overawed people put up a statue of him (which was still there when the Spanish arrived; but some priests took it down). He trudged on to Urcos near Cuzco, sitting on a hill subsequently marked by a second monument, and thence to Cuzco itself. From the future capital of the Incas he made his way to Cajamarca in the north, thence into what is now Ecuador, and down by a river through the provinces of Puerto Viejo and Manta, where some of his companions rejoined him. Thus he reached the Pacific. His last sermon was a warning. False Viracochas would come and the people should not listen to them, but some day he would send his own accredited emissaries. With these words he turned away seaward. According to some, he again spread his mantle and crossed the waves on it; according to others, all the white men simply strode out over the water and faded from view; but if Heyerdahl is right they took advantage of suitable local forests and made rafts. At any rate they departed, looking like wraiths of foam—hence the name Viracocha, sea-foam, bestowed on the god in retrospect. It was thought that he had gone to the isthmus of Panama and so across to the " other sea."

Viracocha's prophecy was fulfilled, since his banished disciple afterwards reappeared posing as the god. The pretender met with ridicule. Nevertheless the white men were remembered without scepticism as the *viracocharuna* or viracocha-people, and the Incas not only expected their return but tried to dignify their own dynasty by connecting it with them. The Inca royal progenitor Manco Capac was alleged to have been a son or descendant of the chief who inherited Viracocha's staff, and the Incas in general professed to trace their ancestry to the " long-ears" of Titicaca. One fifteenth-century emperor who had seen Viracocha in a vision actually assumed his name, thereby becoming a confusing element like Topiltzin in Mexico; and the Inti bird, which was associated with the god, was adopted as an Inca device.

That is the story of Viracocha and his earthly epiphany, a drama worthy of its theatre, and far more impressive than the architectural odds and ends corresponding to it. One wonders what the Peruvians might have given the world if only they had had writing to set their traditions down for themselves. The tale is linked with that of Quetzalcoatl by the motif of superhuman white men, but hardly by anything else, and the impersonal irrelevance of Tiahuanaco reinforced my own suspicion that the motif was simply imported and infused into the mythology of the country. But I still had to ask whether, if only as an aid to the myth-making process, there might actually have been white men in Peru.

This is the crux of Heyerdahl's Polynesian theory. His trump card is the likeness between " Kon-Tiki," the name of the Polynesian divine ancestor, and the title " Con-Ticci-Viracocha " applied to the Peruvian deity. Some of the islanders trace their families back to white voyagers who came over from a land lying toward the sunrise after defeat in war, and about 1900 an Easter Island genealogy was recorded going back fifty-seven generations to the first migrants. Since cross-checking between such genealogies in different archipelagos tells in favour of their reliability, it is worth calculating what date this long pedigree implies. The answer is, very approximately, A.D. 400–500, a conclusion which accords with a radiocarbon dating on Easter Island. Heyerdahl contends that this is an acceptable period for Tiahuanaco; that the place was in fact built by his accomplished nomads from Central America; that they prompted the legend of Viracocha; and that some of them, perhaps the expellees from Titicaca Island, trekked to the coast and went out on rafts to explore the Pacific. He draws parallels between the monolithic statues in highland Peru and those in Polynesia, and discerns significance in the " long-ears." [3]

Now he may be right as to essentials; I am not competent to judge. It may be that members of a pale-skinned Peruvian tribe did sail to Polynesia as refugees, and did carry the cult of Con-Ticci-Viracocha with them. But the rest does not follow by any means, and to survey the Viracocha legend impartially is to realise how little bearing it has. I have no wish to flog specific difficulties, or make an issue of my dissent from an imaginative and invaluable author. My concern is not with the Pacific at all but with Heyerdahl's notion of an important, civilised, influential, yet profoundly alien ethnic group on the American continent, a group with Old World characteristics, moving from country to country over a long period and recalled by the natives in many guises. The existence of such a group would raise the question of its origins, and the possibility of an early European discovery of America followed by colonisation. All the archæology and all the traditions—Mexican, Colombian, Peruvian and so on—would have to be taken into account, a truly alarming prospect.

At Tiahuanaco I was already ceasing to believe such a thing. Among the ruins it struck me that my inspiration in the Oaxaca museum could now be profitably pursued. Mexico had art-objects, bearded faces, that gave the legend of Quetzalcoatl a narrow but incontestable foundation in fact. There had been such men as models in Mexico. But the figure of Viracocha carved on the Tiahuanaco stone had no beard. What about Tiahuanaco sculpture in general? Once again, had the story of Viracocha any comparable support? Had there been such men as models in Peru or Bolivia?

Near the village which I had noticed up the road—San Juan de Tiahuanaco—there was, my guide explained, a museum where some of the material from the site was on display. We drove to it, and he tried to track down the functionary who kept the key, but without success; so we never got in. He conducted me instead through farmyards and fields to another ruined enclosure, but by this time I was taking more interest in the sights of the present, the farm buildings, the thatched roofs with home-made crosses on top, the restless dogs and small shaggy black pigs. The village church had a monolithic statue on each side of the gate, whether genuine or imitation I never found out, but it was good to know that the clergy saw nothing diabolic in Viracocha's stone puppets.

My absorbing purpose now was to go to the other museums in La Paz and look for beards or the absence of beards. Next morning the guide presented himself at my hotel, and before long we reached the Plaza del Hombre, where a kind of sunken garden in the middle of a street-roundabout is the setting for a number of the transplanted statues. One at least of these proved to be a real giant, who did something to counterbalance the earlier impression. If only they had left him where he belonged! But his square hat and square expressionless face conveyed no message, and a square object in his hand could not be confidently interpreted as the " book " carried by Viracocha. We went on to the principal archæological museum, which is behind wrought-iron gates down a side street. The curator offered to sell me a copy of Posnansky's masterpiece with the Phœnicians in it (a volume so bulky that I would have had to buy a new suitcase to take it home) and showed me a basement room with a few chairs and a dust-caked table where, he said, Posnansky had lectured, seemingly without a successor. On the main floors my eye ran down shelf after shelf of sculptures, most of them in the same formal Tiahuanaco style. And there were no beards, except for a couple of exceedingly uncertain fringes on the chins of figures from Titicaca Island, worn almost out of resemblance to humanity.

I had my answer, and the long journey had brought its reward. I could at last safely conclude that Viracocha was not a parallel case to Quetzalcoatl. Nothing stood in the way of my treating his story as fictitious. There was no archæological support for the legend of bearded white men in highland Peru.

That realisation was a turning-point, and it required scarcely any qualification afterwards. Such Peruvian evidence as exists is in fact very weak indeed. The Titicaca statues with the possible fringes are so featureless as to be indecipherable; the fringes may be decorations or chinstraps. The lost statue at Cacha is reputed to have worn a beard, but no drawing of it has been preserved and nothing can be inferred from it. As for the Chimu pottery jars from the north, some are more realistic than others, but all are palpably stereotyped. They are confined to an area which is thought to have been influenced from Central America, and may well be artistic derivatives of the Central American images. No living models are required to account for anything of this kind in Peru.[4]

3

At the risk of iteration I must try to sum up the case as I was led to see it by my American tour.

It seems to me almost incontestable that there were bearded white men south of the Rio Grande before Columbus, before the Vikings. They may have come from Europe or they may have come from some other part of America. They may have been widespread, they may not; the ubiquity of their legend proves very little, since most of the data can be explained by the effect of story-teller upon story-teller and artist upon artist. But whatever their homeland, whatever the extent of their movements, they were really there in the New World—human beings of flesh and blood, not myths.

To the extreme view of Heyerdahl, native tradition lends no solid support. It never speaks of the whites as constituting a fixed clan or society, and never mentions any women or children of theirs. Similarly, the art-objects portraying them are always isolated exceptions. These bearded men are not recognised Americans among other Americans, but interlopers who loom and fade like comets. A few minor bearded tribes do exist in Venezuela and the Pacific North-west, but the facts of geography, plus the improbability that such people would have made such an impression on their more advanced neighbours, rule them out of court. The tradition most likely to be of historical value is the Mexican, and this unambiguously brings the white men in over sea from the Caribbean direction.

Their own culture must have been above the primitive level, not only because of the folk-memories they left behind, but because they were invariably made the heroes of culture-myths. At the same time it is important, here also, not to claim too much. The genetic secret of Mexican civilisation is admittedly obscure, and nobody has quite fathomed its abrupt birth followed by fluctuation rather than a consistent growth. To set up unknown white people as " culture-bearers," however, not only in Mexico but in Peru, removes no difficulties and raises several. It is not a question of any *a priori* dogma about American isolation —on that count the pendulum of opinion is swinging back [5]— but simply of the concrete realities. If culture-bearers, then what culture? The Classic civilisations of Mexico and Peru show no marked affinities; the common factors which are traceable a long way back have little or no relevance to the actual places like Tiahuanaco with which the white men, in legend, are associated. And if from the Old World—again, what culture? Heyerdahl's speculation about people borne across by the Equatorial Current poses a grave dilemma. If they were uncivilised, what culture could they have brought; and if they were civilised, which civilisation did they belong to, and why are there no traces of it in America? The nineteenth-century scholarship expended on demonstrating connections of that sort was lavished in vain.[6] One obstacle virtually fatal in itself is the Americans' comparative backwardness in metallurgy. Mexico had none whatever till about A.D. 900, when copper and gold began to be worked, and iron played no part in the economy till its introduction by the Spanish.

Granted a real contact with overseas visitors of some attainments, it was probably a brief local contact leading to no true communication or comprehension. For this reading of the facts I happened to come upon a notable piece of Mexican evidence, the use made of the wheel. Before entering the American Museum of Natural History I shared the common illusion that the wheel was unknown to pre-Columbian America, and I was therefore amazed to see a wheeled toy dog from Vera Cruz. Excavators have turned up other playthings of the same type, but playthings only. The ancient Mexicans did learn the principle of the wheel, yet despite the appalling transportation problems raised by their architecture they never seriously applied it; a neglect which the label on a similar toy in the Museo Nacional patriotically and excusably calls " inexplicable." While domesticated draught animals were lacking, slaves were abundant, yet still the wheel was not employed. The impression given is that a few Mexicans encountered a people who had it, and that they studied it long enough to grasp its principle but not long enough to grasp its potentialities.[7]

Different lines of thought keep converging on the same hypothesis: that white bearded men visited Mexico with an unforgettable impact, but did not settle there for long, or greatly affect indigenous custom; that a fantastic saga of their doings spread through the New World and was integrated with local mythologies; that portraits of them were made and copied, and the copies were themselves copied and increasingly conventionalised all the way to northern Peru. Where then was the centre of dissemination, the area where the natives did meet them and observe them first-hand? Where (to approach the problem by the artistic route) do the bearded heads look like portraits from life?

To forestall any charge of wishful subjectivism, I will quote Matthew W. Stirling, the principal archæologist at Tres Zapotes and La Venta. In his article " Great Stone Faces of the Mexican Jungle," published in the *National Geographic Magazine* for September 1940, he reproduced the capped clay head from Tres Zapotes, my " Napoleon III," calling it one of the best examples of New World ceramic art, and adding: "Because of its lifelike appearance, it is probably a study of a prominent person." Here then is an impartial pronouncement as a starting-point. About half a dozen other bearded heads are known to me which are not obviously stylised, and suggest eye-witness observation at not too many removes. I have mentioned "Uncle Sam," the unparalleled profile on the La Venta stele; and G. C. Vaillant's "mystery," the hugely bearded pottery face from Rio Balsas, Guerrero; and the squatting Wrestler from Vera Cruz in the Museo Nacional; and the squatting Fire-God in the same place, who comes from the same province. To these might be added a profile on the back of a mirror, also from Vera Cruz, and a relief of a man with a goatee from Tabasco. There are one or two marginal cases.[8] Apart from these last, however, the agreement in tendency is perfect, and Stirling's judgment supplies the key to the whole series. Tres Zapotes, the area where the capped head was dug up, is Olmec . . . and so is La Venta, and so are the Vera Cruz and Tabasco regions generally. Guerrero, while not in the Olmecs' own territory, was deeply under their influence, especially in art.[9]

These clues therefore combine to point to the Olmec country along the Gulf coast, and to the period in the last pre-Christian and first Christian centuries when the Olmecs flourished. La Venta being early, the early portion of the period is much likelier than the late. Confirmation is furnished by the wheeled toys, those apparent legacies of a foreign contact. They come from the same region, and they date back, some of them at least, to the same epoch.[10] Finally, of course, the archæological conclusion tallies with the literary testimony of Ixtlilxochitl, who brings Quetzalcoatl to the Olmecs about the time of Christ. No real alternative is open. This, if any, was the place; this, if any, was the nation; this, if any, was the period. White men came to the Olmecs, who symbolised them in the person of a divine hero, a John Frum; and the hero then underwent the process of fusion which I have already sketched. The Serpent

God was not Olmec, but probably Huaxtec. At some stage, for some reason, the white Olmec hero was identified with him, and the composite Quetzalcoatl began to grow.[11]

To have got so far is something, but unfortunately we cannot at present get much further. If the intruders into Mexico came by sea as the legends assert, they probably came from the West Indies. This deduction may be linked up with Proclus's possible indication that a report of those islands had reached Europe by the early Christian era. But as Proclus gives no hint of the source of his information, merely professing to have copied it from someone else, he has no value as a guide. The Olmec dates would fit in with that hypothetical scattering of refugees from Carthage. However, the Carthaginians were scarcely white, and only a decisive archæological proof would justify invoking them here.

I prefer to turn back instead to the " Cronians," who at least have the merit of shedding a gleam of light on Plato, Plutarch and the rest. Arguably, the white men were Americans after all—European perhaps in their distant ancestry, but fully domiciled—who lived in a part of the continent beyond the Mexicans' horizon. They were descendants of the North Salem builders, or at any rate of early New Englanders or Canadians, who had gradually felt their way to the Indies. Vessels passing between Cuba and Haiti could easily have been carried by wind and current round Jamaica to Yucatan, and thence along the Gulf coast.

It would be cheering to detect likenesses between North Salem and the Olmec remains, but as the interval of slow exploration southward must be supposed to have lasted for several hundred years, no such likenesses are really to be looked for. La Venta has stone altars, and Stirling draws attention to a colossal stone head with a hole through it from the left ear to the mouth, which he says may be an oracular speaking-tube.[12] All that can be affirmed at present about the American legends is that they lead back to an unchronicled stirring in the Atlantic during the last pre-Christian centuries. Ships are faintly discernible on the sea, and the sailors are not Indians. It may be imprudent to say more. But the ships are there.

4

We seem however to be left with a loose end, very much as we were before. What about the traces of Christianity?

Anything from that source must have been superimposed later than the initiation of the main Saga. If Heyerdahl's culture-bearing migrants existed they were of course pagans, and if, as I have preferred to suggest, the Saga arose from transitory local contacts, those contacts can still hardly have been with Christian people. Even St. Thomas as a *deus*—or rather *apostolus*—*ex machina* would probably not be early enough.

Circumspection is necessary here. Most of the supposed Christian vestiges which prompted the friars' Thomas theory can to-day be discarded without misgiving. Their effect depended on Spanish ignorance (not, at the time, culpable or illiterate ignorance) of comparative religion. Deluge-myths and creation-myths and baptismal and eucharistic rites, generally speaking, prove very little. Such features of Christianity can be paralleled after a fashion the world over, and the " fashion " in early America as everywhere else was in any case a highly imperfect one. The cross need not imply anything either. It has had religious or magical connotations in many countries and many periods, and a stress on the compass-points in the cosmology of Mexico made it a natural emblem there. Emphasis is laid on it in some of the legends of Quetzalcoatl and the other white gods, but arguments relying on that emphasis, or indeed on almost any Christian motif in the legends, are open to the further objection that the Indians may have absorbed ideas from the Spanish missionaries and worked them into their own oral mythology during the transitional decades before anybody put it on record. Since the Mexicans thought Cortés was Quetzalcoatl, many of

271

them equated his Christianity with Quetzalcoatl's cult; they could easily have attached bits of it in good faith to their narratives of the god's previous coming.[13] As for Viracocha, part at least of his story was taken down when many Peruvians of the pre-conquest generation were still alive, but although the substance of what was written was doubtless authentic, there had been ample time for the incorporation of Christian details. When Viracocha walks on the water, and when he warns his forsaken people against the false Viracochas who will come to deceive them, I suspect him of acting out the words of some half-understood friar. Indeed these incidents may have been put in as a deliberate retort to the new religion, with a view to making the native god a full equal of Christ.

In the upshot there is still a residue, but its isolation calls for scrupulous care.

First, when all anthropological allowances have been made, the earthly Quetzalcoatl's veto on human sacrifice continues to jar. It runs counter to the whole trend of Mexican theology and ceremony, and reduces the Serpent God himself to such patent incoherence that its concoction in the sixteenth century as an afterthought is not easy to credit. The impression is rather of a discordant tradition which the Aztecs could neither reconcile nor suppress. No parallel exists in any other native religion of America: human sacrifice is known to have been practised by several races, and positively condemned by none. In the veto, and the insistence on it, there is a real hint of outside influence which could well have been Christian influence.

Next, as to Christian traces in pre-Columbian symbolic art, meaning principally the crosses. Here likewise the omnibus rejection is nearly sufficient, but not quite. The Tiahuanaco cross, the Colombian cross of Bochica, and others that are mentioned in Yucatan and Tlaxcala, may all be set aside, while the object in Oaxaca Cathedral is not evidence. The seventh-century Palenque specimen, with its heraldic supporters and its bird on top, has

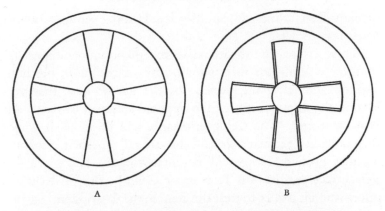

A   B

*Fig.*A Irish type of inscribed cross-circle design
*Fig.*B Cross-circle design on disc carried by Quetzalcoatl

Sketches by the author. The aim is not exact reproduction
but a diagrammatic indication of motifs in a form facilitating
comparison. For variations on A, see e.g. F. Henry, plate 19(c)
and others. For variations on B, see the *Codex Magliabecchiano*
XIII. 3 (Z. Nuttall), page 49, fig. 61, and others; or Vaillant,
plate 59. There is at least one Mexican specimen with arms
extending to the periphery, as is usual in the Irish designs,
and there is at least one with the frequent outward curve
of the arms

features in common with a couple I sketched at Kilmalkedar
near Dingle, though the resemblance is not close enough to
support any guesses at imitation. However, the crosses in the
Codex Magliabecchiano and the Codex Fejervary-Mayer, two
of them borne by Quetzalcoatl, are more arresting. The spreading arms, the hubs, the surrounding circles, the pictorial filling-in
of the outline—these things no doubt can be paralleled in other
places besides Ireland. Yet there is a certain convergence about
them taken together, which might pardonably be viewed as
pointing not merely to Christians in general but to Christians
within the Irish orbit, probably not much before the eighth
century. Thus they enhance the interest attaching to the Maltese

or early-Irish crosses on Sr. Meade's Huaxtec pottery, which, itself, is fairly late.

These crosses in Mexico raise the question of Viracocha's tonsure, a detail not met with in any of the more northerly legends, and intriguing because of the uproar over that very issue in the dispute between the opposed adherent of Celtic and Roman usages. The Celtic monks, it will be recalled, shaved their heads in a peculiar style, and chose to rally for their autonomy on that ground. It would be interesting to know whether Viracocha's tonsure was Roman or Celtic! But in default of information it is safer to treat this item in the description, together with the "book-like object" in Viracocha's hand, as inspired by shaven-crowned Spanish clerics with breviaries.

Nevertheless our loose end has turned out to exist. There actually are signs of an early Christian element interpolated in the Saga of the Wonderful White Men, or rather in the Mexican version of it, since everything farther south can be explained away by influences and coincidences devoid of historical implications. The circle-cross combinations in Mexico suggest other ideas. Inasmuch as they are associated with Quetzalcoatl, either directly or in virtue of his Huaxtec connections, those strange appurtenances of his like the bishop's crook and the cross-marked robe acquire a trifle more weight. The robe could be interpreted as the cloak or *brat* of early medieval Irish religious, which was sometimes starred with crosses embroidered or appliquéed; a *brat* purporting to be St. Brigit's is preserved at Bruges.[14] Secondly, once the Celtic Christian hypothesis is seriously brought in, further considerations begin to arise. When Quetzalcoatl is stated to have sailed from Tabasco on a raft made of snakeskins, the phrase may be pure fantasy; but it is, after all, a translation, and one may glimpse through it the perfectly comprehensible concept of a skin-boat, in other words a curragh. Again, while Dr. Zariquiey's story of the village under the lake may be an offshoot of the American flood-myth, it recalls that recurrent Celtic tale of the town or district submerged for some transgression—Lyonesse, Ker-Is, the Lost Cantref in Wales, the Irish cities under Lough Neagh and the western waves.[15]

I think it should be acknowledged that American mythology may, here and there, have drawn in fragments of religion and legend derived somehow from Celtic Christians, and that Quetzalcoatl in particular may have annexed fragments of this kind as he annexed Topiltzin's career and so much else. Corroborative facts come to hand most curiously. One of the culture-heroes whom we have so far met only briefly is Glooskap, the divine mentor of the Micmacs in the Canadian Maritimes. He is a very humble relation of the splendid southerners, but he does arrive from the Atlantic like them, and the manner of his final departure contributes something extra which they do not. There are two accounts of it. According to the one we have already glanced at, Glooskap terminated his mission by withdrawing into a cave in Cape Breton Island, where he lives still. But according to the alternative account, he went away westward across a body of water (perhaps Lake Ontario) and made his home on an island, approachable by a long roundabout overland route—where likewise he lives still. He is, or was, expected to come back as a deliverer. The ambiguous fate of this hero who does not die, but vanishes *either* into a cave *or* over western waters to an isle in the sunset, is an exact parallel to that of the Celtic Arthur, who is sometimes represented as sleeping in a cavern in Wales, and sometimes as biding his time in the sunset-isle of Avalon, being destined in either case to return. For good measure, Glooskap also rides on a whale, like Brendan.[16]

If these motifs can be matched in other folk-lores, similarly juxtaposed, then they need not mean much; but I am none too sure that they can. Incidentally it is amusing that a Celtic factor would explain what is not otherwise explained, the Mexican identification of the white hero with an irrelevant and incompatible deity. " Pre-Eminent Serpent " is more or less equivalent to " Pendragon," Head Dragon, the familiar

Arthurian title; and a sentence in Gildas makes it clear that kings in Celtic Britain were called "draco" as early as the sixth century.

As it happens, the Micmac legend proves in itself that American folk-lore could digest European matter, since by the time it was taken down it had come to include dealings by Glooskap with the kings of England and France. He was credited with causing the French Revolution. But there is a more apposite case-history. A Celtic tale—the actual tale of Brendan, no less—is definitely known to have been adopted during the Middle Ages, not indeed into the folk-lore of America, but into that of the Canary Islands. The documentation is furnished by Alonso de Espinosa, a friar who worked in Tenerife under Philip II, and whose value as a witness lies in the fact that he manifestly does not understand what he is saying and therefore cannot be accused of tendentiously improving it.

Tenerife was then still populated by the Guanches, a pale-skinned aboriginal race. In 1594 Father Espinosa published a book about them, and mentioned a strange belief of theirs:

> The old Guanches themselves say that they have an im-memorial tradition that sixty people came to this island, but they know not whence they came. They united and formed their settlement near Icod, which is a place on this island, and they gave it this name, which is a word in their language. *Alzanxiquian abcanabac xerax* means "the place of union of the son of the great one."

Espinosa goes on to quote an earlier document, regrettably without giving the exact reference, to the effect that the Canaries were evangelised by "Blandanus," an abbot from "Scotia," together with a "Blessed Maclonius" who resuscitated a dead giant in the reign of Justinian, i.e. between 527 and 565.[17] What the Spanish friar has got hold of here is a slightly garbled version of the legend of Brendan in the form assigned to the ninth and early tenth centuries. The Navigator is made to come from

" Scotia," which meant Ireland then but did not go on meaning it very much longer, and he brings sixty companions (the *Life* crew, not the *Navigatio* crew) including the giant-revivifier Machutus.

Presumably, several generations before Espinosa's arrival, someone came to Tenerife who told the Guanches this version of the legend and asked whether St. Brendan had sailed their way. They obligingly managed to recall that he had; and by the end of the sixteenth century the story had rooted itself among them as an " immemorial tradition " with a singular likeness to the American traditions.

If anything comparable took place among the Americans, it probably did so a long time before Cortés, since the Aztec chroniclers would have taken note of any recent visit by strangers. But the crosses in the manuscripts set a provisional limit in the other direction, since, if they are Irish-inspired, their originals cannot be earlier than the seventh century. The possibility is that between that time and, say, 1000, Irishmen were somewhere in America, and that rumours of their religion and art, of the tales they told and the questions they asked, drifted slowly to various parts of the continent and became mixed up with the existing native saga material. Such Irish Celts, in projecting their mythology outward and inquiring after the heroes of their own race across the western ocean, would only have been imitating those British Celts who talked to Plutarch's Demetrius.

In 1851 Henry R. Schoolcraft, Mississippi explorer and Indian agent, drew attention to a belief current in a tribe of that Algonquin nation to which Glooskap's Micmacs also belonged.

The Shawanoes, an Algonquin tribe, have a tradition of a foreign origin, or a landing from a sea voyage. John Johnston, Esq., who was for many years their agent, prior to 1820, observes, in a letter of July 7th, 1819, published in the first volume of *Archæologia Americana*, p. 273, that they migrated from West Florida, and parts adjacent, to Ohio and Indiana, where the tribe was then located.

"The people of this nation," he observes, "have a tradition that their ancestors crossed the sea. They are the only tribe with which I am acquainted, who admit a foreign origin. Until lately, they kept yearly sacrifices for their safe arrival in this country. From where they came, or at what period they arrived in America, they do not know. *It is a prevailing opinion among them, that Florida had been inhabited by white people, who had the use of iron tools.* Blackhoof (a celebrated chief) affirms that he has often heard it spoken of by old people, that stumps of trees, covered with earth, were frequently found, which had been cut down by edged tools."

John Johnston, Esq., sensibly added that these Indians' own sea-passage might have been nothing more than the crossing of "some great river or an arm of the sea" during the migration. Their account of a white colony in Florida is doubtless flimsy in the extreme—a mere straw which a few enthusiasts have had the temerity to clutch at.[18] The justification for introducing it here is the fact that the American loose end not only exists but can be neatly spliced to the European loose end, so that a mutual reinforcement gives every small clue an interest which it might not otherwise have.

Most of the legendary and archæological evidence from the New World conforms to the hypothesis that unknown people resembling Europeans were in America—in New Hampshire perhaps, in the West Indies perhaps, in Mexico almost certainly—during, say, the pre-Christian millennium and a half; but some residual data would be explained most readily by a second phase of contact and legend-development attributable to the presence of Irish Christians, perhaps in Florida, after A.D. 700 but long before Cortés. Most of the literary evidence from the Old World (Plato etcetera) points to trans-Atlantic links of some sort extending from Britain by way of the northern island-route to Canada and thence to the West Indies during the pre-Christian millennium and a half; but some residual data (the detached *Navigatio* sections about the flat island with Christian inhabitants, the transparent sea, the grape island) would be explained most readily by a more direct Irish acquaintance with the Bahamas and Jamaica, presumably after 840 or so when ocean-going ships were beginning to be available, but not much later than 900. While the coincidence proves nothing, it is incontestably there. The shape of the problem is the same on both sides of the ocean. There are two layers, and they fit together. Moroever the Irish author of the *Navigatio* could have had access via Celtic tradition to whatever remained of the British information tapped by the Greeks, and access of a more immediate kind to the travel reports of his own Irish and Norse contemporaries—in other words to both layers. He would seem to have been in the best possible position to know of America in the tenth century if anybody did.

But it is scarcely easier to get beyond hypothesis with the second layer than it was with the first. Irish seafarers might, I suppose, have reached the New World about 900 by pushing on from Iceland, and the Great Ireland theory may be right in principle after all even though Great Ireland is not America. But I question whether a tiny band of refugee monks could have gone so far or made any lasting impression, and there is the further difficulty of getting them back to Ireland to report. My own guess would be that the Vinland voyages began earlier than the Norse sagas indicate, with expeditions from Ireland comprising large Irish elements in the crews. The explorers followed roughly Columbus's route to America, whether intentionally or not, and some returned while others stayed in Florida and the West Indies. Rumours of the Bahamas and so forth percolated through to the *Navigatio* author, but if there were explicit records they were lost in the Irish chaos after his time. It will be worth asking what signs there are, if any, that such voyages were believed in the Middle Ages to have occurred.

However, the time for a final answer is not yet. On my flight back from South America I woke up one morning and saw the outlines of green islands and promontories below, slowly articulating themselves in the Antillian dawn. After a last stretch of rippled blue the coast of Florida variegated the horizon ahead, and the airliner swung round over the endless houses and private swimming-pools of Miami. That artificial landscape had nothing to tell me, and though the Bahamas themselves lay somewhere on the right, I never caught a glimpse of them. They hid behind the sunlit terrestrial curve, withholding their presence as they withheld their secret.

Epilogue

COLUMBUS'S INHERITANCE

THE IRISH DISCOVERY of America remains, after all, speculative. But the speculation is grounded on fact, the existence in the tenth century of a copious Irish Atlantic-Mythos. This comprised the tradition of the actual sea-pilgrimages of Cormac, Brendan himself, and other monks of the heroic age; the informed exaggerations of that tradition in the *Navigatio Sancti Brendani* and connected literature; the geographical work of scholars like Dicuil; the current oral accounts of more recent Irish voyages, to Iceland indubitably, to Greenland probably, to America possibly; and the Celtic fantasies of Otherworld Quests by water, and island-adventures. All the elements flourished together, mingling in various ways, and undergoing a process of development. Nor was this Atlantic-Mythos devoid of backing in the classical literature which the Irish drew upon. Before Columbus, long before him, an American image existed and evolved in the minds of Europeans.

But this rapid survey I have undertaken . . . can it be said to have settled anything as to the basis of the tale of St. Brendan's Voyage?

I hardly think a short answer, Yes or No, is feasible. " Yes " would imply that an early discovery of America had been proved, which is not the case. " No " would imply that the inquiry had ended in a flat negative, and that is not the case either. It seems to me that the chief outcome has been the definition of certain problems as real problems—authentic mysteries demanding solution, and capable of being solved on the supposition that the Atlantic actually was crossed before the tenth century. None perhaps is very impressive in isolation, but the whole series together cannot be so easily brushed aside.

First (to sum up) there are the classical and related matters. We have Plato's reference to a sea-route from his Atlantis by way of islands to a continent beyond the Atlantic. We have Theopompus's reference to the same continent, and to a "Hyperborean" crossing, hinting at the British Isles. We have Plutarch's further reference, with allusions to Celtic British informants and to a passage from Britain, accompanied by strangely exact particulars. There is Crates's representation of the farther continent as a Perioikean Land surrounded by water; there are the curious paragraphs in Pausanias and Proclus, the latter apparently applicable to the Antilles and nothing else. On the American side, the unexplained North Salem ruins are certainly "megalithic" enough to fit in with early trans-Atlantic contacts, and the central area of these ruins is reminiscent of the chapter in Plutarch and the Cronian cultus which he mentions.

Passing on, we find the *Navigatio Sancti Brendani* itself. Since it has every appearance of being based on competent research and a good map, its quasi-American episodes deserve to be treated with respect. It portrays—as the immrama do not—a land of continental size a long way off across the Atlantic, behind a curtain of fog at about the correct distance from the Faeroes; and it contains descriptive detail apt to the Bahamas and Jamaica.

Lastly we have the American native races, with their pre-Spanish traditions of culture-heroes recalled as bearded and civilised white visitors from over the eastern sea, with a consistency and convergence pointing to an historical origin in Olmec Mexico. And these traditions are supported by Olmec portrayals of bearded men clearly not Indians, and are later elaborated in ways strongly suggestive of Celtic Christendom.

Perhaps I should stress once more that the classical texts are not hand-picked. Their aptitude is not the meaningless aptitude of a few lucky hits in a mass of errors. The topic of the Atlantic beyond the familiar archipelagos is rarely touched on at all in Greek or Latin literature, but whenever it is (apart from a satirical skit by Lucian) we strike something curiously right. I will not insist that the texts, either singly or in combination, amount to proof; but they do amount to a challenge, and pose a question that needs answering.

What, however, could the answer conceivably be? Shall we be registering a concrete gain even if we do postulate early voyages? Or shall we be offending against economy of hypothesis by creating more problems than we solve? It would be wisest to put everything down to chance and leave it there, if the process of "explanation" led us to conjure up a dozen separate discoveries of America, or to invent a discovery by Julius Cæsar and then speculate wildly in the endeavour to "explain" why nobody mentions it.

Perhaps after all the case is not as hopeless as that. No firm conclusion is justified as yet, but the mystery can be got into manageable shape. We can impose limits on the discussion, picking out the few notions that still appear worth investigation, and dismissing others—provisionally at least—as a waste of time. To anyone who has gone over the mass of theorising collected by Gaffarel and Bancroft, and glanced at in several of the books on Columbus, that will not seem a contemptible result.

As to the question of St. Brendan himself, and the Irish generally before the Norse advent among them, I have sadly admitted the obligation to give up my early opinion, or rather hope, and concede that it is no use hunting for the Kerry missionary in Mexico. The hypothesis of a crossing by Brendan or his contemporaries is in any case not helpful in solving the problems as defined. If someone cares to suppose that his written legend was a long-delayed outcome of geographical researches by him, so that he discovered America (as it were) on paper, there is no cogent reason to object. It has emerged as more likely, however, that the legend is a gigantic distension of an actual sea-pilgrimage of his in the Hebrides.

Because of the emphasis on Brendan's guides and informants, I have wondered whether America was reached by European refugees during those troubled centuries after A.D. 300, when Jordanes testifies to an unexplained swarm of Atlantic voyagers. Such a migration could have taken Britons or Irishmen across when ships were still available, while their preliminary discussions at home, and reports brought back afterwards by stragglers, could be made to account for much of the Brendan matter. Moreover, refugee-colonists who pushed on might have entered Peru at the correct time to fill the Kon-Tiki role. When Heyerdahl's *Aku-Aku* was published, one reviewer whimsically suggested that the Easter Islanders were Irish, a conjecture for which the author himself had given the hint.[1] Did either of them appreciate that the partial Irish descent of the islanders is ... just ... arguable? And what about the carved whale Heyerdahl disinterred with a house on his back? But such fancies, however alluring, are better suited to fiction than history, and my sole excuse for airing them is an irrational feeling that the chain of late Imperial coin-finds may some day, quite fortuitously, be prolonged beyond Iceland and the African bulge— prolonged far enough to be evidence.

If it is not quite safe to dismiss Posnansky's Phœnicians, the only ground for hesitation is that the whole Phœnician achievement is so obscure. Recent scholarship tends rather against the view that it was at all spectacular.[2] The reasons are purely negative, and something revolutionary may yet be dug up, but until it is there is no point in bothering with the theory further. Much the same is true, *a fortiori*, of a kindred theory summarised by Gaffarel, that America was discovered in Old Testament times by the Jews. That is a queer thing to ascribe to one of the least nautical nations of antiquity. The gifted Jewish Christian who wrote the last book of the Bible counted it among the glories of the New Jerusalem that there would be no more sea: a prophecy for which he was castigated by Kipling.

Having set aside some of the rubbish, let us ask what " discoveries of America " are still, so to speak, viable. If all the data could be covered by a single hypothesis, that single hypothesis would be very attractive indeed, but none is forthcoming. Any information drawn on by Plato must be earlier than his death, which took place in 347 B.C. Any Celtic cross-circle design imitated in Mexico must be a product of the seventh century A.D., or later than that. American folk-lore and archæology bring up parallel difficulties, and might almost lead us to despair if it were not for the fact that the difficulties actually are parallel, and span the ocean with a faint chronological echo.

Some of the data on both sides of the Atlantic can be accounted for by Irish participation in early " Vinland voyages " to the West Indies about 900, and subsequent American wanderings by Irish settlers or castaways—a theory which introduces nothing radically new, but simply extends a recognised movement of American exploration a hundred years or so farther back. Whether such a West Indian discovery should be counted as Irish or Norse. would depend on the composition and leadership of the crews involved, an unprofitable theme for debate.

The rest of the facts can be arranged in a sort of pattern, but they still cannot all be covered by a single expedition or even migration from the Old World, Carthaginian for example. There is no direct evidence that any such exodus occurred in the historical pre-Christian era, and, if it had, we would expect classical authors to speak of it in plain terms. On the other hand, the recurrent pointers to Britain or the British Isles are in favour of trans-Atlantic contacts of some kind along the northern route. Something can be made of the " Cronian " supposition that a seafaring race of people with European characteristics (ultimately Iberian perhaps) lived once in eastern North America, built North Salem, made their way round to Britain passing on information of which a little percolated through to the Greeks, and also got to the West Indies and Mexico. "Cronian" traditions lingering among the British Celts, as among the Mexicans, would explain not only the classical items but the subsequent notions of the related Irish Celts. We might ask whether perhaps the visionary isles of the immrama are cousins of Aztlan; whether the vivid immram ocean-dwellers and sea-borne messengers possess a common ancestry with the white gods of the Americans; whether we have been catching glimpses of a single reality from a series of diverse aspects.

There is *something there*. For the present I go no further in assertion. I simply toss out the challenge for any investigator to pick up who cares.

What in fact are the potentialities for future research? Chance archæological finds may transform the scene at any moment, but manifestly nobody can plan or predict them, or do much more than recommend further sifting of North Salem, of Olmec sites, and, if Sr. Meade is on the right track, of Huaxtec sites. The discovery of a cave like the North Salem Y-chamber in the Gulf of St. Lawrence area, where Plutarch's Cronian sanctuary might have been, would open up vistas, as indeed would the discovery of any fresh traces of a maritime "Cronian" culture. There is, however, another side of this topic. I have a suspicion that evidence may already have been found, and gone unrecognised. All archæological workers are specialists nowadays, and it would be interesting to ascertain how many authorities on Celtic antiquities have even looked at American antiquities, or vice versa. As Professor Evans remarked to me, " they would be afraid people would think they were cranks." No doubt a justified fear, but what a pity! In another field, the Far East, Sir Mortimer Wheeler has underlined the same difficulty: the mapping-out of Greek and Roman penetration of Asia is retarded by the fact that the orientalist may not know a classical object when he sees it.[3] I am not disputing the need to specialise; I am entering a plea for collaboration. It is perfectly possible that the vital clue is staring us in the face, only the proper expert has not yet been induced to stare back.

A second type of investigation is the experimental attempt to do what others may or may not have done before, in the manner of the Kon-Tiki expedition. The value of such adventures can, of course, be overrated. Heyerdahl's demonstration that a raft could sail from Peru to Polynesia deflated ethnologists who had ignored his theory on the ground that it was physically impossible. But it did not prove, and could not prove, that enough Peruvians ever drifted westward to make up a substantial part of the island populations—or indeed that any did. The utmost it could effect was to clear the way for arguments of a positive sort, should these be forthcoming. Yet that in itself was much, and there is a strong case for similar tests with replicas of Irish and other vessels. A fuller knowledge of the practice of ancient and medieval navigation, with due allowance made for changes in the climate and ocean currents, could not fail to be illuminating. Not enough is established about the ocean-going capacities of the large curragh: T. C. Lethbridge, speaking with some authority, has expressed views on the subject,[4] but we cannot be sure. Practical trial could show what the sea-pilgrimages to the Faeroes and Iceland were really like, and how fast and under what handicaps the curragh could travel—information of value for checking the distances in the *Navigatio* and hence the proposed map. If it turned out that an Atlantic crossing might have been accomplished, well and good. Whether it did or not, a proof that at least some of the journeys described could have been performed by a large curragh at the right season would reinforce the presumption that the author of the *Navigatio* was a knowledgeable person and no mere architect of mirage.

2

I set myself the task of interpreting St. Brendan's Voyage, and my conclusion is affirmative . . . as far as it goes. The *Navigatio*

Sancti Brendani is a compendium of marvels which are sometimes incredible and sometimes hard to construe, but seldom wholly without basis. There were Irishmen in the tenth century who knew that America was there; who regarded the farther continent of classical authors in the light of Celtic tradition, as something more than a figment; who collected intelligible rumours of the New World. I cannot say how. They did.

Nothing else remains but one question, the greatest of all, nevertheless, from the point of view of immediately ascertainable history—whether the Irish Atlantic-Mythos had any influence on Columbus.

This can be answered. To answer it properly involves recognising that while in one sense the tenth century was an end, in another sense it was a beginning. The Irish imagery and legends went on flourishing through the Middle Ages, affecting the thoughts, writings and actions of medieval men inside and outside Ireland, and mingling with a broader stream of ideas. Within that expanded context we can trace a line from the Celt to the Genoese, and, in so doing, make a few final adjustments to our evaluation of the Atlantic-Mythos generally.

Brendan's own literary fortunes, after the tenth century, slide into a morass of muddle and corruption. Clerical authors persist in trying to fit pieces of the *Navigatio* into the framework of the *Life*, with painful consequences, whether in Latin or in Irish. The extreme point is reached in an Irish text that simply incorporates everything, and also makes use of a poetic alternative legend in which the Voyage is prompted by the apparition of a wonderful flower from the Land of Promise.[5] Its author or editor treats the *Navigatio* as a mere quarry of unconnected incidents, and jumbles them shamelessly, destroying the crucial relationships of time and space. His loss of touch is quite characteristic of these rehandlings. All possibility of recovering the map is wiped out, and meanwhile the descriptions tend to grow more extravagant, with scenes of pure immram type, which nobody would dream of trying to reconcile with any reality, creeping in among the rest. There is also a concurrent involvement with the secular immrama themselves, which the *Navigatio* infiltrates. Brendan's popularisation abroad extended the process. It seems to have begun very early, even before the major domestic developments. His adoption by the Celts of Wales and Brittany, which injected the Voyage into the *Life of St. Machutus*, afterwards generated a longer romance now lost. Another diffusion from the lower Rhine valley may have started before 950 through the enthusiasm of Irish monks who frequented that area. In due course an Anglo-Norman verse paraphrase of the *Navigatio* publicised Brendan among the literate subjects of the Plantagenets; this poem reproduced the original more or less fairly, but with many un-Irish excrescences. Further medieval versions were in Old French, Middle English, Dutch, Flemish, German, Provençal, Norse, and Italian. St. Brendan's Voyage became, in fact, a favourite literary theme. But this fame was the fame of a general idea and little more. The specific geography was almost entirely dissipated.[6]

Yet the shape of the idea, the confused medieval conception of Irish discovery in the Atlantic, still has a certain interest for its corroboration of a suggestion already made, that Irishmen somehow or other learned directly of the West Indies in the later ninth century. The authentic thread which runs through in spite of all, and leads forward to Columbus, has an air of leading back to that.

A recurrent topic has been the relation between the Irish and Norse, and in taking leave of it we should note that the Vinland narratives themselves are probably not uninfluenced by the cluster of traditions associated with Brendan. Vinland, " the Good " as the Vikings called it, was somewhere in North America and about the year 1000 they did get across; yet even at that extremity the Gaelic ghosts which had hovered over Iceland and Greenland continued to haunt their steps. The name of the place means Wine-land, and the attached epithet " good " carries an implication that it counts as a Fortunate Isle. The first description of it,

Adam of Bremen's, confirms the implication by a direct paraphrase from Isidore of Seville, referring to wild vines and self-sown corn.[7] The thirteenth-century written sagas that deal with the Norse discoveries repeat the corn-and-vine motif, and I have cited the Norse geographer who puts forward the astonishing theory that Vinland is an outpost of Africa, presumably in the same region as the Fortunate Isles of Ptolemy and Isidore, the Canaries. Wild berries and wild corn in America could have given the Viking imagination something to build on, and parallels occur in the memoirs of more recent explorers such as Jacques Cartier. Still it is perplexing that such practised navigators should have perpetrated such a geographical howler, and it is rather more than perplexing that people who had camped out through a winter in New England or the Maritime Provinces (as Leif and Thorfinn apparently did) should have conceived themselves to be in the Fortunate Isles, even allowing for alterations of climate. The sagas allege that the Vinland winters were free from frost or snow. For some coastal areas such a statement could still, in a mild year, be true, but nowhere is the weather Elysian.

Hence it has long been suspected that when the voyagers' stories came to be elaborated by literary men at home, a fallacious Hibernian preconception took hold. This in essence was the opinion of Nansen, who pointed out the affinity between Vinland and the tropical grape-island of St. Brendan, and argued that while the Norse doubtless reached the New World, Vinland itself as well as White-Men's-Land was a bookish fancy of Irish provenance. Nansen's hypercritical view is now generally rejected, but Vinland does make better sense on the supposition that Norse authors identified Leif's discovery with a warm western isle which the Irish, or other Norse in close touch with them, had long been talking about. They knew, or at any rate they thought, that Irishmen had gone over, and we may picture them putting two and two together erroneously, just as Columbus was to force his own discoveries into conformity with Asia, making out Cuba to be Japan, and so forth. To say so is not to belittle the achievements of Leif and those who came after him, or to cast fundamental doubt on the claims made for them. It is to suggest that the interpretation of what they did was in some degree falsified by a tradition of slightly previous voyages from Ireland south-westward, resulting in a West Indian landfall.

Certainly in the medieval maps, where the notions of Atlantic islands spread by Irish literature are chiefly preserved, we detect hints of such a preoccupation.[8] An allusion in Honorius of Autun's *De Imagine Mundi*, about 1130, shows the way in which maritime speculation was by then operating outside Ireland.

> There lies in the Ocean an island which is called the Lost (Perdita); in charm and all kinds of fertility it far surpasses every other land, but it is unknown to men. Now and again it may be found by chance; but if one seeks for it, it cannot be found, and therefore it is called " the Lost." Men say that it was this island that Brandanus came to.[9]

Pursuing the concept further, however, we find an oddity in it. The " St. Brandan's Isle " of maps and derivative legend is not portrayed as the continent of the *Navigatio* but simply as another island, nor, in general, as a very big one. It is seemingly not the Promised Land but one of the tropical sub-paradises visited by the saint during the quest. So violent a displacement of focus indicates that here, as with Vinland, imagination may well have seized on an actual reputed discovery by the southern route, an actual adventure fictionalised in the *Navigatio* rather than a pure fiction.

At any rate medieval maps are unanimous in placing St. Brandan's Isle to the south rather than the north, and it is sometimes referred to as a Fortunate Isle. Several early authorities accordingly put St. Brandan's among the Canaries—an idea reflected in the document quoted by Espinosa—and that location is allotted in the famous Hereford map of 1275. Dulcert's chart drawn in 1339, a better-informed, less academic piece of work, pushes St. Brandan's toward Madeira; in the maps of Pizigani (1367), Beccario (1426, 1435), and others, it has drifted on till it is not far from the Azores region. Dulcert and Pizigani betray Irish mythical influence by giving it the alternative name " Isle of Maidens," which recalls Bran.[10] Then the discovery or rediscovery of the Azores themselves prompts Bianco (1448) to show " St. Brandan's or the Fortunate Isles " as two groups lying west of them. Finally Behaim in 1492, on the eve of Columbus's departure, sketches a large St. Brandan's Isle just north of the Equator, close to the position occupied in reality by the coast of South America.

Subsequently the Isle ceases to be noteworthy, surviving only as a phantom that flits about in an altogether demented manner. But attention must be paid also to the inscrutable " Brazil," another Irish-inspired figment which appears on maps compiled long before anybody had reached the country now called so. It is not the elusive Hy-Brasil of romance, it is an Atlantic island seriously held to exist. The Genoese Dalorto marks it in 1325 as a fair-sized circle in the latitude of southern Ireland, and so do several later cartographers. But its position and conformation are always open to much doubt. On a Catalan map it lies south of Greenland; on another Catalan map dated 1375 it is not a single island at all, but a ring of land enclosing a sea with nine smaller islands.

The name is variously spelt, and its application to the red dyewood of America has confused the etymological issue. However, it is said to be originally the Irish breas-ail, meaning " very good " or " blessed," another gesture toward the Fortunate Isles. Its shape on the 1375 map has been adduced as evidence that Brazil is Newfoundland and that the inside-out version is a reminiscence of the Gulf of St. Lawrence, entered by Irish sailors at some undetermined period. But Brazil is never mentioned under that name by the medieval Irish themselves, and even if it does bear a faint impression of the Canadian approaches, the explanation is likely to be Norse-Irish misunderstanding in

another form, *breas til* being equivalent to Vinland the Good.
Both St. Brandan's *Isle* and Brazil, however indistinct they
might be, were relics of Irish geographical learning with a
potential value for explorers. Their impact was undeservedly
and unfortunately weakened by a proliferation of fancy that
dotted the Atlantic with other and less respectable islands. While
the diffusion of the Brendan saga had set many minds working
in a fruitful way, the ignorant nature of that diffusion led to
endless diversions and irrelevancies. Elsewhere in the quoted
paragraph of Honorius we already confront islands of sheep
among the Hesperides which are not the saint's, but doubtless
take a hint from his. Honorius also revives Atlantis, and his
Perdita, though he thinks it is the same as St. Brandan's Isle, is
in fact a new ghost-land. The spawning has started. Soon
after him the Arab Idrisi, whom we met in connection with the
Sargasso and Great Ireland, sets down his ideas on the geography
of other parts of the Atlantic, stating that there are twenty-seven
thousand islands in it A small selection fantastically described
by him [11] includes an Island of Sheep and a nearby Island of
Birds. The implied acquaintance with Irish sources is a nodding
one only: Idrisi tells us that the sheep are unpalatable because
their flesh is too bitter, and that the birds are red fish-eaters
similar to eagles—details that do not agree at all with the *Navigatio*.
Also he situates the Island of Sheep, and hence its avian neighbour,
in a vacant expanse of sea south of the Azores, incompatible
both with the *Navigatio* and with real geography. He seems
to have simply picked up the names, or little more than the names,
and to have added the rest himself.

The point here is that Idrisi's fictitious catalogue is typical, a
true foretaste of later maps. These depict such spectres as a
crescent-shaped " Mayda " of Moorish inspiration south-west of
Ireland (it bobbed up again in the Bay of Biscay on an American
map published in 1906 [12]); " Daculi " west of Scotland; " Frisland " and " Stokafixa " (i.e. Stockfish), allegedly repetitions of
Iceland; the " Island of the Hand of Satan " and other diabolic

abodes; "Drogio" and "Estotiland" in the north; several
scattered "Green Islands"; and, in the sixteenth century, the
"Sunken Land of Buss"—Atlantis in miniature—and a number
of phantasmal islets named after other saints than Brendan,
including "Saint X." Most famous was the Isle of the Seven
Cities. The Cities, peopled, according to legend, by descendants
of eighth-century Portuguese escaping from the Moors, were
sometimes located in the imaginary Brazil, more often in a
distinct "Antillia." [13]

But in spite of all competition the two veterans, Brazil and
St. Brandan's Isle, did perpetuate a little of the Irish insight,
thereby throwing a bridge, frail but unbroken, over the gap
between two epochs of Atlantic discovery. These two islands
clung to the maps and refused to be dislodged, they elbowed their
way through the thicket of less reputable phantom-isles, and by
the eve of the Renaissance they at last attained, after all, a dignity
shared by Antillia alone.

Whereupon, the ineffectual centuries ended, and the ideas
which the pair expressed began once again to mould the thinking
of seamen—the thinking, and the action too. In 1498 Pedro de
Ayala, the Spanish ambassador to England, wrote to Ferdinand
and Isabella:

> The people of Bristol have, for the last seven years, sent out
> every year two, three, or four light ships in search of the
> island of Brazil and the seven Cities. [14]

Hence the expedition of Cabot and the rediscovery of North
America.

Lastly, Columbus himself. By the time of the first English
probings for Brazil, the Genoese was satisfied that land lay to
the west. It is an old story how he underestimated the distances
and thought the land to be Asiatic. As to what else he thought,
there has been copious controversy; but among the few certainties and near-certainties, three in particular stand out. It is
almost certain that he made inquiries in Galway, trying to

fathom the secret of the Gulf Stream Drift, and perhaps also gathering local lore. It is almost certain that one of the crew on his first American voyage was a Galway man. It is absolutely certain that he heard of St. Brendan and chased him westward beyond all charts. His son relates how he was inspired to sail partly by reports of "the islands of St. Brendan of which wonderful things are told"; and the Admiral himself, aboard ship in 1492, recorded how he had heard eight years previously of Portuguese searches for the land Brendan found, subjoining his own conviction that "therein lay the Earthly Paradise." [15]

Flying homeward with my note-books and photographs and tourist's paraphernalia, I knew already that nothing I could do, nothing anybody could do, would ever detract from Columbus's essential glory. Before 1492 America was a matter of hints and legends, accidental glimpses almost forgotten, ephemeral realisations never communicated. Columbus's vocation was not to broach the question of "land to the west," but to settle it for ever. Sweeping back the curtain of mist and sunset-cloud, he opened a path for all future generations, and joined two worlds into one. But where Columbus himself acknowledged a debt, it is only fitting that credit should be given. The Irish conquest of the Atlantic was a contributory cause of his own, even if it never happened; and while Brendan may not have discovered America, he has no rival as the patron saint of American discovery.

APPENDICES

Possible Sources of the Navigatio Sancti Brendani

This is a summary of the main findings of Chapters Four, Five and Six, together with one or two suggestions made elsewhere. Citations in square brackets refer to works which the author, for chronological reasons, could not have used, but which shed light on the nature of the knowledge and ideas likely to have been available to him.

1. *The Island of Sheep and the Paradise of Birds (identified with Faeroes)*
   Dicuil, and oral accounts from the Norse and from Irish monks.

2. *The Island of Smiths and the rock of Judas (Iceland)*
   Same as No. 1, supported in a general way by the classical tradition of Thule.

3. *The steep island (St. Kilda), the islet of Paul the hermit (Rockall), the second volcanic island (Jan Mayen)*
   Oral accounts from Norse and Irish. [For Jan Mayen, cp. Ari Frode's *Landnamabok*.]

4. *The Gulf Stream Drift and prevailing westerlies*
   Irish observation [cp. *Snedgus*, and Columbus's notes], probably supplemented by Norse.

5. *The western region of whales, "sea-cats," stunted vegetation, etc. (Greenland area)*
   Reports of Gunnbjörn's voyage, as known to Eric; perhaps also reports from Irish settlements in "White-Men's-Land," i.e. Greenland [cp. Idrisi].

6. *The crystal column (iceberg)*
   Reports from off-course Vikings and Irish associated with them?

7. *The fog (Newfoundland Banks)*
   As No. 6, or the " Sea of Gloom " conception derived from the Carthaginians and recorded by Avienus [cp. Idrisi].
8. *The nearer Atlantic islands to the southward—St. Ailbe's (Madeira), the island of bad water (St. Michaels)*
   (a) In general: Martianus Capella, Isidore of Seville, Pliny, etc. [and cp. Honorius of Autun, and Idrisi].
   (b) Madeira: Plutarch, Ptolemy, Diodorus Siculus, Pseudo-Aristotle, and information of Carthaginian provenance partially known to them.
   (c) St. Michaels: Seafaring tradition, ultimately Carthaginian; Atlantic voyages during last phase of Western Empire, noted by Jordanes.
9. *Currents and winds outside Gibraltar*
   As 8c; also Diodorus regarding Madeira.
10. *The " thick " sea (Sargasso)*
   Avienus, Jordanes [and cp. Idrisi].
11. *The trans-Oceanic continent*
   Plato, Theopompus (text preserved by Aelian), Plutarch; or British traditions used by them, as indicated by Plutarch.
12. *The Hyperborean route to this continent, north-westward from the British Isles*
   Theopompus, Plutarch, Ptolemy.
13. *The insular character of the farther continent*
   Macrobius, Martianus Capella.
14. *The trans-Oceanic Paradise*
   Cosmas Indicopleustes.
15. *The sphericity of the Earth, as apparently implied in the location of Paradise*
   Plato and other Greeks, Macrobius, Martianus Capella, Bede, Virgil of Salzburg, Dicuil.
16. *The flat Island of Strong Men and transparent sea (Bahamas), the grape island (Jamaica?)*
   No known source; conjecturally, early " Vinland voyages " via the southern route.

Atlantis

In considering the overdone topic of Plato's lost continent, it is as well to get rid at once of any notion that it may have existed as described. That was not the view of the Greeks themselves, apart from one or two deferential Platonic commentators. In Hakluyt's time, the myth was thought to have expressed a hazy Greek idea of America. Yet the literal reality of Atlantis was affirmed in 1882 by Ignatius Donnelly, an American politician who also discovered Baconian cryptograms in Shakespeare, and it has since been championed by a school of " Atlantologists " of whom the best known are Lewis Spence and Egerton Sykes. They claim (or some of them do) that Atlantis lay precisely where Plato says; that it was the site of Eden and all other earthly paradises; that the gods and goddesses of mythology were once inhabitants of Atlantis; that the Egyptian, Mexican and Peruvian civilisations started from Atlantean colonies; and that Atlantis actually was ruined by flood and earthquake nine thousand years before Solon's visit to Egypt, i.e. about 9564 B.C., the Azores being the last remnant.

This theory is entirely overthrown by chronology. No sizeable part of the mid-Atlantic sea-bed has been above the water for millions of years, and no inundation large enough can be assigned to the right period. Donnelly indeed found no satisfactory way of explaining how the disaster could have happened at all. His modern disciples have adopted Hoerbiger's hypothesis, according to which the Moon is a minor planet captured by Earth in comparatively recent times, an event which produced immense tidal convulsions before the satellite settled into orbit. Hoerbiger's hypothesis has not found much favour with astronomers. Even if we shift Atlantis to some area geologically more tractable, the date is still refutation enough. Atlantologists urge that the civilisations of Egypt and Meso-America seem to have sprung from nowhere without adequate traces of prior evolution. So they do, but not in the tenth millennium before Christ, or even simultaneously. Atlantis itself is portrayed by Plato as the home of an advanced bronze-age society which could not have flourished in 9564 B.C., quite apart from the unlikelihood of its history having been preserved for so long through millennia which are otherwise blank.

The solution of the Atlantis problem is that there is no solution. The tale is a composite, a collection of themes, moulded into unity by Plato's poetic genius and love of myth-making. In this instance he is stressing the ability of Hellenic city-states to withstand " barbarian " empires. At the same time there are objections to dismissing his story as a personal fancy and nothing more. Admittedly it is unfinished, but it is too elaborate for any moral that can be drawn, and too circumstantial to be let pass without scrutiny. While recognising always that Plato is writing fiction, we may still ask, as with the *Navigatio*, what his raw materials are.

His assertion about an Egyptian source is perhaps true, since he may have used Egyptian traditions of the " Keftiu " and the " Sea Peoples." The Keftiu meant, roughly, the Ægean nations under the hegemony of Minoan Crete; the Sea Peoples meant the Achæans and others who succeeded to the Minoan maritime power, and undertook widespread raids and invasions throughout the eastern Mediterranean, allied, significantly, with the Tyrrhenians and Libyans, both named by Plato as Atlantean auxiliaries. The Sea Peoples' final repulse at the gates of Egypt by Rameses III is commemorated in an inscription at Medinet Habu.

Plato's narrative of the great conflict has in fact a kernel of authenticity. Several bronze-age wars, spread over several centuries, have been telescoped by his own or Egyptian imagination into one tremendous campaign, but they did occur, and Crete at least is a common factor. Atlantis has unmistakable Cretan attributes: its warm baths and bull-sacrifices are both characteristic of the high Minoan culture, and its marked resemblance to the land of the Phæacians in Homer tends the same way, inasmuch as the Phæacians themselves are more Minoan than anything. One episode in semi-legendary Cretan affairs was an attack on Athens followed by earthquakes, and the Atlantean assault on the city with its cataclysmic sequel may be the same incident seen through Egyptian eyes. If the absurd "nine thousand years" is amended to "nine hundred," the Athenian war is placed exactly where Greek legend places it, in the fifteenth century B.C.

But no such piling-up of genuine historical oddments can result in history. Plato's myth is a gorgeous literary patchwork with just enough history in it to be provoking—rather like the medieval romances of Arthur and Charlemagne. The major difficulty is to see why his amalgam of Egyptian and Homeric details is grafted on to the fantasy of an Atlantic empire; why, indeed, this fantasy should have taken shape at all. References by Herodotus and Diodorus to an "Atlantian" nation in Morocco do not seem to me to settle anything. I think it likeliest that Solon heard a legend arising from the early Ægean contacts with Wessex, in which a Britain exaggerated like the kingdom of Prester John was brought, at the appropriate date, into relationship with the Cretans and their neighbours.[1]

Dante's Paradise

It is debatable whether the *Divine Comedy* owes any actual debt to Celtic vision-literature and voyage-literature, but several affinities are manifest. Here our attention may be confined to a single topic. When Dante, like the *Navigatio* author, has to decide where to place the Earthly Paradise, he puts it at the top of the Mount of Purgatory on the other side of a spherical Earth. The Mount rises from an island in the otherwise empty ocean at the antipodes of Jerusalem. Dante is aware, not only that such an island's day would be Europe's night, but that it would lie in the southern hemisphere under alien skies: he speaks of a constellation of four bright stars, which could well be the principal members of the Southern Cross. The verses dealing with these things are *Inferno* xxxiv. 112–15, 118; *Purgatorio* i. 22–30, 100–1, and iv. 61–84. Most remarkable of all, he follows the *Navigatio* by describing a voyage toward the Earthly Paradise across the Atlantic —not eastward. In *Inferno* xxvi. 94–142, Odysseus (whom Dante of course calls by the Latin name Ulysses) is made to recount his last adventure, his final ocean-quest that brought him within sight of the Mount of Purgatory. Laurence Binyon translates as follows; readers of Tennyson will recognise the source of an anthology piece.

> Not sweet son, nor revered old father, nor
>   The long-due love which was to have made glad
>   Penelope for all the pain she bore,
> Could conquer the inward hunger that I had
>   To master earth's experience, and to attain
>   Knowledge of man's mind, both the good and bad.

But I put out on the deep, open main
  With one ship only, and with that little band
  Which chose not to desert me; far as Spain,
Far as Morocco, either shore I scanned.
  Sardinia's isle I coasted, steering true,
  And the isles of which that water bathes the strand.
I and my crew were stiff and old of thew
  When, at the narrow pass, we could discern
  The marks that Hercules set far in view
That none should dare beyond, or further learn.
  Already I had Sevilla on the right,
  And on the larboard Ceuta lay astern.
" Brothers," I said, " who manfully, despite
  Ten thousand perils, have attained the West,
  In the brief vigil that remains of light
To feel in, stoop not to renounce the quest
  Of what may in the sun's path be essayed,
  The world that never mankind hath possessed.
Think on the seed ye spring from! Ye were made
  Not to live life of brute beasts of the field
  But follow virtue and knowledge unafraid."
With such few words their spirit so I steel'd,
  That I thereafter scarce could have contained
  My comrades from the voyage, had I willed.
And, our poop turned to where the Morning reigned,
  We made, for the mad flight, wings of our oars,
  And on the left continually we gained.
By now the Night beheld within her course
  All stars of the other pole, and ours so low,
  It was not lifted from the ocean-floors.
Five times beneath the moon rekindled slow
  The light had been, and quenched as oft, since we
  Broached the hard issue we were sworn to know,
When there arose a mountain in the sea,
  Dimm'd by the distance: loftier than aught
  That ever I beheld, it seemed to be.
Then we rejoiced; but soon to grief were brought.
  A storm came out of the strange land, and found
  The ship, and violently the forepart caught.

> Three times it made her to spin round and round
>> With all the waves; and, as Another chose,
>>> The fourth time, heaved the poop up, the prow drowned,
>> Till over us we heard the waters close.

Five months at sea. Let no one imagine that Dante conceived the globe as small.

King Arthur and Prince Madoc

The legend of Brendan was recognised in the Middle Ages to be connected with the legend of Arthur. In both the basic material was Celtic, in both the historical element belonged to the sixth century, and in both an important part of the development was due to the Celts of Brittany. A different use of mythological imagery in the British cycle masked the relationship but did not altogether efface it.

About the year 900—that is, before the existing Irish sea-stories, apart from the *Voyage of Bran*—an unknown Welsh poet wrote a Welsh immram or near-immram with Arthur as its hero. It was entitled *The Spoils of Annwn*, and was supposed to be narrated by Taliesin, the great northern bard of the sixth century. Annwn is a Welsh Otherworld which in this case is reached by sea. But it is not exactly an island. It is a fairy realm invisible to everyday sight, and entry is by way of obscure secret openings from the familiar world. The island containing the particular opening used by Arthur is not far from the shore, and may be Gresholm or Bardsey; thus the theatre of action is much closer to the mainland than it is in the immrama. The verses are condensed, allusive, and most uncommunicative, but what seems to happen is that Arthur invades Annwn with a contingent of knights to find and carry off a cauldron. This cauldron is a talisman with wonderful powers; nine virgin prophetesses have it in keeping. The raiders are ferried over in three boatloads, but ghostly garrisons contest their advance, and only seven escape the trap of the fortifications.

Celtic quest-imagery as accommodated to Arthur branched out later in the romance of the Grail, which was not at first a Christian relic but a talisman akin to the cauldron. A persistent presence through all the developments, associated somehow with the goal of the quest, was the voyager Bran in his British guise. The adaptation of themes, however, was not all. A complex rearrangement occurred. Annwn in Welsh myth was at best an indistinct sort of Otherworld, disclosing itself in various ways at various places, but one of its more intense manifestations—perhaps only a late and poetic manifestation, perhaps not—was Avalon, the Elysian "apple-orchard," a blissful island with attributes like those of Bran's islands. It lay somewhere, though not always anywhere in particular, in the direction of sunset; and it became celebrated as the retreat to which Arthur was borne away after his last battle "to be healed of his wounds."

The authority for that event is the exuberant Celtic antiquarian Geoffrey of Monmouth, who, in the 1130's, did so much to promote romance and bedevil history by his book making Arthur out to have been a mighty monarch and overlord of western Europe. Elsewhere, in a metrical *Life of Merlin*, he reintroduces Taliesin and makes the bard deliver a speech about the Atlantic islands. Having described the Gorgades and Hesperides, Taliesin passes to Avalon, the "Isle of Apples which is called Fortunate." He mentions the Isidorean self-sown corn and vines, and says the island is governed by nine sisters, evidently the same as the nine maidens of Annwn. Then he continues:

> Thither after the battle of Camlan we took the wounded Arthur, guided by Barinthus to whom the waters and the stars of heaven were well known.

Barinthus is Arthur's guide as well as Brendan's; Geoffrey keeps us in contact with Ireland.

At some stage in these literary transformations Glastonbury entered the scene. Celtic legend was much studied at the famous abbey, and its library is thought to have possessed manuscripts of St. Brendan's Voyage. In those days the abbey stood on an island encircled by rivers and lagoons—the marshes had not yet been fully drained—and at a date unknown, for reasons unknown but probably connected with local folk-lore, the island came to be identified as the real Avalon. Another Celtic name for it was reputed to be Ynys-witrin, the Isle of Glass, and this was reminiscent of a "Glass Fort" in *The Spoils of Annwn*. Once publicly established, such Somerset localisations ensured that the focus of otherworldly fancy in Britain would be transferred from the open sea to relatively landlocked waters. Moreover, a legend of Glastonbury's inception as a Christian site played a part (it now seems agreed) in that strange imaginative process by which the magic vessel searched for by Arthur's knights was reinterpreted as the cup or dish of the Last Supper, conveyed to Britain through the agency of St. Joseph of Arimathea.

Thus the ultimate British counterpart of St. Brendan's Voyage was something superficially quite unlike it, the Quest of the Holy Grail. Here too is a Christian religious romance drawing on Celtic mythology about an Otherworld Quest by water, and both legends have the pagan figure of Bran in the background. While Bran may or may not be Cronus, Plutarch's dreaming god certainly anticipates not only Arthur but the maimed king, custodian of the Grail, who lies in a state of suspended animation in the castle that houses it. The atmosphere of initiation surrounding Cronus is also noticeable in the romances. Furthermore the castle must still be approached over water; the name of the companion to whom St. Joseph entrusts the Grail is Brons, a corruption of Bran; and its first British resting-place is the Vale of Avalon. The Grail romance *Perlesvaus*, written about 1220, includes a kind of *imram* in which episodes from Irish tales are imitated with little change, and Malory's better-known Grail story, adapted from a French book of the early thirteenth century, has the sea passage to " Sarras " in it.[1]

Despite their Irish borrowings, the Arthurian tales never hinted at Atlantic crossings traceable on a map. Where the water-transits were not made indecipherably indefinite they were made very short, mere ferry trips from the beaches of Wales, or across glorified moats. Throughout the Middle Ages this feature was accepted without comment, and no geography was extorted which was not there. But in Tudor England, when a partly Welsh dynasty was on the throne and politicians were anxious to counter Spain in the New World, several attempts were made to prove that something tangible about " land to the west " could be wrung out of Celtic tradition in its British form. The potential utility of such a proof was clear. If somebody from Britain had got there first, his priority could be urged to undermine the Spanish pretensions.

Two such attempts have left their mark on Hakluyt's *Voyages*. The astrologer John Dee, an active patron of exploration and one of the earliest authors to use the phrase " British Empire," sought a basis for his political propaganda in the history of Arthur. The British King, according to Geoffrey of Monmouth, had conquered Iceland.

This expedition obviously carried the sixth-century Britons far along the northern route; was it credible that they had gone even farther? Dee decided affirmatively. In 1578 he put it to Hakluyt that Arthur's realm had embraced "Frisland," an island then supposed to exist south of Greenland, and publicists under his influence took the final step and credited Arthur with annexing part of America. It followed that Queen Elizabeth, by right of succession, had a valid claim in the New World. But the theory was too far-fetched. Hakluyt preferred a more moderate position, citing the alleged Arthurian empire only as a general precedent for English expansion; and soon afterwards we find George Abbot dismissing "vain shows out of the British antiquities," and adding with reference to the American notion that "the wisdom of our State hath been such as to neglect that opinion." [2]

Contemporary caution, however, did not extend to a second fable. Abbot himself was willing to believe in the discovery of America by Madoc, a medieval prince of North Wales. Madoc's legend was not connected with Arthur's, but the sort of guesswork indulged in by Dee helped to foster it, and the British antiquarian Camden had a share in its popularisation. Prince Madoc did actually exist, and some Welsh verses indicate that he went to sea. But he never became, like Brendan, a hero of folk-lore, and his exploits cannot be documented till after Columbus, a most suspicious circumstance. Elizabethans declared that he took ship in 1170 to escape from a dynastic feud, and sailed westward round the south of Ireland; that he came at last to a country with unfamiliar people; that he returned to Wales and equipped a fleet; and that this fleet disappeared for ever across the Atlantic. Hakluyt says, quoting a history of Wales by David Powel:

> This land must needs be some part of that country of which the Spaniards affirm themselves to be the first finders since Hanno's time. Whereupon it is manifest that that country was by Britons discovered, long before Columbus led any Spaniards thither. . . . I am of the opinion that the land whereunto he came was some part of the West Indies. [3]

The allusion to Hanno, implying a current Carthaginian theory, is intriguing but unexplained; the rest speaks for itself. Hakluyt's continuator Purchas bestows a similar endorsement.

Madoc was still prospering two hundred years later, when the indefatigable Southey composed an epic about him. His collapse as a serious proposition was comic. Before the 1858 Eisteddfod a prize was offered for the best essay on " The Welsh Discovery of America." The sole entry of any value was handed in by Thomas Stephens, who distinguished two classes of alleged proof. The meagre Welsh literary matter he rejected as worthless. It was necessary also, however, to look into a long-standing belief that somewhere in America travellers had come across a Welsh-speaking tribe. This latter evidence was more interesting, but it turned out to be another case of the rope-trick phenomenon. The Welsh Indians had always been placed by rumour outside the zone of settlement, and every time it had become practicable to check the report, they had been transferred somewhere else. After sifting a large quantity of unauthenticated hearsay Stephens abandoned the pursuit, and concluded that there was no case for Madoc whatsoever.

His essay was disqualified by the horrified Eisteddfod judges on the ground that it was not on the set subject. The subject was " The Welsh Discovery of America," and he had written on " The Welsh Non-Discovery of America." As a result Madoc lingered on for thirty years more, and the essay was not published till 1893.

So expired, for practical purposes, a claim which was almost certainly nothing but a Tudor invention. Even in their heyday these Celtic fancies of the sixteenth-century English had not been of much profit to them. It is possible that one permanent thing, the designation of the south-east peninsula of Newfoundland as " Avalon," was a consequence; otherwise the effects were small. At first glance it is surprising that they never exploited the far more promising Brendan legend. But they could hardly have used anything which gave credit to the subjugated papists of Erin, or which might have been construed as conceding American rights to them. The principle thus implied in the conduct of the founders of English-speaking America was upheld in the presidential election of 1928, but repudiated in that of 1960.

NOTES AND BIBLIOGRAPHY

Notes

Works are designated in these notes by their heading in the Bibliography, usually the author's name.

Chapter One

1. For the historical St. Brendan, see BUTLER, DUNN, O'DONOGHUE, O'HANLON, PLUMMER (I).
2. DE PAOR, page 76; DILLON, xi; LINDSAY, 254–6; JONES, 248 ff.
3. PTOLEMY, II. I; WEBB, 5–7; LINDSAY, 248.
4. GOGARTY, 22–4, 31–3, 51; O'KELLY and WILSON; DE PAOR, 50.
5. BIELER *passim*; KENNEY, 310; LINDSAY, 173.
6. N. K. CHADWICK (2), I–3; DE PAOR, 48–50; GOUGAUD, 67; WILLIAMS, 363.
7. DE PAOR, 31–2, 73–4, 108–9.
8. DE PAOR, 73, 77, 79–80, 87–8; GOGARTY, 116–17.
9. DE PAOR, 39–46, 61–2, 96–7, 102, 106–8, 116 ff.
10. DE PAOR, 98–100, 106–8.
11. DE PAOR, 33, 50, 71–2; GOUGAUD, 75; THRALL, 277.
12. DE PAOR, 50–4, 68, 71; BOSWELL, 113–14; GOUGAUD, 36, 58, 129 ff.; FLOWER, 21.
13. DE PAOR, 33, 53–6; GOUGAUD, 149.
14. DE PAOR, 45, 62, 124–6; HENRY, 50-60; LETHBRIDGE (2), 84. Additional information from the National Museum in Dublin.
15. ADAMNAN, Book I, chapters vi, xiv; Book II, chapter xliii; Book III, chapter viii. Further, GOUGAUD, 131 ff.; THRALL, 279–83; DUNN, 449; DE PAOR, 52; LETHBRIDGE (2), 72, and (4), 78 ff.
16. MEYER, 5–10; LINDSAY, 248.
17. DE PAOR, 50, 64–5; BOSWELL, 113–14; MEYER, 12, 26 n.35; WESTROPP, 236; *Cambridge Medieval History* (M. R. James), 502 ff.; LINDSAY, 324.
18. DE PAOR, 65, 112.

19. GOUGAUD, 71; BOSWELL, 119 n., 135 ff.; LOOMIS (2), 21, 138; FLOWER, 14–15; JACKSON, 153–54.
20. GOUGAUD, 275; BUTLER, vol. I, 228. GOUGAUD also discusses the allusions to St. Brigit, noting their unorthodox character, and quotes a hymn calling her " the mother of Jesus " (271–2).
21. DE PAOR, 66; FLOWER, 13; MURPHY, xv–xvii; BOSWELL, 135 ff.
22. FLOWER, 1–4; DE PAOR, 74; DILLON, xvi; JACKSON, 63, 183. The Tara seating plan is in the National Museum.
23. MURPHY, xiii–xv; MEYER, 13 ff.; DE PAOR, 66–8, 74.
24. DILLON, xii, 73 ff.; FLOWER, 5, 14–15. Cp. GRAVES (1), 296; (2), 103, 130.
25. DUNN, 437; BOSWELL, 120, 127 ff., 136, 143, 146 ff.; DILLON, 101 ff., 124 ff.; FLOWER, 16, 29. For Lives of Saints, see KENNEY and PLUMMER passim.
26. CRONE, 17; THOMSON, III, 114; MERRIEN, 51; GAFFAREL, 144–5; WRIGHT, 18–19.
27. NEWTON, 5, 25; RYAN, 24; NANSEN, vol. I, 151; WRIGHT, 56.
28. RYAN, 15–24; DE PAOR, 140–1.
29. GAFFAREL, 149; THOMSON, 166, 326–7; RUSSELL, 281–2.
30. KENNEY, 545–8; TOOLEY, 47–8.
31. NEWTON, 86–7; TURVILLE-PETRE, 60–6, 100–1, 167.

Chapter Two

1. ADAMNAN, Book III, chapter xviii. With regard to Hebridean voyages by St. Brendan, cp. O'DONOGHUE, 212; MARCUS, 110.
2. KENNEY, 410–11, 481–2, 728; DUNN, 411–19; O'DONOGHUE, 84, 90; THRALL, 282.
3. KENNEY, 410, 417–18; THRALL, 283; O'DONOGHUE, 210 ff. Cp. N. K. CHADWICK (1).
4. KENNEY, 410–17; PLUMMER (1), I. xvii ff.; DUNN, 418–19; THRALL, 283.
5. NANSEN, passim.
6. Cp. LOOMIS (2), viii, 35, 47, etc.
7. MEYER and NUTT, passim; MURPHY, 93–101, 216–17; FLOWER, 16.
8. Tom Moore challenged Jeffrey, who had reviewed his poems unfavourably, to a duel. Bow Street officers arrived to prevent it, and Moore had a change of heart and cried out what a shame

the whole business was. They held a banquet of reconciliation. But somebody who examined the pistols found that they were not loaded.

9. BOSWELL, 146 ff., 165; DILLON, 101, 124 ff.; DUNN, 446; KENNEY, 411–15; MURPHY, 216–20; THRALL, 276–83. Neither DILLON nor MURPHY whole-heartedly endorses the conjectural early dating of *Mael Duin* which the theory of clerical imitation demands, whilst THRALL'S argument is subversive of the theory in principle. Statements of the "Christianised immram" view as e.g. in WATERS, lxxxi–lxxxii, will always (I think) be found superficial and oversimplified.

10. DUNN, 399.

11. BOSWELL, 127 ff.; LOOMIS (2), 30–1.

12. BOSWELL, 146 ff.; DILLON, 101, 124 ff.; WESTROPP.

13. KENNEY, 410–11; PLUMMER (1), I. xvii–xviii.

14. STOKES, 247–61; KENNEY, 412–14.

15. In the *Annals of the Four Masters* an event recorded for the year 887 is the stranding of a white mermaid 195 feet long on the coast of "Alba." The *Life of St. Brendan* may have taken a hint from this report.

16. SCHRÖDER, 51; cp. WRIGHT, 159.

17. HORNELL, 111–12, 176–9.

18. HORNELL, 111–14, 138–40; GOGARTY, 33–41; LITTLE, 58–61; MARCUS.

19. GOGARTY, 33; HORNELL, 179; MARCUS, 105–7; VILLIERS, 45–6; LETHBRIDGE (2), 76.

20. HORNELL, 142–7.

21. HORNELL, 141; ADAMNAN, 280–1; DE PAOR, 99–100.

22. DUNN, 439; MARCUS, 114; LITTLE, 109–25; LETHBRIDGE (1), 136–7, 153–7; DE PAOR, 99–100.

23. MARCUS, 107; LETHBRIDGE (2), 77; NANSEN, vol. I, 248–51; HOVGAARD, 64 ff.; GATTY, *passim*.

Chapter Three

1. On the manuscripts and the general literary aspect, see KENNEY, 411–17.

2. Cp. WRIGHT, 197, 351. WRIGHT quotes an interesting tribute paid to this authenticity by Renan.

3. Or east to west—the reading is uncertain.

4. Or fifteen.
5. At the beginning of the episode his direction is not given. But the whale which pursues the boat, i.e. travels the same way, is met by the second monster coming *from* the west.
6. The text is corrupt. One version gives 60 years and 20, another 40 and 30. But 60 and 30 must be correct: when Paul gives his own account he states the times thus, repeats them, and confirms them by adding them together.
7. So O'DONOGHUE construes a somewhat vague phrase.
8. BEAZLEY, 230.
9. NANSEN, vol. I, 362; DUNN, 458; BABCOCK, 37; WRIGHT, 351–2; TURVILLE-PETRE, 94–5; LITTLE, 69–70. Cp. KENNEY, 411–12. In the following paragraphs on the Faeroes I have used chiefly O'DELL, 62, 304–21; KENDRICK, 328; and WILLIAMSON. The good fishing in the streams was noted in a travel article in the *Sunday Express*, 6th March, 1960.
10. WRIGHT, 220, 224–5; also DUNN, and authors cited in next note.
11. NANSEN, vol. I, 362; WRIGHT, 224–5; cp. TURVILLE-PETRE, 94–5.
12. O'DELL, 329, abridged. Italics mine.
13. Thus WRIGHT, 197–8, 351; BABCOCK, 36; O'HANLON, 432 n.; LITTLE, 134–5; and others. There are textual ambiguities in the " column " passage. I have used SCHRÖDER to amend O'DONOGHUE's translation slightly.
14. WESTROPP, 249 ff.
15. See JOYCE. The appropriate sections of *Mael Duin* are XXI–XXIII, XXVI.
16. DUNN, 412–13; OENGUS, 402.
17. Winds: see map in VILLIERS, x. The St. Kilda identification: WRIGHT, 351–2; SCHRÖDER, 37; LITTLE, 68. Particulars of St. Kilda: BELL, 367–71; WILLIAMSON and BOYD; FISHER, 44–5; ADAMNAN, lxiv.
18. I have no wish to insist that oriental stories had no influence at all on the *Navigatio*. I do not think such influence is relevant to any of the basic conceptions which the author has embellished, but it may possibly have suggested some of the embellishments. The case is stated as strongly as it can be by ASIN, 206–14. As for the whale himself, see DUNN, 426–31. Cp. WALLIS, 322–3, 333; HEYERDAHL (1), 316, and plate between 256–7. At

Brandon Creek I was struck (without immediately noticing the connection) by the resemblance between the inverted tar-covered curraghs and the backs of whales as they appear at sea. Did the Brendan fancy originate from this?

19. BROWN, p-14, p-15, e-27. An Anglo-Norman metrical version of St. Brendan's Voyage speaks of the water as *embetumée* by flowing over poisonous ores.

20. BABCOCK, 28. See further Chapter Four. The possible relevance of the Azores-Madeira area to the legend is recognised by BABCOCK himself, 5, 48; also by DUNN, 459; BEAZLEY, 230; GAFFAREL, 259.

21. RENAULT, 64.

22. STOKES, 354; BUTLER, art. "Ailbe."

23. LOOMIS (2), 56–7, 138.

24. VILLIERS, X, 26, 30.

25. NANSEN, vol. II, 10 ff., 17, 75.

26. ENGLAND, 198–9; LITTLE, 135–6.

27. VILLIERS, X. In some parts of this region of the world, and in some respects, the climate has deteriorated since the dark ages. But O'DELL indicates that the characteristics mentioned used, in south-west Greenland, to be worse rather than better.

28. The Purple Islands of Pliny are the nearer Canaries, but in HONORIUS of Autun in the twelfth century the "purpleness" has shifted far out into an indefinite west. See NANSEN, vol. I, 375–6. The other mythical islands are discussed in subsequent chapters.

29. Cp. O'HANLON, 431; LITTLE, 142.

30. FORBES, 13 ff.; GELLHORN, 3, 4, 31–62, 120; GOULD (1), 101–7; *Encyclopædia Britannica*, art. "Bahamas."

31. FORBES, 52, 54–5, 61, 65.

32. FORBES, 16, 37, 73. Cp. LITTLE, 146.

33. This identification of Brendan's volcanic island is suggested by GAFFAREL, 255. For Jan Mayen generally, see O'DELL, 297–301.

34. VILLIERS, X.

35. FISHER, *passim*.

36. The direction of this final sail is unfortunately obscured by an early confusion. Cp. DUNN, 458. O'DONOGHUE'S version says "west," but in the good text printed by JUBINAL no compass-bearing is given at all. SCHRÖDER'S text has a sentence making

the saint sail east; so has the British Museum copy (Add. Ms. 36736), which is the oldest, though demonstrably erroneous in several respects. But the two sentences are quite different and do not suggest a common original. Probably JUBINAL's version is the true one. The author himself did not specify the direction here, wishing perhaps to keep an air of mystery, but scribes and revisers afterwards put it in, and in some cases those outside Ireland and lacking contact with Irish concepts were misled by the conventional notion of an eastern paradise. There seems to be no other hypothesis that will preserve the hitherto unbroken consistency of the story, since " east " cannot be made to square with the rest. Brendan eventually reaches the same place as his informant Barinthus, who started from the *west* side of Mernoc's island, and sailed *west* (the British Museum copy is definite on that point). The Lismore *Life*, in which Brendan takes the last step toward his goal from what appears to be the Greenland zone, carries the same implication. I conclude that the crossing is vaguely westward, but not here stated by the author to be so.

37. Cp. HOVGAARD, 61–3; NANSEN, vol. I, 322, 335; KENDRICK, 26.
38. For this information I am indebted to Mr. Lethbridge personally.
39. BEAZLEY, 230; WRIGHT, 197–8, 220, 224–5, 351–2; BABCOCK, 48, 187.
40. *The Month*, July 1958.
41. STOKES, 354.

Chapter Four

1. LETHBRIDGE (5), 110–11, 149–51.
2. BELL, 368.
3. Cp. KENNEY, 412.
4. DUNN, 449.
5. See NANSEN, vol. I, 44–70; CARY and WARMINGTON, 33–7; THOMSON, 143–50; and references to classical authors given by these. THOMSON, the most recent authority, favours Iceland. Cp. LETHBRIDGE (2), 76.
6. WESTROPP, 236.
7. LETHBRIDGE (5), 110–11; JORDANES, I. 9; ISIDORE, XIV. vi. 4. On the other hand the sixth-century Byzantine PROCOPIUS

equates Thule with Scandinavia. But writers in western Europe would probably have been better informed about Atlantic islands and any recent visits to them.

8. DICUIL, VII. ii. 3, 6; NANSEN, vol. I, 164–5.

9. NANSEN, vol. I, 166–7; KENDRICK, 336.

10. *Landnamabok*, Prologue. ELLWOOD, the translator, notes several islands in the Hebrides, Orkneys and Shetlands called Pabba or Papa after the Irish hermits who lived on them.

11. NANSEN, vol. I, 261 ff.; KENDRICK, 361.

12. DIODORUS SICULUS, V. 19–20. For the identification, see CARY and WARMINGTON, 53; THOMSON, 78.

13. CARY and WARMINGTON, 52–4; NANSEN, vol. I, 345–51.

14. PLINY, VI. 36.

15. For the Corvo problems, see BABCOCK, 164–73; CARY and WARMINGTON, 54; THOMSON, 78; HARDEN, 141 n.

16. SMITH (2), art. " Atlanticum Mare "; THOMSON, 89. Compare the policy of the Hudson's Bay Company, which protected its trading monopoly north-west of Ontario by assuring prospective settlers that they had nothing to hope for from a barren soil and an intolerable climate.

17. MERRIEN, 66–8; BABCOCK, 28. For the passages quoted from Psudo-Scylax and Avienus, see BABCOCK, 27; CARY and WARMINGTON, 31–2, 48–50.

18. Cp. NANSEN, vol. I, 69. For the myths, see Chapters Six and Seven.

19. NANSEN, vol. I, 37–8. Cp. B. H. WARMINGTON, 209: when the Romans destroyed Carthage they handed over the contents of the libraries to the King of Numidia.

20. MARTIANUS CAPELLA, VI. (page 349); ISIDORE, XIV. vi. 8–10; DICUIL, VII. 1. 5.

21. JORDANES, I. 4, 7. Italics mine.

22. LETHBRIDGE (5), 110–11.

23. IDRISI (1), 223–5; (2) IV. 1 (vol. II. 26–9). IDRISI says that a street " still exists in Lisbon " named after the Magrurins. But the story makes it clear that their language was Arabic.

24. HONORIUS, I. 36; see NANSEN, vol. I, 375–6.

25. TOOLEY, 9–10.

26. NANSEN, vol. II, 54.

27. MERRIEN, 59–60, 64–5. Over the medieval door of the church

at Clonfert, where St. Brendan founded his last community, there are some carved faces of which several have a distinctly Red Indian look. I wonder if they were copied from the dead features of presumed natives of the country he visited!

28. HOVGAARD, 75–6; IDRISI (2), III. I (vol. I, 197), VII. 10 (vol. 2, 440).
29. MERRIEN, 64.

Chapter Five

1. DUNN, 449; KENDRICK, 328, 338.
2. NANSEN, vol. I, 166–7; KENDRICK, 328, 336–9; TURVILLE-PETRE, 97–8, 100–2.
3. Quoted in HOVGAARD, 75–6.
4. HOVGAARD, 77.
5. DUNN, 452.
6. HOVGAARD, III–12. Cp. KENDRICK, 338.
7. NANSEN, vol. 2, 48–50. The full text may be read in the translation of the saga by WILLIAM MORRIS and E. MAGNUSSON.
8. NANSEN, vol. I, 331–2. His aim was not to establish the reality of White-Men's-Land but to discredit the sagas. The argument, however, cuts either way.
9. HOVGAARD, 75–9; NANSEN, vol. 2, 1–2.
10. See e.g. DUNN, 451 ff.; Catholic Encyclopædia, art. "Brendan"; LITTLE, 181; MERRIEN, 65.
11. IDRISI (2), VII. 2 (vol. 2, 426).
12. TOOLEY, 123.
13. Landnamabok, I. i; cp. NANSEN, vol. 2, 166–7.
14. NANSEN, vol. I, 259–60, vol. 2, 77–8; HOVGAARD, 76. The authority is ARI FRODE'S Islendingabok.

Chapter Six

1. Oecumene and Ocean: ROSE, 17–18; SMITH (2), art. " Atlanticum Mare "; NANSEN, vol. I, 8–10, 76, 79, 86. Direction of flow: ROSE, 32–3 (the Sun plunges into the western Ocean and returns to the east with the stream, presumably round Africa since Africa is hot). The whirlpool: GRAVES (I), 284–5. Caspian Sea as an inlet: NANSEN, vol. I, 10, 76. HERODOTUS refers to the cosmographical ideas several times (II. 21, 23; IV. 8, 36), his tone indicating that while he was sceptical himself, they were

commonly accepted. His accuracy about the Caspian (I. 203) is centuries ahead of his time. PTOLEMY also disputes the conception of a world-girdling Ocean.

2. HESIOD, *Works and Days*, lines 170–3.

3. HOMER, *Odyssey*, IV, lines 563 ff. Trans. E. V Rieu.

4. Cronus: FARNELL, 23–34. Exile of Titans: HESIOD, *Theogony*, lines 729–48. There are allusions in Homer, *Iliad*, VIII, line 477, and Pindar, *Olympian Odes*, II, lines 77 ff. Cp. DIODORUS SICULUS, III. 56; GRAVES (I), 40–1. Cronian Sea: NANSEN, vol. I, 65, 121. Gorgons and Hesperides: KERENYI, 46, 48–9; GRAVES (I), 507, 512.

5. UNGER, 312–14. There are other explanations, for which see THOMSON, 39.

6. ROSE, 182.

7. WEBSTER, *passim*; COTTRELL, 211; THOMSON, 26–7.

8. KERENYI, 248–9; THOMSON, 40–1; WEBSTER, 88.

9. THOMSON, 19, 30.

10. STONE, 98–9, 113–20; ROSE, 203; GRAVES (I), 603–4; ATKINSON, 4, 31, 83–5, 115, 122–3, 161–5. For the information about the rings I am indebted to Professor Atkinson personally.

11. GRAVES (I), 495–6, 504; (2), 231, 301.

12. But Hercules's indentification with the Phœnician god Melkart, who was worshipped in those regions, may have been a contributory factor; the priority is uncertain. See B. H. Warmington, 67.

13. HOMER, *Odyssey*, X, lines 506–11, and XI, lines 13–19, 636–40.

14. Northerly and Atlantic Cimmerians: CARY and WARMINGTON, 30. Myth regarding Britain: PROCOPIUS, VIII. xx. 47 ff.

15. SMITH (2), arts. " Corcyra," " Ogygia." Cp. SPANUTH, 143–50.

16. THOMSON, 91.

17. See further Appendix B.

18. DANIEL, 15–18; BROMWICH; AMMIANUS MARCELLINUS, XV. ix. 2–6.

19. DIODORUS SICULUS, II. 47; translation quoted from GRAVES (2), 283–4. The identity of the island with Britain is fairly generally accepted; cp. THOMSON, 150.

20. AELIAN, III. 18.

21. Cp. GRAVES (I), 284–5.

22. PTOLEMY, II. I.

23. PAUSANIAS, I. xxiii. 5–6.

24. GAFFAREL, 161–2; CARY and WARMINGTON, 55; THOMSON, 281.
25. PLUTARCH (2), Chapter 26.
26. Cp. GRAVES (2), 231.
27. NANSEN, vol. I, 65; HESIOD, *Theogony*, lines 729–48; Homer, *Iliad*, VIII, line 477.
28. PLUTARCH (I), 76–8, Chapter 18; RHYS, 367–9.
29. THOMSON, 237–8; NANSEN, vol. I, 363.
30. GRAVES (I), 38, 193–4; (2), 50–2, 65, 123, 171, 232, 280, 395, 416.
31. PLUTARCH (3), 136; cp. GAFFAREL, 137–8.
32. See note I.
33. PLINY, VI. 36.
34. See MACROBIUS, 49 n., 214–15; THOMSON, 166, 202–3, 322, 383; WRIGHT, 18–19, 56, 158–9; SCHRÖDER, 51.
35. COSMAS, Introduction *passim*, 33, 43, 75–6, 376, and fig. 6 at end of book.
36. NANSEN, vol. I, 377, and vol. 2, 56–7.
37. NEWTON, 164–5. See further Appendix C.
38. SMITH (I), art. "Proclus."
39. PROCLUS, 148.
40. GAFFAREL, 18–19; FRAZER, 281.

Chapter Seven

1. B. H. WARMINGTON, 25–7, 29.
2. DANIEL, 15–18; ATKINSON, 183–5. After finishing this book I discovered that Heinrich Schliemann, the great archæologist who unearthed Troy and the Aegean civilisation, later became interested in Atlantis and Odysseus's Ocean crossing. He even planned an expedition to the Canaries and Mexico, but did not live to attempt it (Robert Payne, *The Gold of Troy*, page 173). In view of the vindication of his intuitions in other cases the fact is notable, though he evidently favoured the southern route rather than the northern.
3. NANSEN, vol. I, 45; THOMSON, 143.
4. GAFFAREL, 42–88; HAKLUYT, vol. 7, 133–5; and see further Appendix D.
5. It is uncertain, of course, whether this is all British information or whether Plutarch's "stranger" was a real person who actually contributed. But Flacelières, the French editor of the *Oracles*

dialogue, thinks that most of the passage is based on Demetrius's report, and his view is the simplest. See PLUTARCH (1), 76–8.

6. COTTRELL, 140–2.

7. ENGLAND, Chapters III, VII.

8. WALLIS, 305–6, 366.

9. GRAVES (1), 495–6; (2), 230–1.

10. I am not concerned here with the problem of a drifting boatload of " Indians " which is mentioned by one or two classical authors. See GAFFAREL, 167–71; CARY and WARMINGTON, 54–5.

Chapter Eight

1. HEYERDAHL (2), 286–93, and plates XVII–XXV; cp. PETERSON, 223–4. Dr. Gordon F. Ekholm of the American Museum of Natural History tells me that he doubts whether the Rio Balsas head is, as hitherto supposed, pre-Columbian. But he cites no evidence of Spanish artistic influence; his only ground for disputing VAILLANT's dating seems to be that the head does not fit into the " known styles." With all respect to Dr. Ekholm, surely this is a kind of question-begging? The object, like some of the others mentioned, is exceptional; that is precisely the point.

2. STIRLING, 327.

3. COLLIS, 54–60, 77, 84, 95; MACNUTT, 64–6, 79, 95, 128–9; RADIN, 174; SCHOOLCRAFT, 19 ff.

4. For Quetzalcoatl as god, see BRINTON, *passim*; THOMPSON (1), 109, 157 ff., 205; COLLIS, 55, 56, 66, 110; HEYERDAHL (2), 274–5; MACNUTT, 215–16; PETERSON, 127–9; VAILLANT, 170; COVARRUBIAS, 134; SWAN, 124.

5. COLLIS, 51–4, 118–19, 137, 162, 179; PETERSON, 152–3; RADIN, 62, 91–7, 116, 175 ff.; THOMPSON (2), 94.

6. COLLIS, 58–9; *Encyclopædia Britannica*, art. " Aztecs "; PETERSON, 86; DONNELLY, 89, 270; RADIN, 61; GELLHORN, 96.

7. BRINTON, 129–33, etc.; COLLIS, 54, 77, 110; MACNUTT, 64–6; THOMPSON (1), 157 ff.; HEYERDAHL (2), 275–7.

8. THOMPSON (1), 20–2, and (2), 98–100; COVARRUBIAS, 133. Cp. IXTLILXOCHITL, SAHAGUN.

9. For cult-centres and crosses, see GUIDEBOOK (3); COLLIS, 55, 107; PETERSON, 63; MACNUTT, 31, 153; *Catholic Encyclopædia*, art. " Mexico "; NUTTALL, xix, 21, 49, 50 (diagrams 33, 61, 62); KINGSBOROUGH, vol. 3, part 3, No. 44; VAILLANT, plate 59;

COVARRRUBIAS, 134. VAILLANT, in his *Aztecs of Mexico* (endpapers in the original volume, page 9 in the revised Pelican edition of 1953), decorates a map with an artist's simplified version of the Fejervary design. It resembles an Irish ring-cross, and the caption says it is taken from another Mexican text, the Codex Vaticanus B. The elliptical wording—due no doubt to considerations of space—creates an impression of facsimile reproduction. Actually, while the cosmological themes do occur in the Vaticanus, the cross as printed is not to be found there, or in any Mexican manuscript so far as I know.

10. COLLIS, 56; MACNUTT, 215–16; THOMPSON (2), 94.
11. THOMPSON (2), 97–104, 108, 111–12, 129; BRINTON, 145–67; HEYERDAHL (2), 277–8; RADIN, 63–4.
12. BRINTON, 207–24; HEYERDAHL (2), 279–83.
13. MASON, 16–17, 110, 117, 131, 202–7; HUBER, 99–100, 127, 171–2; BUSHNELL, 130; BRINTON, 170–207; HEYERDAHL (2), 230–68.
14. BRINTON, 224; RADIN, 277–9; RAND, 228, 232, 252, 293; WALLIS, 42, 51, 153, 154, 205–6, 321–37.
15. HEYERDAHL (2), 291–2 and elsewhere. Part V of this book is entirely devoted to the problem of the white men.
16. RADIN, 37; MASON, 202–3.
17. VAILLANT, 170.
18. PETERSON, 127, 129.
19. COLLIS, 233.
20. ATTENBOROUGH, 141–59.
21. Cp. O'DONOGHUE, LITTLE. In extenuation of my own past dalliance with the same theory I can at least plead that I took account of Viracocha.
22. As "Dietrich of Bern," alias Theodoric, was made responsible for a good deal of ancient architecture in German legend. See H. M. and N. K. CHADWICK, 295; and cp. Chapter VIII of that work generally.
23. BUSHNELL, 52–3; HEYERDAHL (2), 306.
24. GUIDEBOOK (2); PETERSON, 61–2; VAILLANT, 6, 71, 79, 273; THOMPSON (1), 204. Regarding archæological imitations and fakes, see PETERSON, 278.
25. IXTLILXOCHITL, 1–13; cp. VAILLANT, 68.

Chapter Nine

1. MASON, 13–17, 66–7, 86 ff.; BUSHNELL, 24–5, 31, 85–9; HUBER, 24, 28–9; HEYERDAHL (2), 222–3.
2. Regarding the Incas and their editing of the past, see HUBER, 53, 56, 72; MASON, 108–10, 117. Legends of Viracocha were collected by a number of Spanish scholars in the sixteenth and seventeenth centuries. Abstracts of their findings are in BRINTON, 170–207, and HEYERDAHL (2), 230–68. See also BANDELIER, II, 293 ff.; HUBER, 35–9, 55, 76, 171–2; MASON, 113–14, 232–3; BUSHNELL, 116.
3. HEYERDAHL (1), 127, and (2), 35–7, 221–3.
4. HEYERDAHL (2), 306, and plates XXIII–XXV; and see further the discussion on pages 295–303, where Heyerdahl gives some alleged examples and second-hand descriptions. But I am not convinced that these "beards" actually are beards; it seems to me that the legend of Viracocha has put the notion in people's heads. Certainly Heyerdahl produces nothing from anywhere near Tiahuanaco comparable to the obvious and various beards of Meso-American art, and nothing that in the least suggests portraiture from life. He acknowledges the workings of artistic convention (299) and the scarcity of arguable specimens (300).
5. MASON, 20, 23.
6. For some picturesque examples of the results, see BANCROFT, 63–129, and DONNELLY, 257–8, 274–6, etc. The most remarkable of the eccentrics in this field was Lord Kingsborough, who produced a monumental work of genuine and lasting value in an effort to prove that the Mexicans were the Lost Tribes of Israel.
7. GUIDEBOOK (1), 38; PETERSON, 266–7.
8. HEYERDAHL (2), plates XIX. XXI, XXII.
9. PETERSON, 56–9; GUIDEBOOK (1), 29.
10. STIRLING, 314; GUIDEBOOK (1), 38; PETERSON, 266–7.
11. PETERSON, 58; THOMPSON (1), 157; GUIDEBOOK (1), 35. I hereby retract my previous exploratory notes toward dating Quetzalcoatl (*The Month*, July 1958), which the pressure of additional facts has forced me to regard as erroneous.
12. STIRLING, 327–8.
13. Cp. COLLIS, 232; THOMPSON (2), 140–2.
14. LITTLE, 65.

15. BROMWICH; WESTROPP, 249 ff.
16. RAND, 228, 232, 252, 293; WALLIS, 154, 305–6, 322–3, 333, 366.
17. ESPINOSA, 27–8, 31.
18. For example O'HANLON, 439–41. SCHOOLCRAFT'S paragraph (italics mine) occurs in a miscellany of pre-Columbian traditions in his *Historical and Statistical Information*, 19 ff. I have been told of mysterious "forts" in Florida, and a Viking sword in Mexico, but have not attempted to evaluate these items.

Epilogue

1. HEYERDAHL (1), 313.
2. THOMSON, 30; B. H. WARMINGTON, 25–7, 29, 69.
3. WHEELER, V.
4. LETHBRIDGE (2), 76, and (4), 78–91.
5. KENNEY, 412–17; PLUMMER (1), I. xvi–xxv, II. 44–98.
6. KENNEY, 412.
7. For the written materials on the Norse voyages to America, and their interpretation, see BABCOCK, GATHORNE-HARDY, HOV-GAARD, KENDRICK, NANSEN. The passage about the vines and corn of the Fortunate Isles is in ISIDORE, XIV. vi. 8; translation in NANSEN, vol. I, 345–6. A controversial question left unexamined here, but possibly relevant, is the report of the Italian Zeno, for which see BABCOCK, 124–36; BRUCE, chapter 1; MAJOR.
8. The cartography and the legendary Atlantic islands are discussed by BABCOCK and WESTROPP. See also NEWTON, 162–3; DUNN, 459–61; LITTLE, 183.
9. HONORIUS, I. 36; translation in NANSEN, vol. I, 375–6.
10. RAVENSTEIN, 77.
11. IDRISI (1), 60–5, and (2), III. 1 (vol. I, 197–202). The Arab's "Island of Sheep" is approximately placed by his account of the Magrurins' voyage: (1), 223–5, and (2), IV. 1 (vol. 2, 26–9).
12. GOULD (2), 194.
13. For certain other medieval and post-medieval developments, see Appendices C and D.
14. BABCOCK, 68; NANSEN, vol. 2, 228–30, 294–5.
15. DUNN, 469–70.

Appendix B

1. See DONNELLY; THOMSON, 90–2; *Cambridge Ancient History*,
   vol. 2, 172–7, 274 ff.; GLANVILLE, 40–2, 118; GRAVES (I),
   308–10, 345 note 1, 639 note 4, 715 note 6; also GRAVES'S
   discussion of Atlantis on pages 146–8, with which, however, I am
   only partly in agreement. SPANUTH raises some interesting
   issues, though his conclusion seems to me incredible.

Appendix D

1. See KENNEY, 412; PARRY; LITTLE, 30; BOSWELL, 131;
   LOOMIS (2), 35, 37–9, 47, 56–7, 74, 152 ff.; and LOOMIS (1),
   285–6, the same author's observations on the Glastonbury legend
   of St. Joseph of Arimathea.
2. TAYLOR, 10; PARKS, 47; ABBOT, section "Of America or the
   New World."
3. HAKLUYT, vol. 7, 133–5.

Bibliography

ABBOT, George, *A Briefe Description of the Whole World.* 1620.
ADAMNAN, *Life of St. Columba.* Ed. and trans. William Reeves. 1874.
AELIAN, *Varia Historia.* Trans. Thomas Stanley. 1665.
AMMIANUS MARCELLINUS, *Res Gestae.* Trans. John C. Rolfe (Loeb Classical Library). 1956.
Annals of the Four Masters. See O'DONOVAN.
ARI FRODE. See ELLWOOD.
ASIN, Miguel, *Islam and the Divine Comedy.* 1926.
ATKINSON, R. J. C., *Stonehenge.* 1956.
ATTENBOROUGH, David, *Quest in Paradise.* 1960.

BABCOCK, William H., *Legendary Islands of the Atlantic.* 1922.
BANCROFT, H. H., *The Native Races of the Pacific States,* vol. 5. 1876.
BANDELIER, A. F., *The Islands of Titicaca and Koati.* 1910.
BEAZLEY, C. R., *The Dawn of Modern Geography,* vol. 1. 1897.
BELL, J. J., *The Glory of Scotland.* 1932.
BIELER, Ludwig, *The Life and Legend of St. Patrick.* 1949.
BOSWELL, C. S., *An Irish Precursor of Dante.* 1908.
BRADFORD, John, " The ' Lost Continent ' of Atlantis." In *Myth or Legend?* cited under DANIEL.
Bran, The Voyage of. See MEYER and NUTT.
BRENDAN, SAINT. The *Life*: see O'DONOGHUE, O'HANLON, PLUMMER, STOKES.
    The *Voyage*: see JUBINAL, O'DONOGHUE, O'HANLON, SCHRÖDER.
BRINTON, D. G., *American Hero-Myths.* 1882.
BROMWICH, Rachel, " Cantre'r Gwaelod and Ker-Is." In *The Early Cultures of North-West Europe,* ed. Cyril Fox and Bruce Dickins. 1950.
BROWN, A. Samler, *Madeira, the Canary Islands and the Azores.* 1932.

BRUCE, Erroll, *Challenge to Poseidon.* 1956.
BUSHNELL, G. H. S., *Peru.* 1956.
BUTLER, Alban, *Lives of the Saints.* Revised and ed. by H. Thurston and D. Attwater. 4 vols. 1956.

Cambridge Ancient History, vol. 2. 1924.
Cambridge Medieval History, vol. 3. 1936.
CARY, M., and WARMINGTON, E. H., *The Ancient Explorers.* 1929.
Catholic Encyclopædia, arts. " America, Pre-Columbian Discovery of," " Brendan," " Mexico."
CHADWICK, H. M. and N. K., *The Growth of Literature,* vol. 1. 1932.
CHADWICK, N. K., (1) " The Lost Literature of Celtic Scotland." *Scottish Gaelic Studies,* August 1953.
(2) Ed., *Studies in Early British History.* 1954.
CICERO, *The Dream of Scipio.* Ed. and trans. E. H. Blakeney. 1927.
COLLIS, Maurice, *Cortes and Montezuma.* 1954.
COSMAS INDICOPLEUSTES, *Christian Topography.* Ed. and trans. J. W. McCrindle. 1897.
COTTRELL, Leonard, *The Bull of Minos.* 1953.
COVARRUBIAS, M., *Mexico South.* 1947.
CRONE, G. R., *Maps and their Makers.* 1953.

DANIEL, G. E., " Lyonesse and the Lost Lands of England." In *Myth or Legend?* 1955.
DANTE, *Inferno* and *Purgatorio.* Trans. Laurence Binyon. 1933, 1938.
DE PAOR, Maire and Liam, *Early Christian Ireland.* 1958.
DICUIL. See LETRONNE.
DILLON, Myles, *Early Irish Literature.* 1948.
DIODORUS SICULUS, *The Library.* Trans. C. H. Oldfather and others (Loeb Classical Library). 1933, etc.
DONNELLY, Ignatius, *Atlantis: the Antediluvian World.* Edited and augmented by Egerton Sykes. 1950.
DUNN, Joseph, " The Brendan Problem." *Catholic Historical Review,* January 1921.

ELLWOOD, T., *The Book of the Settlement of Iceland* (i.e. the *Land-namabok*). 1898.
Encyclopædia Britannica, arts. " Aztecs," " Bahamas," " Cronus," " Cross."

BIBLIOGRAPHY

Encyclopædia of Religion and Ethics, art. " Cross."

ENGLAND, G. A., *Isles of Romance.* 1929.

ESPINOSA, Alonso de, *The Guanches of Tenerife.* Ed. and trans. Sir Clements Markham. 1907.

Eyrbyggja Saga. See MORRIS.

FARNELL, Lewis Richard, *The Cults of the Greek States*, vol. 1. 1896.

FISHER, James, *Rockall.* 1956.

FLOWER, Robin, *The Irish Tradition.* 1947.

FORBES, Rosita, *Islands in the Sun.* 1949.

FRAZER, Sir James, *Folk-Lore in the Old Testament*, vol. 1. 1918.

GAFFAREL, Paul, *Histoire de la Découverte de l'Amérique*, vol. 1. 1892.

GATHORNE-HARDY, G. M., *The Norse Discoverers of America.* 1921.

GATTY, Harold, *Nature is your Guide.* 1958.

GELLHORN, Eleanor Cowles, *McKay's Guide to Bermuda, the Bahamas and the Caribbean.* 1958.

GLANVILLE, S. R. K. (ed.), *The Legacy of Egypt.* 1942.

GOGARTY, Oliver St. John, *I Follow St. Patrick.* 1950.

GOODWIN, William B., *The Ruins of Great Ireland in New England.* 1946.

GOUGAUD, Louis, *Christianity in Celtic Lands.* 1932.

GOULD, R. T., (1) *Enigmas.* 1929.
(2) *Oddities.* 1928.

GRAVES, Robert, (1) *Greek Myths.* 1958.
(2) *The White Goddess.* 1952.

GUIDEBOOKS. (1) *Official Guide to the Museo Nacional de Antropologia* (Mexico City). English. 1956.
(2) *Teotihuacan.* Official Guide published by the Instituto Nacional de Antropologia e Historia, Mexico. English. 1958.
(3) *Tula.* As (2). English. 1957.

HAKLUYT, Richard, *The Principal Navigations, Voyages, Traffiques and Discoveries of the English Nation.* 12 vols. 1903–5 edition.

HARDEN, D. B., " The Phœnicians on the West Coast of Africa." *Antiquity*, September 1948.

HENRY, Françoise, *Irish Art in the Early Christian Period.* 1947.

HERODOTUS, *History*. Trans. G. Rawlinson. 2 vols. 1907.

HESIOD, *The Poems and Fragments*. Trans. A. W. Mair. 1908.

HEYERDAHL, Thor, (1) *Aku-Aku*. 1958.

(2) *American Indians in the Pacific*. 1952.

HILL, Evan, "The North Salem Mystery." *Saturday Evening Post*, August 8th, 1959.

HOMER, *The Odyssey*. Trans. E. V. Rieu. 1945.

HONORIUS (of Autun), *De Imagine Mundi*. In P. Migne, *Patrologiae Cursus Completus* (Latin series), vol. 172. 1854.

HORNELL, James, *Water Transport*. 1946.

HOVGAARD, William, *The Voyages of the Norsemen to America*. 1914.

HUBER, Siegfried, *The Realm of the Incas*. 1959.

IDRISI, (1) *Description de l'Afrique et de l'Espagne par Édrisi*. Ed. and trans. R. Dozy and M. J. de Goeje. 1866.

(2) *Géographie d'Édrisi*. Ed. and trans. P. Amédée Jaubert. 2 vols. 1836, 1840.

ISIDORE (of Seville), *Etymologiae*. Ed. W. M. Lindsay. 1911.

IXTLILXOCHITL, *Histoire des Chichimèques*. Trans. H. Ternaux-Compans. 1840.

JACKSON, Kenneth H., *A Celtic Miscellany*. 1951.

JONES, J. Morris, *Taliesin*. 1918.

JORDANES, *The Gothic History*. Trans. C. C. Mierow. 1915.

JOYCE, Patrick, *Old Celtic Romances*. 1894.

JUBINAL, M., *La Légende Latine de S. Brandaines*. 1836.

KENDRICK, T. D., *A History of the Vikings*. 1930.

KENNEY, James F., *The Sources for the Early History of Ireland*, vol. 1. 1929.

KERENYI, C., *The Gods of the Greeks*. 1951.

KINGSBOROUGH, Lord, *The Antiquities of Mexico*, 9 vols. 1830-48.

Landnamabok. See ELLWOOD.

LETHBRIDGE, T. C., (1) *Boats and Boatmen*. 1952.

(2) *Herdsmen and Hermits*. 1950.

(3) "The Isles of the Bless'd." In *Myth or Legend?* cited under DANIEL.

(4) *Merlin's Island*. 1948.

(5) *The Painted Men*. 1954.

LETRONNE, A., *Récherches géographiques et critiques sur le livre De Mensura Orbis Terræ . . . par Dicuil, suivies du texte restitué.* 1814.

LINDSAY, Jack, *Arthur and his Times.* 1958.

LITTLE, George A., *Brendan the Navigator.* 1945.

LOOMIS, R. S., (1) Ed., *Arthurian Literature in the Middle Ages.* 1959. (2) *Wales and the Arthurian Legend.* 1956.

MACNUTT, Francis Augustus, *Fernando Cortes.* 1909.

MACROBIUS, *Commentary on the Dream of Scipio.* Ed. and trans. William Harris Stahl. 1952.

Mael Duin, The Voyage of. See JOYCE.

MAJOR, R. H., *The Voyages of the Venetian Brothers Nicolo and Antonio Zeno.* 1873.

MARCUS, G. J., " The Scotic Curach." *Scottish Gaelic Studies,* August 1953.

MARTIANUS CAPELLA, *De Nuptiis Philologiae et Mercurii.* Ed. Adolfus Dick. 1925.

MASON, J. Alden, *The Ancient Civilizations of Peru.* 1957.

MEADE, Joaquin, *La Huasteca.* 1942.

MERRIEN, Jean, *Christopher Columbus.* 1958.

MEYER, Kuno, *Learning in Ireland in the Fifth Century.* 1913.

MEYER, Kuno, and NUTT, Alfred, *The Voyage of Bran.* 2 vols. 1895-7.

MORRIS, William, and MAGNUSSON, E., *The Story of the Ere-dwellers* (i.e. *Eyrbyggja Saga*). 1891.

MURPHY, Gerard, *Early Irish Lyrics.* 1956.

NANSEN, Fridtjof, *In Northern Mists.* 2 vols. 1911.

Navigatio Sancti Brendani. See JUBINAL, O'DONOGHUE, SCHRÖDER.

NEWTON, A. P., ed., *Travel and Travellers of the Middle Ages.* 1926.

NUTTALL, Zelia, *The Book of the Life of the Ancient Mexicans* (i.e. the Codex Magliabecchiono xiii. 3). 1903.

O'DELL, Andrew C., *The Scandinavian World.* 1957.

O'DONOGHUE, Denis, *Brendaniana.* 1893. (Contains translation of the *Navigatio.*)

O'DONOVAN, John, ed. and trans., *Annals of the Kingdom of Ireland by the Four Masters.* 7 vols. 1851.

OENGUS, *Félire.* Ed. and trans. Whitley Stokes. 1905.

O'HANLON, John, *Lives of the Irish Saints,* vol. 5. 1875.

BIBLIOGRAPHY

o'kelly, m. j., and wilson, David, "The Celtic West and the Near East" (broadcast). B.B.C. Network Three, October 20th, 1959.

parks, George Bruner, *Richard Hakluyt and the English Voyages*. 1928.
parry, j. j., *The Vita Merlini of Geoffrey of Monmouth*. 1925.
pausanias, *Description of Greece*. Trans. W. H. S. Jones (Loeb Classical Library). 5 vols. 1918–35.
peterson, Frederick, *Ancient Mexico*. 1959.
pliny, *Natural History*. Trans. H. Rackham (Loeb Classical Library). 1938, etc.
plummer, Charles, (1) *Bethada Naem nErenn* (i.e. Lives of the Saints of Ireland). 2 vols. 1922.
    (2) *Vitae Sanctorum Hiberniae*. 1910.
plutarch, (1) *Sur la Disparition des Oracles*. Ed. and trans. Robert Flacelières. 1947.
    (2) *The Face which appears in the Orb of the Moon*. Ed. and trans. A. O. Prickard. 1911.
    (3) *Le Περιτον Προδωπου de Plutarque*. Ed. and trans. P. Raingeard. 1935.
posnansky, Arthur, *Tihuanacu: the Cradle of American Man*. 3 vols. 1945.
proclus, *Commentary on the Timæus of Plato*. Trans. Thomas Taylor. 1820.
procopius, *History of the Wars*. Trans. H. B. Dewing (Loeb Classical Library). 1915–40.
ptolemy, *Geography*. Trans. E. L. Stevenson. 1932.

radin, Paul, *The Story of the American Indian*. 1944.
rand, Silas T., *Legends of the Micmacs*. 1894.
ravenstein, e. g., *Martin Behaim*. 1908.
renault, Gilbert, *The Caravels of Christ*. 1959.
rhys, John, *Studies in the Arthurian Legend*. 1891.
rose, h. j., *A Handbook of Greek Mythology*. 1958.
russell, Bertrand, *A History of Western Philosophy*. 1940.
ryan, John, *Early Irish Missionaries on the Continent and St. Vergil of Salzburg*. 1924.

338

BIBLIOGRAPHY

SAHAGUN, Bernardino de, *General History of the Things of New Spain.* Trans. Arthur Anderson and Charles E. Dibble. 1950.

SCHOOLCRAFT, Henry R., *Historical and Statistical Information respecting . . . the Indian Tribes of the United States*, vol. 1. 1851.

SCHRÖDER, Carl, *Sanct Brandan.* 1871. (Contains Latin text of the *Navigatio*, and some later versions.)

SMITH, William, (1) *Dictionary of Greek and Roman Biography and Mythology.* 1849.

(2) *Dictionary of Greek and Roman Geography.* 1878.

SPANUTH, Jürgen, *Atlantis—the Mystery Unravelled.* 1956.

STEPHENS, Thomas, *Madoc.* 1893.

STIRLING, M. W., "Great Stone Faces of the Mexican Jungle." *National Geographic Magazine*, September 1940.

STOKES, Whitley, *Lives of Saints from the Book of Lismore.* 1890.

STONE, J. F. S., *Wessex before the Celts.* 1958.

SWAN, Michael, *Temples of the Sun and Moon.* 1954.

TAYLOR, E. G. R., *Late Tudor and Early Stuart Geography.* 1934.

THOMPSON, J. Eric, (1) *Mexico before Cortez.* 1933.

(2) *The Rise and Fall of Maya Civilization.* 1954.

THOMSON, J. Oliver, *History of Ancient Geography.* 1948.

THRALL, William Flint, "Clerical Sea Pilgrimages and the Immrama." *Manly Anniversary Studies in Language and Literature.* 1923.

TOOLEY, R. V., *Maps and Map-makers.* 1952.

TURVILLE-PETRE, G., *The Heroic Age of Scandinavia.* 1951

UNGER, Eckhard, "Ancient Babylonian Maps and Plans." *Antiquity*, September 1935.

VAILLANT, George C., *The Aztecs of Mexico.* 1953.

VILLIERS, Alan, *The Western Ocean.* 1957.

WALLIS, W. D. and R. S., *The Micmac Indians of Eastern Canada.* 1955.

WARMINGTON, B. H., *Carthage.* 1960.

WATERS, E. G. R., *The Anglo-Norman Voyage of St. Brendan.* 1928.

WEBB, Percy H., *The Reign and Coinage of Carausius.* 1908.

WEBSTER, T. B. L., *From Mycenæ to Homer.* 1958.

WESTROPP, T. J., *Brasil and the Legendary Islands of the North Atlantic.* 1912.

WHEELER, Sir Mortimer, *Rome beyond the Imperial Frontiers*. 1955.

WILLIAMS, Hugh, *Christianity in Early Britain*. 1912.

WILLIAMSON, Kenneth, *The Atlantic Islands*. 1948.

WILLIAMSON, Kenneth, and BOYD, J. Morton, *St. Kilda Summer*. 1960.

WRIGHT, John Kirtland, *The Geographical Lore of the Time of the Crusades*. 1925.

ZENO. See MAJOR.

INDEX